THE GREAT EXPATRIATE WRITERS

Also by Stoddard Martin

WAGNER TO *THE WASTE LAND*: A Study of the
   Relationship of Wagner to English Literature
CALIFORNIA WRITERS: Jack London, John Steinbeck, The
   Tough Guys
ART, MESSIANISM AND CRIME
ORTHODOX HERESY: The Rise of 'Magic' as Religion and its
   Relation to Literature
THE SAYINGS OF LORD BYRON (*editor*)

The Great Expatriate Writers

STODDARD MARTIN

St. Martin's Press   New York

First published in the United States of America in 1992

Printed in Hong Kong

ISBN 0–312–06861–1

Library of Congress Cataloging-in-Publication Data
Martin, Stoddard, 1948–
    The great expatriate writers / Stoddard Martin.
        p.   cm.
    Includes bibliographical references and index.
    ISBN 0–312–06861–1
    1. English literature—Foreign countries—History and criticism.
  2. American literature—Foreign countries—History and criticism.
  3. Literature—Exiled authors—History and criticism.   4. Authors,
  Exiled—Biography.   5. Stendhal, 1783–1842.   I. Title.
PR125.M37   1992
820.9'920694—dc20   91–25431
                                                                        CIP

Nor is there singing school but studying
Monuments of its own magnificence;
And therefore I have sailed the seas and come
To the holy city of Byzantium

W. B. Yeats

Contents

Author's Note

This book concentrates on what Henry James called 'the international theme'. It represents a further development of, and complement to, studies undertaken in my previous critical books. The first of these explored important motifs in European modernism, the second the literary tradition of my native American state, the third various strands of immorality from the French Revolution to the present, the fourth some movements toward enlightenment. The reader of all five books may see a cumulative development in them. The reader of this book on its own may find in it too a progressive interweaving of themes, echo-patterns and perhaps even fugal elements.

I note this in warning. An academic book is not ordinarily expected to have style; perhaps it is not even desired. Be that as it may, I have attempted a kind of symphonic development here; and the reader is left to judge whether that is not appropriate to a work which follows certain continuities through the works and careers of a succession of great writers. Like all my books, the present volume may be read best at speed. The reader should get the effect of a *sweep* of tradition as it passes through time; for the expatriate idea has never been a static one, it has been and remains in dynamic motion – as, indeed, the mind of the enthusiastic reader and critic should be as well.

Of work by previous scholars, I have tried to follow in the steps of F. R. Leavis and his successors, as well as other critics who have favoured the panoramic view, such as Edmund Wilson. Down here below Parnassus, I have been helped by suggestions from Virginia Smyers and Roger Stoddard of Harvard University, Deirdre Toomey and Warwick Gould of Royal Holloway and Bedford New College, University of London, Anna and Colin Haycraft, the late Virginia Moriconi, Gay Clifford, and a number of other friends who have given moral support, including Sarah Shuckburgh, Christine Salmon, James and Daphne Jameson, Lynne and William Wilkins and not least my publisher's editor.

1

The Expatriate Tradition

According to the Oxford English Dictionary, the first definition of an expatriate might be[1] someone who is driven or banished from his native country. This definition dates from the latter half of the eighteenth century and conjures visions of Casanova thrown out of Venice or aristocratic *émigrés* fleeing the Reign of Terror. In the nineteenth century, it became fashionable for romantics to dabble in revolution, be hounded out of their fatherlands and roam across Europe like the Wandering Jew. Jews themselves contributed to this fashion by the spectacle of their flight from prejudice and pogrom. In the early twentieth century the fashion continued, becoming more widespread as actual revolution and war sent aristocrats, Jews, kulaks, socialists, communists and finally old fascists scurrying away from regimes bent on wiping them out, or at least muzzling their expressionistic urges. Still, when we speak of an expatriate nowadays, most of us have in mind the second OED definition: that is, a person who withdraws from his native country and/or has renounced his allegiance. An expatriate is a voluntary exile in our view. He has decided to live in Spain because it is sunny, or the taxes are lower, or he finds some deep attraction in the culture of bullfighting. He is not remotely similar to the Iranians who fled Khomeini or the Nicaraguans who left their own country with the advent of the Sandanistas. These are the driven and banished of now: inheritors of traditions of *ancien régime émigrés* or White Russian exiles from the Soviet state. We do not, as a rule, refer to them as expatriates. That term is reserved for rich Europeans living in Manhattan or rich Americans living in Switzerland, or northern Europeans who have left for the south, or artists who for the sake of individual expression have seen fit to live away from where they were born.

It is this type of expatriate that this book is about. As a result, it does not directly concern Karl Marx or Wagner, thrown out of Germany; Lenin or Solzenitsyn, in exile from Russia; Schoenberg or Thomas Mann or scores of artists in flight from the Nazis. While there was an element of elective withdrawal and renouncing alle-

1

giance in such cases, these figures were principally unwilling exiles: men driven or banished from their countries. Most continued to concern themselves with the affairs of those countries, devoting years to brooding over the national *hubris* which had driven them hence. Forced *émigrés* of this kind do not become citizens of the world easily or quickly, if ever. Citizenship of the world is not what they are looking for so much as triumphant return in the third act of their hero's progress and vindication of their true patriotism over the aberrant kind which made their homelands foreign to them. An exile is a Russian or German or Jew living in another country but dreaming of going back to Russia or Germany or Israel. An expatriate in the pure sense is someone who has left his country behind and does not long to go back to reform it but wants to establish a new life elsewhere with other loyalties. Tax exiles from England who intend to go back when the rates are favourable fall out of the category. Americans who left their country in the 1950s in disgust at McCarthy, or in the 1960s because of the Vietnam War, are moral exiles rather than expatriates proper: shades of the Victor Hugos and Bakunins who went to far places the better to rail against antipathetic regimes. Most of them have gone home long ago. And going home constitutes cancellation of one's visa to the new land of expatriation. It proves that what might have appeared as aspiration to transnational detachment actually boils down to temporal exile or an extended voyage of discovery.

A traveller, in short, is not an expatriate. Among novelists, then, there are many we can exclude. E. M. Forster, for instance. *A Room with a View* is about tourists. They go to Florence, long to live there, yet come back to England in the end. Being abroad appears to help them arrive at a better understanding of themselves; but it is as Englishmen that they went and as Englishmen that they return, if somewhat broadened by the experience. Something similar applies to *A Passage to India*, which is not a novel about expatriates either, though it may be closer to it. The book is about colonialism; and again the effect of being abroad is measured by whether it helps to achieve better Englishness. Forster is engaged in a critique of his own people. Foreign behaviour and experience are used as standards of contrast and, as such, have secondary importance. Forster is not concerned principally with what it might be like to become a citizen of another land, nor did he live out of England for an extended period himself. Thus he is little more of an expatriate writer than he was an expatriate.

His friend and contemporary D. H. Lawrence may be closer to the type. Lawrence too was a traveller: he took up the persona of the Wandering Jew; and owing to some persecution in England during the First World War (he had married a German and was under surveillance as a pacifist), he could argue that he was hounded out of the country. But this would be no more precisely accurate than in the cases of Shelley and Byron (which we shall come to). Lawrence did want to become a citizen of a new world and experimented in living in Australia and New Mexico before returning to Europe to spend his last years in Italy and southern France after doing the *de rigueur* stint for 1920s writers in Paris. He wrote at least one story, 'Things', which is unambiguously about the effects of expatriation. Several other stories, novellas and books touch on the expatriate experience to greater or lesser degree, notably *Sun* (which was published by Harry and Caresse Crosby's trendy expatriate press) and the novels about Australia and Mexico, *Kangaroo* and *The Plumed Serpent*. Unquestionably Lawrence was aware of and fascinated by the new ways of life that twentieth-century expatriation might bring. No doubt he foresaw that expatriation would become an increasingly important theme. Unquestionably too he rejected the little England experience, or at least the conventional Englishness of his time, enshrined at its most sophisticated level by Bloomsbury. But was he finally, on balance, an expatriate himself? I think not. His obsessions remained individual, psychosexual and English; and his last several books either returned to specifically British scenes – *Lady Chatterley, St Mawr, The Virgin and the Gypsy* – or were transcendental and unconcerned with national matters or settings – *Apocalypse* and *The Man Who Died*.

Lawrence then also seems to belong principally to this category of traveller. So too, more clearly, does a writer like Evelyn Waugh. He never lived for an appreciable time out of England and when dealing with expatriate matters (as he frequently does), does so in the context of describing a larger English whole. Consider, for instance, the wanderings of Sebastian Flyte in *Brideshead Revisited*. These may constitute a picture of expatriation proper, but if so, the condition must be seen as pathetic: a reaction to failure and ostracism in England. The same is true of the expatriation of Sebastian's father, Lord Marchmain, who has lived in Venice for decades, owing to sexual scandal in England, but returns to die at Brideshead. Waugh himself became an insular, perhaps even provincial English country gentleman in middle life, a role he had sentimentalised in his early novel, *A Handful of Dust*, in which an instinctive suspicion of expatriation is also apparent. The demise of the book's hero comes as a result of his leaving his Gothic country estate for Amazonia, again driven hence for pathetic reasons; and the character who presides over this demise caricatures Waugh's fear of what may arise from a type of expatriation. He is a half-breed Englishman who has lived his entire life in the bush and reveres his ancestral culture (in this case the novels of Dickens) with a fanatical zeal no educated Englishman would share, but without any sense of the essential morality at the heart of it.

'I will show you fear in a handful of dust' is the book's epigraph. This is taken from T. S. Eliot's *The Waste Land*, which in turn took its epigraph originally from Joseph Conrad's *Heart of Darkness*; and a 'heart of darkness' – locus for psychological implosion and demoralisation – is where Waugh, like Conrad, fears that expatriation must end: at least that kind of expatriation which leads from north to south, from civilisation into the primitive. In book after book Conrad had explored the moral meltdown experienced by European man when on land or at sea in the tropics. The classic instance of this after *Heart of Darkness* is *Lord Jim*; another example is the third Conrad work narrated by Marlow, *Youth*. But while the experience pictured in these books involves expatriation, would it be right to call them expatriate novels? Specifically, expatriate novels in a 'great tradition'? I think not. Conrad himself left his native country, it is true; and much of his opus deals in expatriate kinds of problems – the expatriate as international anarchist in *The Secret Agent* or as capitalist bringer-of-progress in *Nostromo*. But these are expatriate problems of a colonial and refugee type. Conrad almost never considers the situation of characters who have conscientiously chosen to uproot themselves and change their homeland in order to become citizens of a new and perhaps better world. Lord Jim is a fugitive; Kurtz in *Heart of Darkness* is a renegade. Even Conrad himself may appear, on closer inspection, to be less an expatriate proper than an emigrant who sets out deliberately to replace one *patria* with another.

This brings us to the case of the figure who might leap to most Anglo-Saxon minds as the classic expatriate of this century: T. S. Eliot. But was Eliot an expatriate in the most thoroughgoing sense of the term? Should a man who gives up one country only to become a citizen – indeed, a *patriot* – of another be viewed, strictly speaking, as an *ex-patriate*? Shouldn't the term finally be taken to imply a fundamental discontent with the status of belonging to a *patria* altogether? If so, then Eliot must drop off the list. His travels were brief; he settled in England; even more than Conrad he became a fixed part of the literary establishment and later of the national establishment at large. Eliot wanted to *belong*. An expatriate in the great tradition longs to be free of belonging to anything but his own destiny and ideals. Some province of the mind or soul is his proper country, and this province will probably finally have no fixed objective correlative on earth. As for Eliot, if the fixity of his progress in a geographical sense does not seem sufficient to disqualify him from principal consideration, then a glance at his opus must. Where in any of his works, except possibly *The Waste Land* (and then only by precarious extrapolation), does an expatriate problem or theme command important attention? I can think of nowhere and would venture to say that in the end Eliot found the idea of permanent expatriation *à la* his friends Pound and Joyce of dubious moral value. The urge for fixity, so contrary to the expatriate impulse, came to dominate in him. Ironically, this may be in part because he had become what was unnatural to his nature in the first place: an expatriate: uprooted, wandering, ever unbelonging.

Going away from home may create an impulse to reproduce one's national characteristics more intensely. This is the colonial syndrome: the explanation for why the British in India or Kenya could seem a caricature of the Home Counties English, or the Americans in the Philippines or Vietnam could seem even more lawless and 'Wild West' than back home in California or Texas. It is also the reason why James Joyce does not seem an expatriate in the grand tradition either. 'I go to encounter for the millionth time the reality of experience and to forge in the smithy of my soul the uncreated conscience of *my race*' (italics mine), says Stephen Dedalus at the end of *A Portrait of the Artist as a Young Man*. And what does Dedalus/Joyce produce in the course of thirty years' wandering across Europe? *Dubliners*, *Portrait*, *Exiles*, *Ulysses* – all books set in Ireland: indeed, the most intensely Irish books ever written. Joyce went away in order to see his homeland better. In *Exiles* he treats an expatriate subject, but it is the subject of the expatriate coming home – that is, ending his expatriation. *Finnegans Wake* may be the ultimate international exercise in language; but as novel, its setting and characters, such as they are, are Dubliners again, and the mentality involved might be described as the apotheosis of drunken Irish conversational brilliance. Joyce belongs to a period and *Zeitgeist* preoccupied with expressionistic exploration of one's racial identity. He is symptomatic of that inward-looking process of self-definition which grew up in the arts before and during the heyday of psychoanalysis. Bloom may be Everyman, but he is Everyman in intensified Irish-Jewish guise; and it would remain to Joyce's disciple, Samuel Beckett, to bring the master's modernist methods and subject matter out into unequivocally universal characters and situations.

Is Beckett then an expatriate proper? Probably. Most of his work was written in French; he lived predominantly out of his homeland; his content, as said, transcends nationality. The argument might be raised that he too falls into the category of trading one *patria* for another: he left Ireland not to wander critically but to settle in Paris. This, however, does not disqualify him: he did not become French in the way that Eliot or even Conrad became English. Nor did he take up writing exclusively or even principally for the French. The real question about Beckett in this context is not whether he became an expatriate but whether his work is distinguished enough to qualify as representative of a '*great* tradition'. Does it have roots in the great expatriate work preceding it? Does it show a way forward, or does it rake over motifs of a decaying modernist movement and do the final gravedigging for them begun by Joyce and Gertrude Stein? The way I state these questions indicates my prejudice. Beckett seems a minor figure and endpoint, not a robust and *great* or successful expatriate. Indeed, it might be said that what he demonstrates best about expatriation is how at its worst it can winnow away specificity of subject, setting and character, until the process of writing becomes too abstract and philosophical to hold any but the most rarefied reader's attention.

Beckett and Joyce, being Irish, bring up the matter of Irish expatriation in general. Certainly it was widespread among men-of-letters, particularly in the late nineteenth century. But in this period, Ireland was so closely attached to Britain that she had representatives in the Westminster parliament; and to call Wilde and Shaw expatriates because they lived and wrote in London seems no more appropriate than to call various American writers expatriates because they came from Mississippi or Nevada to settle in New York. In his attachment to French aestheticism, Wilde showed a transnational tendency typical of English writers of his type at the time; and his self-exile on leaving Reading Gaol is expatriation of a kind. But the first is little more than an educated man's admiration of things foreign; and the second is an instance of pathetic flight – an exaggerated preview of Sebastian Flyte's form of expatriation, produced by ostracism and resulting in disintegration. Wilde's and Shaw's garrulous contemporary George Moore is a better example of true expatriation. Going to Paris as a young man, he anticipated the Left-Bankism of Anglo-Saxon and Irish writers of the 1920s; and his *Confessions of a Young Man*, with its devotions to Verlaine and Mallarmé, is an expatriate book of a type which would have several descendants – even, in vulgar form, works of Henry Miller's. But Moore returned to London and Dublin in middle years; and his genial approach to life and literature altogether bespeaks the disposition of tourist, which is what he finally might be seen to be, though of a committed and active type, unlike Forster, and on a civilising rather than primitivising mission, unlike D. H. Lawrence. In any case, Moore seems a marginal figure nowadays: hardly a candidate to represent a great tradition.

What then of those who, following Moore, most literature-dabblers of the twentieth century might think of first when the word expatriate comes up? I mean here Gertrude Stein's 'lost generation': all the Americans and Brits who swarmed around Montparnasse in the 1920s adding their bits to the mélange of the modernist avant-garde and imagining, while drunk or drug-high or recovering from sexual depletion, that they were helping to inaugurate a new age of perception and expression. Here we have Hemingway and Fitzgerald, the above-mentioned Miller and Lawrence Durrell, Anaïs Nin, Djuna Barnes, Bryher, Hilda Doolittle (who wrote as 'H.D.'), Robert McAlmon with his Contact Editions, Harry Crosby and his Black Sun Press, Nancy Cunard and her Hours Press, so on and so forth – all the well-chronicled 'published in Paris' crowd, and their descendants like Lawrence Ferlinghetti and Jack Kerouac, who sought to bring Left-Bankism 'back home' to North Beach (San Francisco) or Greenwich Village (New York), recognising perhaps the substantially American character of the phenomenon in the first place. The enduring interest of this period may be that it was the first time that a great number of writers, artists and others self-consciously turned their backs on the provinces they had come from and tried to forge a single-world ethos, or at least, aesthetic. Paris of the 1920s was the first and perhaps the last great capital of world expatriation. As such, it has become a kind of archetype for a state of mind, a condition of life, that artists, writers and others of succeeding generations have tried to imitate. And like any phenomenon so mythologised, it has a wealth of bogus as well as legitimate elements.

In terms of expatriation, it must be said that the effect of living in Paris turned out in most cases to make writers, like Joyce, more intensely provincial in their subject matter, if avant-garde in approach. For Americans, Left-Bank expatriation was principally a means of seeing the Middle West better – indeed, for the first time. Robert McAlmon, by all accounts a central figure of the period, dedicated himself to publishing American writing: *real* American writing, as it was thought, not the American experience filtered through English English *à la* Henry James. Beyond his own provincial tales, McAlmon was responsible for bringing out in this way Gertrude Stein's magnum opus, *The Making of Americans*, and Hemingway's early stories about his youth in Michigan. Can we call this expatriate writing? Only in the sense that it was written away from home. Stein was a better expatriate when championing Picasso or writing her various 'autobiographies'. McAlmon was an expatriate writer proper when his subjects were homosexuals in Berlin or his literary peregrinations in Paris, later revised by Kay Boyle, in *Being Geniuses Together*. Hemingway alone of these three came to qualify in subject matter as a great expatriate. His big books, *The Sun Also Rises*, *A Farewell to Arms*, *Death in the Afternoon*, *For Whom the Bell Tolls* and *Across the River and into the Trees*, are all about European expatriation. Some of his finest stories are on expatriate subjects. Most of his later, non European-located books might be viewed as concerned with expatriate matters too: *The Green Hills of Africa*, *To Have and Have Not*, even *The Old Man and the Sea*. Finally there is his posthumous memoir of Paris in the 1920s, the most memorable text about this overwritten-about period, *A Moveable Feast*.

Hemingway was a great expatriate writer, one who understood the tradition preceding him, carried it on and influenced what was to come after. In *The Green Hills of Africa*, the authors he gossips about are mostly expatriate predecessors or contemporaries: Turgenev and James, George Moore, D. H. Lawrence and Joyce. His tutelage by Stein and Pound and another partial expatriate, Ford Madox Ford, are principal subjects of *A Moveable Feast*. Of all novels of the period, by Americans anyway, only Scott Fitzgerald's *Tender is the Night* deals as directly with expatriate motives and effects. Why then do I balk at including Hemingway in this study as one of the great expatriates? The reasons are various. First, we live in a period which doubts Hemingway's durability and quality of achievement, and for good reason. His subject matter is as restricted as his prose is spare. There is an undercurrent of whining, special pleading, even bottled-up hysteria about his work at its worst; this suggests permanent emotional immaturity. Through his various wanderings he was a misfit, with few close friends and a well-chronicled tendency to fall out with lovers and wives. His education, and thus sense of tradition, was limited, with the result that – in comparison to James or Maugham or even Pound – he remains a temporal provincial in the historical panorama of 'monuments of unageing intellect'. His ending in suicide casts a shadow of failure back across his career and famous 'code'; and this shadow falls over his accomplishment as expatriate along with everything else. Hemingway did not 'beat out his exile'. He did not achieve a higher sense of civilisation or citizenship of a better world. In the end he came home, first to Key West, then to the *de facto* American colony of Havana, finally to Ketchum, Idaho. His reputation may have been born in Paris, but it was brought up by a Madison Avenue-type publicity machine. And it was very much as an American that he returned to Europe when he did: as a journalist during the Spanish Civil War and liberation of Paris; later as a tourist and jet-set celebrity.

As much as any American writer, Hemingway seems to represent an imperial impulse. He does not write about colonial subjects, like Kipling. But his focus, while predominantly on abroad, is on Americans abroad; and the ethos he imposes on his material could be described as an American orthodoxy. In this way, he seems a successor to Jack London, writing about the East End of London or the South Seas, or a precursor to a writer like Paul Theroux, whose tone and values are those of an American abroad rather than of an individual becoming free from nationality. Were all this not sufficient, I would finally, reluctantly, drop Hemingway from a short list of great expatriates in the interests of variety of geography and genre. Byron, Maugham and Greene are British; James and Pound, American; Stendhal, French. In the West in the post-imperialist period, this seems a proper mix. The British have been the great wanderers; the Americans have been their successors and fellow-travellers, as have the French to a lesser degree. Other nationalities, while producing no dearth of exiles, have not figured as prominently to date in producing distinguished elective expatriate traditions. As to genre, Byron and Pound were poets, the rest novelists. All were critics and/ or journalists as well; and this seems an appropriate mix too. The great tradition of expatriate writing belongs to a period dominated by the novel and the novel's breakdown into pastiche, critique, disguised memoir and 'text'. It is not a tradition that includes many dramatists. Poets, however, have persisted, and among them names with as much claim to consideration as Hemingway – Robert Browning's, for instance.

One book cannot include everything. Moreover, as F. R. Leavis taught those who taught me, the job of a critic is to distinguish the greater from the lesser: to set up a standard, which becomes a point of departure and argument for other readers, not merely to entertain with gossip and fact, as in an historicist survey. Leavis was Olympian, for better or worse. He was attempting to establish the great texts for study in a new classical tradition, in which English literature would replace works of Latin and Greek taught in previous centuries. We live now in something approaching a global village and accept that the study of English literature alone may be a relic of imperialism and that some more international approach should be sought. Thus in discussing an expatriate tradition, one must remain aware that one is not talking about something fixed or exclusive. Time will add more and remove the Anglo-American bias, which in this case is also in part a function of the author's origins and culture as well as the difficulty all scholars still have of achieving competence in literatures of other languages. Works of Latin Americans, East Asians and so on will find their way into prominence eventually. Meanwhile, one should not resist trying to distinguish the great from the good and the bad for fear of getting it wrong or of being inadequate to a vast subject. Leavis would not have given way to any such pusillanimity. Nor would have Oscar Wilde, who declared in a reference to Goethe that discourse and opinion – that is, *criticism* – would be the method by which race prejudice was eradicated finally.[2]

Browning would have accepted that there might be valid reasons for him not being considered in this study. Gertrude Stein, who had an inflated view of her position, would probably have not. McAlmon depicts the monumental lady as saying that she represented the only significant advance in writing in English since Shakespeare;[3] nor was this meant to be witty, as was a similar statement from G. B. Shaw. Stein was great in ego but too narrow in content and eccentric in style to be considered a great writer. The result of her experiments in word-formation was the early Hemingway and, by extension, his 'school'. Otherwise, her influence appears to have been nil and her place as a personality of her times rather than as a useful innovator. She retains some appeal to some women perhaps, lesbians particularly. But even women who have written books about her confess that they do not know what to make of her writing; and one of them at least would not rate her work as highly as that of Pound's friend H.D.[4] Thus the great female candidate for inclusion in this volume must be passed over, despite the fact (as I am told) that one would be wise to include a woman for the text to be representative.

Representative or not, the question remains: what female writer could be ranked in the company as a great expatriate? Jean Rhys? Bryher? Nancy Cunard? Anaïs Nin or Djuna Barnes, mentioned above? Mary Butts? But are these really *great* female writers in the tradition of Austen, Georges Sand, George Eliot and Virginia Woolf (as Stendhal and James *are* great writers in anyone's tradition)? Or are they oddities and footnotes: representatives of a school of thought and way of life to be collected and considered in the aggregate, as Gillian Hanscombe and Virginia Smyers have done in their engaging study *Writing for their Lives*?[5] Again, the way I pose the question suggests my prejudice. There is, alas, no great female expatriate writer yet – not even Pearl Buck, though she won the Nobel Prize. Katherine Mansfield, originating from New Zealand, may have had the promise to become one: that depends on how you view the admiration of Virginia Woolf and hagiographising of Middleton Murry. Germaine Greer in our own time might be one, but to include her would involve extending the discussion to include critics who were never novelists or poets first, academics, philosophers – writers of all kinds. Such expansion might also let in figures such as Nietzsche, who became an expatriate and was certainly a great writer, or at least an influential one. But one must stop somewhere lest the field become so broad as to include Wagner – also an expatriate (for a time), great and (among other things) a writer. And then there are the painters and even politicians who have left their own countries – Whistler and Sargent, Hitler for goodness sake! Couldn't they qualify as 'great expatriates' too?

Setting up categories may seem proscriptive, even somewhat reactionary, in this tolerant, democratic, all-merging age. This is especially true when dealing with subjects like expatriation, which by their nature are internationalist and universalising. Still, distinctions must be made if civilised discourse is to continue: if indeed we are to preserve language at all. This may seem a principle the 'published-in-Paris' crowd did not admire, with their preoccupations with 'nightspeak' and forms of *esperanto*. But time has shown up the adolescence of some of their antics, and we are coming to accept that their form of modernism led up as many blind alleys as it broke productive new ground. *Finnegans Wake* was an endpoint. Succeeding generations have learned to do exactly the opposite of what it involved: to pursue universal subject matter in conventional forms, not provincial self-expression in avant-garde regalia. And so we arrive at a writer like Graham Greene, a master of complex moral situations described in everyday language. And in Greene (and to a lesser degree Maugham) we touch on another branch of the expatriate tradition – that is, the manly (if you will) type of expatriation which leads out of Europe (or America) to the south and east: Conrad's tropics, Lawrence's new worlds, the Second and Third Worlds of our day. This type of expatriation may begin by being civilising or escapist but its result is often primitivising.

I have mentioned it already in connection with Conrad, Lawrence and Waugh. But the sub-genre is larger. There is of course Kipling, the bard of colonialism. There is the 'Kipling of the Klondike', Jack London, who depicts colonial/pioneer life in books on the South Seas such as *Adventure*. There are in fact many writers in this mode, the big game-hunting Hemingway of Africa being one too. (Perhaps we should also mention here one of the best of female writers passed over, Isak Dinesen.) Within the sub-genre there is the particular matter of writers seeking for what Jack Kerouac called *satori* in Mexico: Lawrence as mentioned, London ('The Mexican'and so on), Antonin Artaud (see my *Art, Messianism and Crime*), Kerouac himself (especially in *On the Road*) and his friend William Burroughs, who also lived and wrote for some years in Morocco, as did the not inconsiderable American expatriate Paul Bowles. Mexican expatriation was also the principal preoccupation of two of the greatest practitioners of this sub-genre, the German, B. Traven, and the Anglo-Canadian, Malcolm Lowry; and if there were space in this study, both would deserve to be included, the latter having written perhaps the most penetrating of all texts about retrograde expatriation, *Under the Volcano*.

I say 'retrograde'. The reader will have realised by now that my 'great tradition' involves achieving, or at least pursuit of, some idea of higher civilisation; and this customarily requires turning toward the 'monuments of unageing intellect' of Europe, classicism, Italy and Mediterranean culture. But some Europeans – Artaud is an example – were propelled out of Europe by the idea that European civilisation was not *high* in a true sense, but corrupt, and that exemplary civilisation might only be found in some faraway, overgrown Atlantis – that is, among Aztec or Mayan ruins. In the case of Lawrence Durrell, a similar impulse provoked quest amid the stones of ancient Cyprus and Egypt. Thus in one aspect Mediterranean expatriation is not so different from what sent Lawrence romanticising among plumed serpents. *Sea and Sardinia* and *Etruscan Places* are also books in quest of the higher in the long-decayed. And while Durrell excavated the eastern Mediterranean for clues to a better, purer life, Robert Graves set himself up in service to the White Goddess in Majorca. The impulse to the south – whether to Mexico, the old Mediterranean, or the India of so many hippies' journey to the East – is always a drive toward the sun, out of an overcivilised north, into an ethos dominated by older, stranger, pagan gods It is also, almost always, semi-consciously motivated by a desire to resurrect and glorify phallic energy. This was, for instance, behind Harry Crosby's obsessive sun-worship in Egypt and the setting up of the Black Sun Press. It was a large part of what drove Aleister Crowley (another eccentric writer of the period, though hardly great) to Mexico, Ceylon and finally Sicily, to set up his notorious Abbey of Thelema. And then of course there is Henry Miller, always in pursuit of sun and sex throughout his self-indulgently overchronicled wanderings, through France, to Greece and finally back to a quite foreign (for a New Yorker) Big Sur.

This 'manly' or phallically motivated expatriation may have its origins in part in the nineteenth-century literature of the high seas. Melville and Richard Henry Dana (*Two Years before the Mast*) are certainly precursors of London's *The Sea Wolf*, Traven's *The Death Ship* and Lowry's first novel, *Ultramarine*. Miller and Kerouac ride freighters in their peregrinations to Europe; and the ethos of the Ancient Mariner (another version of the Wandering Jew) is never far from the voices of their quasi-existentialist first-person narrators. Lonesome travellers of this genre view the world through the prism of a melancholy stream-of-consciousness, often enlivened and extended by drink. Philosophising is irresistible. The music of endless motion through space and time is a long, slow jazz or blues of broken melodies, strange voices, exotic languages. The quest in this genre may be superficially to find riches, as in Traven's *The Treasure of the Sierra Madre*. But characteristically, material wealth is spurned as part of the decadent city left behind. Society, polite women, man-

nered men, family values and children are not sought. The grail
seems to be individual energy, perfect equilibrium in the face of an
ever-changing world, and then all-accepting entropy – a kind of salt-
of-the-earth resignation to the supervening force of the All. It is no
mistake that this genre takes as its principal images the sea, which is
endless, and the sun, which always rises again. It is a genre in which
man wishes finally to go to ground: back to nature: into 'the heart of
the light / the silence'. And to expatriates of the great, civilisation-
seeking tradition, it must seem that what these seekers too often
discover is 'the horror! the horror!' – Mr Todd's or Mr Kurtz's
spiritual waste lands. But that may be in part the city-dwellers'
blindness. There is an odd, organic fulfilment even in the Consul's
grotesque death at the end of *Under the Volcano*. Stripping away
civilisation, becoming a creature of jungle and sun and going back to
the earth without illusions of transcendence must have a permanent
attraction to most of us and remain a significant motive for expatriation even when all the overgrown Atlantises have been paved over
and the only 'hearts of darkness' left to explore are in outer space.

But this study will stop short of science fiction, which is mental
expatriation, if expatriation at all, or perhaps expatriation in its
'astral' form: a fantasy of escape. Such fantasy may not be bad *ipso
facto*. Utopia may be a worthy destination; and in the sense that they
are seeking a better home-land, all types of expatriates are trying to
get to it. But for the sake of concision and coherence, we shall leave
out consideration of travellers to Dune or wherever, pointing out
that – while authors may have spent entire careers imagining such
places – none has actually lived there. A writer's expatriation in
body is one of the chief standards by which we are classifying those
discussed here (the others are attention to expatriation as theme and
greatness as writers at large). For all considered, expatriation was
neither a mental game nor a temporal choice to be unmade at whim.
As befits seekers after a better mode of living, each undertook his
own expatriation with serious purpose and a sense of higher moral
and artistic responsibilities. This is a criterion. We are not talking
about writers as mere entertainers but as workers within a tradition
implicitly based on Shelley's dictum that the poet is the true legislator of mankind. And so writers of sci-fi thrillers or other forms of
airport news-stand pulp, however universalist, are out of the window.
Nor can one admit fine writers whose principal concerns remain

'lifestyle' or frivolity. Some 'gay' writers might be eliminated on this basis. Others such as Auden and Isherwood, and even (briefly) Tennessee Williams, merit more consideration.

Williams needs mention because of *The Night of the Iguana* and *The Roman Spring of Mrs Stone* among other works. Here expatriation is dealt with as a symptom of an impulse to liberation and self-expression analogous to what homosexuals (and other sexual eccentrics) are driven by when they 'come out'. Attention to this theme qualifies Williams (perhaps along with Tom Stoppard) as the important playwright to figure in a study of this kind. But like so many others dismissed, Williams did not live out of his country for long; and he remains an American in essence, however in sympathy with the idea of citizenry in a new and better world. Auden and Isherwood, propelled out of England in part by fear of the laws which had condemned Wilde but mostly by sexual and political curiosity, really did make much of their expatriation, first in Berlin and later in New York and California. Of the two, Isherwood is the more worthy of discussion in this context. Auden went home to England in the end; nor does expatriation to New York involve quite the same cultural sea-change for an Englishman of his time that expatriation to California did. In any case, Auden's poems are sufficiently eclectic to give the impression that they would have turned out much the same wherever they had been written. This cannot be said of *Berlin Stories* or indeed most of Isherwood's so-called fiction, in which sense of place is an essential component. Unequivocally, Isherwood qualifies as an expatriate. Better than anyone – Chandler, Huxley, or going back further Stevenson – he typifies the situation of those who left Europe for America, in search of more freedom, in both lifestyle and mental activity. In particular, Isherwood sought a better, more tolerant world as a homosexual: something Wilde had been after and, among those considered in this study, Maugham may also have been motivated by. At the same time, he was seeking a new spiritual environment: more open, experimental and speculative than old Europe seemed able to offer – something akin to what poor, mad Artaud was seeking among the drug-taking Indians of Mexico.

This second impulse relates in part to the exploratory urge which drove religious seekers like Madame Blavatsky and Krishnamurti to America, as it had also sent the former and Annie Besant to India at the turn of the century. And the case of Isherwood reminds us that the search for a new religious understanding may be an important motive for expatriation: a fact also confirmed by the preoccupations

of some members of the 'manly' tradition essayed above. Henry
Miller introduces theosophical speculations into *The Colossus of
Maroussi* among other books; Lowry makes the Consul in *Under the
Volcano* dream of writing a book about cabalism; and Kerouac fills
his tales with pop Buddhism – indeed, he makes the expatriation to
Japan of his friend Gary Snyder, the poet, the central focus of *The
Dharma Bums*. Isherwood's attachment to an Eastern guru, recorded
in *Down There on a Visit*, is as central to his reputation as his dedication to 'the homintern', spoken of openly in *Christopher and his Kind*.
Homosexuals in general may feel themselves in quest of some other,
better country: they are probably expatriates in imagination always,
dreaming of places where they may be with each other in peace,
without being discriminated against. But religious seekers must also,
almost always, feel some alienation from single countries: their
homeland is nirvana, Christian heaven, the Grail chapel or some
more artificial paradise. Thus the sub-genre of expatriation to California such as Isherwood represents: a locale which has appeared to
be especially tolerant of gays and – as the geographical endpoint for
Western Man's pioneering – a natural starting-point for dreams of
the Beyond.

Isherwood's importance as expatriate is as the exemplar of how
these strands of the tradition come together. The problem is that they
do so in such a matter-of-fact, unimaginative context. 'I am a cam-
era', Herr Issyvoo wrote at the beginning of his career; and so he
remained to the end: a chronicler of what existed rather than a maker
of these grand metaphors we call novels. Fine as he was as a stylist,
Isherwood is not great in the Leavisite, traditional sense. The book
he might have written about expatriation as religious quest was
largely accomplished by Maugham in *The Razor's Edge*; and the imaginative work he might have created out of the expatriate homosexual artist's view of the twentieth century was finally written by
Anthony Burgess in *Earthly Powers*. Both are great expatriate novels.
None of Isherwood's books are, finally, though *Berlin Stories* will retain
its unique place and memorability. Maugham and his novel we shall
go into later. Burgess, alas, is one more to pass over. For, though he
has lived out of his country and written this towering expatriate
book, Burgess's motives for expatriation have been called into
question (doesn't he live in Monaco for tax purposes?); his attachment
to England remains profound (doesn't he write nearly weekly for an
English paper and don't most of his books still have English subjects?);
and his consistent quality as a writer is a matter of great debate (isn't

he profligate and sloppy?). Thus without even invoking the matters of geography and genre mentioned in connection with Hemingway, Burgess must be dismissed – confined to a category with Scott Fitzgerald perhaps, as author of a great novel of the south of France but not himself a great expatriate.

Isherwood, Burgess – the list goes on. Among recent contemporaries there is, for instance, Marguerite Yourcenar, who went to Maine from Belgium in the 1930s and wrote at least one fine book concerned with expatriate wanderings in her mediaeval tale *The Abyss*. But we must not go on further. The day may come soon when we are all expatriates of a kind – indeed, when expatriation has been made irrelevant because culture world-wide has been homogenised. Meanwhile, to repeat, in undertaking this book I am concerned not only with writers who are great and who have lived away from their homelands by choice, but also those who elected to expatriate themselves precisely because they were in quest of some higher, better and perhaps finally unrealisable idea of civilisation. And civilisation is the key word here. I am not talking about a tradition of immature protest, of petulant sneering at one's own kind by individuals who were misfits, but of mature – or at least maturing – pursuit. Nor is this pursuit for something other-worldly like the Holy Grail, but for something that just may be able to be constructed out of the 'monuments of unageing intellect' and 'monuments of its own magnificence' of *this* world. The great tradition in Leavis was imbued with a sense of civil responsibility, not escapism, mere aestheticism, cultism or other forms of self-indulgence. It required attention to society, its shortcomings and needs, and a high moral attitude. Thus it could not be filled up by authors mainly in pursuit of 'liberation'. Liberty perhaps. Generosity of spirit. But not revolutionary romantic or modernist mania for breaking down barriers, only to go wandering off through the rubble without thought of what is likely to take their place.

To discuss great expatriates, as to value any form of greatness or tradition, may seem to imply conservative views. This book, however, is conservative only in the sense that Yeats, that perfect modern hybrid between the provincial and the cosmopolitan, meant it in the poem from which I take my epigraph. In 'Sailing to Byzantium' Yeats suggests an ideal correlative for the homeland that expatriates of the great tradition are seeking: a city of timeless values of art and thought; a culture in which natural things may be transmuted into their golden counterparts, to shine forth and inspire future generations to create finer cities and more glorious transmutations, until what the human imagination calls eternity has been reached. In this sense, the great tradition is transcendental as well as civic. But the urge to transcendence is neither resigned, as in Buddhism, nor abstract, as in cults of the Grail. It is active and concrete in the best Western tradition of engagement. It involves the individual achieving the right balance between private contemplation and social relation. It is animated by wonder amid myriad cultural patterns, so that in the end – if prejudice remains – it is the educated prejudice of those who have come, seen and connected, rather than of those who have only heard and imagined from afar and, because it is easier, dismissed. I say this realising as I do that inclusion of Pound in a company meant to be so exemplary may seem offensive to some. But then none of my 'great expatriates' is perfect. And it may be that their individual failures are all in proportion to the difficulty each found in achieving citizenship of the world in the first place.

2
Byron

Byron is the prototype of the Romantic expatriate. He left England in 1809 at the age of 21 and wandered the Mediterranean for two years; then he left again in 1816, took up the only permanent residence of his adult career in Italy and died struggling for liberation of the land which he claimed had made him a poet, Greece.[1] The motives of his expatriation have been speculated upon ever since the mythical 'Byron' achieved a kind of rock-star fame with publication of the first two cantos of *Childe Harold's Pilgrimage* in 1812. Byron himself weaved mystery around the question. 'If the consequences of my leaving England were ten times as ruinous as you describe', he wrote to his lawyer, 'I have no alternative, there are circumstances which render it absolutely indispensible, and quit the country I must immediately.'[2] Such outbursts just prior to his 1809 departure are sometimes taken to refute the theory that he went principally to escape debts run up at Cambridge. But what are the 'circumstances'? One kind of cynic might argue that they amounted to little more than a desire to get away from a vulgar, widowed mother, whom Byron, as an only child, found a meddlesome bore. Another might assert that the young rake simply wanted to continue his debaucheries in far places, where pleasure was cheap and censorious eyes could only see what he chose to show.

This second argument, allied with letters to university chums about pederasty, has led Byron's most painstaking biographer, Leslie Marchand, to suggest that Byron simultaneously wanted to escape scandal over a liaison with a King's College choirboy (John Edleston) and to explore homoeroticism further among the sherbet-eaters and sodomists of the East.[3] This explanation has some basis, especially considering the illegality of homosexuality in the England of the day; and Byron did enjoy gay companionship in Athens, at least until his principal catamite made himself ridiculous by carrying a parasol when riding.[4] But Byron was put off by the overtures of the devoted pederast, Ali Pasha; and apart from Edleston at Cambridge and the Greek boy Loukas Chalandritsanos at Missolonghi at the

end of his life, he never entertained a serious homosexual relationship, nor wished to. On the evidence of his last poem 'On This Day
I Complete My Thirty-Sixth Year',[5] he found such urges unworthy of
the code he wanted to embody; and in general, it seems the distor-
tion of a later, Freud-obsessed age to make him out as a precursor of
Auden and Isherwood in pursuit of cheap boys in Berlin.

The Romantic was more sentimental than his Modernist counterparts. He was looking for love more than sex. Several other of his
biographers argue that he was still pining over teenaged rejection by
his neighbour, Mary Chaworth, and that he had undertaken his
travels in part to prove his attractiveness to foreign women so that
he might appear sufficiently dashing not to be rejected again on
return.[6] There is some support in *Childe Harold* for this theory. In the
middle of the first canto he breaks off to address a lyric 'To Inez'; to
the first two cantos as a whole he appended a dedication 'To Ianthe'.
Both are general enough to suggest that he has been in search of an
earthly incarnation of the muse; and his letters of the time are full of
paeans to young women met in his travels, suggesting that heterosexual longings were not just a poetic pose. In Malta, he had his first
experience with a married woman of his class. In Athens, he became
sentimentally involved with one of the daughters of his landlady
and penned the famous lines, 'Maid of Athens, ere we part / Give, oh
give me back my heart'. Passages of this kind were just the sort of
thing to appeal to young ladies back home, and they lend force to the
argument that establishing such an appeal was a principal reason for
Byron's 'flight'.

This has more psychological credibility than the idea that he was
after easy access to boys, or even to female prostitutes. He had had
more than his fill of the latter at Cambridge and at his Gothic feudal
estate, Newstead Abbey. Besides, while tales of sexual buccaneering
might add spice to letters to male friends, they could hardly impress
reputable women. For them, tragic love was the drug in this era of
Lady Hamilton, pathetic parting the fond reality. For Byron, the
latter had peculiar attractiveness. He had watched his own mother
pine for his absent, ne'er-do-well father who had died in debauchery
on the Continent when the boy was only three. Perhaps from that
age, but certainly from the time of his departure for Harrow, Byron
had learned the power and attraction of the emotive farewell. Apart
from 'To Inez', the other significant break in the first canto of *Childe
Harold* comes with the lyric 'Adieu, Adieu! my native shore'. Here as
elsewhere throughout the poem, Byron implies that the real reason

he has gone away is that there is no one to love him at home. This is preposterous, but revealing. The Childe goes away partly in demand that some worthy, protective muse remain behind watching his progress.

Memories of mama and nannies waving him off to school no doubt inform this. But nannies were lower class and mama plump and tricky; and the young lord had learned as early as at Harrow that they were neither good enough nor enough for him. Perhaps the Mary Chaworth affair did provide a glimpse of what he thought he required. Perhaps rejection did exaggerate the requirement, so that what the Childe really craved in his mind was memory of a clutch of pretty young women standing at the dockside, waving tear-stained handkerchiefs in his slipstream. That Byron went away to evoke such reaction is indicated by the immense number of letters he trailed behind him, as well as the intensely autobiographical poetry. These parade his *feelings* to an extent unsurpassed in serious literature to that date. The romantic wanderer must be reassured that there will always be someone who cares to hear about his every sensation. During this early period it remains his mother *faute de mieux*. Later, in London after her death, it would become the more congenial mother (and notional lover) figure, Lady Melbourne. Finally, in the later, more serious stage of his expatriation, it would become that private version of the triple goddess, his half-sister Augusta: part mother, part lover, part friend.

The grand tour can thus be seen as a quest for love from two sources: those suitable ladies he meets en route and those doting presences who follow his progress from home. This is a first purpose for it. A second is linked to Byron's other chief correspondents: his male friends, such as John Cam Hobhouse, who had gone to university with him and shared in his two lifelong professional interests, literature and politics. This category of correspondent would later include Byron's publisher, John Murray, and his approved poet contemporaries such as Tom Moore. They filled the places of the brothers and father he never had and clearly were more than mere professional friends. For them, the fare was not sentiment and feeling so much as anecdote, boasting, political and literary opinion – in general, bold views of a kind to command attention, if not respect, and ultimately manly love. With male confidants Byron could also excoriate those who neither respected nor loved him, nor were likely to. Chief enemies of this type were the establishment figures who could determine his success or failure at home: the critics he feared would attack anything new he might publish and the politicians he would have to confront if and when he took an active part in Parliament.

Such attention as the poetasting young lord had received before his departure made him view with trepidation his likely reception on return. His first published book, *Hours of Idleness* (subsuming the portentously named 'Fugitive Pieces'), had provoked an attack from the *Edinburgh Review* berating the teenager for his lack of experience, his apparent lassitude and air of privileged irresponsibility. Byron had responded with a satire against virtually all the established literary lions of the day, *English Bards and Scotch Reviewers* (1808). Because of his obvious gift for prosody, he had earned more applause than might have been expected for a work of such immature over-reaction and of unrepentant *lèse-majesté*. But a neophyte who mocks the high priests of the profession he proposes to enter had better have genius with which to defend himself; and Byron was undoubtedly conscious that he had to develop some justification for his persona, or at least rationale, and a subject-matter more compelling than drinking out of a skull-mug at Newstead. He had, in short, to become an authority in his own, unique sphere. And since the detested Southeys and Wordsworths had appropriated England from London to the Lakes, why not take on the classical world of his childhood reading and adolescent education: the Mediterranean, whose poetic productions of the past made Albion's of the present seem measly, even wimpish?

He had argued himself into this position in the conclusion to *English Bards*. *Childe Harold* thus becomes a staking-out of the new man's territory; and the choice of abroad carries implicit within it criticism, even rejection, of home. When Baudelaire was tried for obscenity, Sainte-Beuve observed that the French descendant of Byron *had* to write about Hell because Lamartine had appropriated Heaven and Hugo the Earth.[7] Every writer's milieu is dictated not only by what he chooses but by what he can do which has not been done before; thus writers must begin by rejecting father figures (as Harold Bloom has taught us). One method of doing this might be to invoke the superior authority of grandfather figures: thus Byron's lifelong championing of Pope and Dryden. Another might be invocation of even more ancient, noble traditions: thus the paeans to Homer in Greece. But finally the Romantic method must be glorification of self: its superior youth, energy, insight and (in Byron's case) rank. Young Byron epitomises such glorification. Psychologically it was the doted-on child's natural bent, one that had been reinforced by popularity at Harrow and Cambridge. *Childe Harold* fixes the instinct into its first serviceable form. Navel-gazing is the proper study of mankind; outer authority becomes fair game for attack. As the spoiled child confuses mother with the world, so the spoiled adult confuses the world with mother and responds with petulance when it does not attend to his every whim.

Byron's instant, instinctive rejection of England and its establishment might be seen in this light, both as a successful literary strategy and as a psychological imperative. Of course, the objective is the reverse of the appearance: Byron wants the acceptance, indeed love, of the *haut monde* he professes to despise. Nevertheless, Childe Harold extols every country he visits at the expense of his own. Portugal is debased by 'licking the hand' of her ally in the fight against the French. Spain degrades herself by putting her fate in the hands of the antipathetic Wellington. Greece, that nation symbolic of the best in man – liberty, classical beauty, poetry and so on – is diminished not only by her own decline and occupation by the Turks but also by the civilised rapine of Lord Elgin who – even while Byron frolics with his catamite – is dismantling the frieze of the Parthenon. England to these Europeans represents reaction, bullying and self-righteousness; and so it must seem to the renegade lord. His civic task – his version of *noblesse oblige* – is to show his kind the unattractive figure it cuts in the world. This may mature one day into a sincere reforming instinct, but at the moment it is chiefly a way to establish instant superior morality and vision, rather like Auden and Isherwood taking up fashionable Marxism in the 1930s.

Byron aligns himself with the radical liberalism of his day. Lambasting anything Tory, he depicts his progress to be the literary counterpart of Napoleon's as liberator of Europe from detested *anciens régimes*. The posture is ironic. Byron is offended when an official procession in Constantinople fails to make a special place for him on account of his rank.[8] And while extolling liberty and the revolt of nations 'enslaved', he travels ever with servants. The fanciful identification with Bonaparte is apt: in later years, Byron would travel in a replica of the carriage which had sped the French Emperor across Europe; he would sign himself 'NB' once the Noel family title had come to him through his wife; and like the conquering tyrant who had begun his career as the saviour of the liberal revolution, Byron contained from the first contradictory impulses to radical change and ultra-conservative formalism. There is a respect too in which

Byron's partisanship for favoured countries constitutes an imperial urge to promote his own *gloire*, rather than mere sentimental attachment to their mores and struggle for self-determination. He takes Greece on as his own, for instance, rather as Bonaparte had taken on Italy or – returning to the poetic sphere – that Tory bore Wordsworth had taken on the English lakes.

Byron wears his sympathy for the Greek cause as an emblem of his precocious understanding of worldly affairs. The superiority implicit is the liberal obverse of Lord Elgin's belief that British scholars will take better care of the marbles. Then too there is an element of simple post-adolescent dress-up: Byron with the Greeks is a precursor of the flower-children of the 1960s who – eager to identify with a noble, oppressed, ancient people – kitted themselves out like American Indians. Thus Harold revels in the feasts and war-songs of the Suliotes, who would frustrate the mature Byron to death when he actually tried to liberate them. For the young man, however, it is all part of an elaborate masquerade: of donning Turkish garb for a portrait; of pretending that he has incorporated the 'noble savage' into himself; of establishing in any case a personality more colourful than would have been possible in a homeland overly secure, wealthy, conventional, boring, unrevolutionised and unrevolutionising. Imagine how deadly it might have been to have stayed at Newstead through dull, provincial winters! One can only do so much reading, worrying over debt and fornicating of local 'Paphian girls'.

Frederic Raphael finds important motivation for Byron's early journeys in what he calls 'the chronic canker of boredom'.[9] Byron himself provides support for this theory. In *Childe Harold*, he depicts Newstead as either the scene for debauches leading to satiety and existential malaise or a hermitage where the lonely inhabitant was reduced to 'finding ways to conjugate the verb *ennuyer*'.[10] Byron was a surprisingly domestic creature attached to routine and privacy; but throughout his career he had a thirst for movement – for the feel of a horse under him, a carriage careening or a ship bucking the waves. In this aspect of his personality, the books, guests and spiritual presences of his solitude were no match for new sights passing, foreign colours and gorgeous landscapes topped with dramatic sunsets. The motives for Childe Harold's departures were not just emotional or Machiavellian: Byron was taken periodically by a kind of rage to transform passivity into action. He had to escape out of sedentary brooding into new experience and thought: to move outward into a personal attachment to that classical world of great passions, which had first enlivened his secluded childhood and later constituted a principal study at public school (which itself had been his first significant escape from smothering domesticity).

In *Childe Harold* the cloistered and the active, the scholarly and adventurous, reveal themselves as the two poles of Byron's character. Neither were provided by literary and social life in London, which is what he had to confront on return to England. It was either this or retreat to Newstead, a cloister made the more ghastly by the deaths in quick succession of his mother, Edleston and another Cambridge friend. Newstead too meant debt and debauchery of the kind Harold had already fled. So Childe Burun[11] faced destiny, went up to the metropolis and proceeded with publication of his poem. First, however, the Harrow and Cambridge alumnus appended copious notes to explain geographical details, appendices to elaborate literary references, even translations of languages he could not speak – Greek and Albanian. These show his concern not to be taken as a mere irresponsible adventurer. But few were fooled. The neophyte's self-defensive scholarly pose was overwhelmed by his persona's unrestrained taste for exotic excitements. The latter is what impressed the jades of the great city; and soon the lionised author found himself half-pandering to them with ever wilder expressions of it:

> O'er the glad waters of the dark blue sea,
> Our thoughts as boundless, and our souls as free,
> Far as the breeze can bear, the billows foam,
> Survey our empire, and behold our home!
> Our flag the sceptre all who meet obey.
> Ours the wild life in tumult still to range
> From toil to rest, and joy in every change.
> Oh, who can tell? not thou, luxurious slave!
> Whose soul would sicken o'er the heaving wave;
> Not thou, vain lord of wantonness and ease!
> Whom slumber soothes not – pleasure cannot please –
> Oh, who can tell, save he whose heart hath tried,
> And danced in triumph o'er the waters wide,
> The exulting sense – the pulse's maddening play,
> That thrills the wanderer of that trackless way?

Thus *The Corsair*, greatest of the several 'Eastern tales' Byron composed during his years back in England, glamourising what he had seen and felt even more than *Childe Harold* and establishing his persona firmly in the public mind as a moody, daring lover of action. To the *haut monde* he continued to try to pose as a scholar-recluse: 'In the spring of 1813 I shall leave England forever. . . . Neither my habits nor constitution are improved by your customs or your climate. I shall find employment in making myself a good Oriental scholar. I shall retain a mansion in one of the fairest islands, and retrace, at intervals, the most interesting portions of the East.'[12] But this is another defence. The young man has succeeded beyond his wildest dreams. London has given him the greatest literary and social cachet anyone can remember. Great ladies are falling over one another to become his lovers. The very establishment he has scorned has suddenly made him its cynosure. He has got what he subconsciously went away to achieve. But now that he has it, new questions arise: what to do with it and how to protect himself against the fall which may come as swiftly as the unforeseen ascent.

In answer, the Childe becomes father to the public figure. As young Byron established his authority by expatriation, so the literary lion is now obliged – some might say condemned – to return to expatriation as his most reliable theme. The *haut monde* is daunting, antipathetic, too sophisticated for him. He cannot glorify his progress in it in the way he had glorified his previous travels: to do so would show up his sentimentality, his tendency to idealise and the wish-fulfilling aspect of his point of view. Tales of London were for wits, like his new drinking-companion, the playwright Sheridan. Byron went to the theatre: he longed to dazzle the literary world in this mode. But he sensed his limits: his type of literary man had to keep separation and affect surly petulance – the spoiled child's instinctive posture. He had to write Eastern tales: only under the guise of such learned fictions could he continue to wrap mystery and glory around himself. Had he really known characters like the daring Giaour, they would ask? or the 'renegado' Selim, or the pirate Conrad, or the heroic Lara who dies fighting to better the condition of his people who have suffered while he's been away?

Of course Byron had fantasised most of these: they were hardly the fruits of scholarly research; they were essentially masks, grand disguises he put on to keep the *haut monde* at arm's length, so that he could continue his daydreams of escape into seclusion and adventure. Thus the prototypical Byronic hero is born. He is detached, misanthropic, very private. He makes his own laws and does not worry if in conventional terms he is called 'evil'. He is an outsider living by a Robin Hood code. He is high-born yet somehow removed from his birthright. He lives for one thing: love for a particular woman. He finds himself typically rescuing a damsel in distress. The events of his life – his vaunted destiny – lead inexorably toward some tragic finis. And like the Wandering Jew, or perhaps the Lone Ranger, he is fated to disappear in the end, leaving sad ladies and tearful retainers scouring the horizon for some sign of his return:

'Tis morn – to venture on *[Conrad's]* lonely hour
Few dare; though now Anselmo sought his tower.
[Conrad] was not there – nor seen along the shore;
Ere night, alarm'd their isle is traversed o'er:
Another morn – another bids them seek
And shout his name till echo waxeth weak;
Mount – grotto – cavern – valley search'd in vain,
They found on shore a sea-boat's broken chain:
Their hope revives – they follow o'er the main.
'Tis idle all – moons roll on moons away,
And Conrad comes not – came not since that day:
Nor trace, nor tidings of his doom declare
Where lives his grief, or perish'd his despair!
Long mourn'd his band whom none could mourn beside;
And the fair monument they gave his bride:
For him they raise not the recording stone –
His death yet dubious, deeds too widely known;
He left a Corsair's name to other times,
Link'd with one virtue, and a thousand crimes.[13]

The affectation of sinning, of committing crimes, preoccupied the poet at this stage. Why? It seems that he was feeling trapped, domesticated, overmothered by London; and as the child expresses rebellion by acts of naughtiness, so the man goes in for more late nights and carousing than he had done since Newstead. As the earlier debauchery was a declaration of independence from the Calvinism of his background, so this phase involves a subtle declaration of the same from the moral code of his present milieu. The lionised hero has become involved in dangerous liaisons, which he despises for their insincerity. The presiding figure over them is Lady Melbourne, mother-in-law of Caroline Lamb with whom Byron has a scandalous adultery, and aunt of the prim Annabella Milbanke whom he marries in a vain attempt to reform. Herself an adulteress in early years and never prim about Byron's affairs, Lady M would seem an unlikely candidate for the poet to rebel against; but the spirit that was 'born for opposition' (his description of himself at this time)[14] finds a way to appal even her. He commits incest with his half-sister. Semiconsciously he realises that such a 'crime' is the only means to shock the unshockable. The ultimate *liaison dangereuse*, it is the one sure method he has to separate himself from those who have had the temerity to smother him with their attentions.

The affair with Augusta had its positive use in this way. It also provided Byron with something else that the Eastern tales show us he craved: an object of obsession. In Childe Harold's early wanderings, as in Don Juan's later ones, love and sex are taken as they come, in a series of adventures which may cause some tears at parting but in general can be remembered as happy for all, rather like Casanova's in his recently published memoirs. But in Byron's affairs once back in England we see yet again the tendency to unhappy obsession which had afflicted him with Mary Chaworth. The great love for the forbidden Augusta, dommed to failure, is one face of this; the ill-fated marriage to the humourless Annabella is another. Both are prefigured in the obsessive attachments of Byron's Eastern heroes: the Giaour bleeds his soul for Leila; Selim dies for Zuleika; Conrad almost destroys himself to free Gulnare, whereupon Gulnare risks her all to free Conrad, whereupon Conrad returns to his beloved Medora only to find that she has killed herself pining for him. The argument can be made that Byron was just writing racy, passionate stuff to please the tragic tastes of an age used to death in war. But Byron could write nothing which did not involve his own *feelings*; and the feelings these obsessive love-stories reflect are decidedly pathological.

The truth was that single-focused love such as convention hypocritically demanded in England was designed to make this man unhappy. Inasmuch as he was a product of the society, he perhaps needed it. But if so, he needed it most as the wrong norm against which a rebel needs to rebel. For rebel Byron had to if he was to retain hope that he might still find happiness and full self-realisation. The great outer world was what promised this, not the 'tight little island' of Britain. Having to get back to it, he departed for the second and last time in the spring of 1816. Shortly before, Annabella had left him amid accusations of madness. Well, if madness is defined as terminal dissatisfaction with a situation one feels trapped in, then mad Byron had indeed become. He had managed to reproduce most of the negative factors contributing to his original flight: groaning debt, nagging and unsympathetic women, fear of scandal over an illicit liaison (Augusta and incest replacing Edleston and homoeroticism), and a sedentary domestic routine, chased by town tarts, carousing and gloom. Meanwhile, everything he wrote evoked the beauties of the East, which – as Marchand states – worked 'like an intermittent malaria in Byron's mind'.[15] He had not found his destiny by conquering London. In coming home he had discovered that home was the enemy. Expatriation was his only hope.

One should not treat lightly the disappointment to Byron of the failure of his life in England. For all his self-defensive rejection of his homeland, his ostentatious description of it as 'your country' and the rest, he always marked his own progress by its standards; and it is telling that he had introduced *Childe Harold* with an epigraph (from *Le Cosmopolite*) suggesting that the principal reason for travel was to reconcile one with one's own land. Byron was British – indeed, a British peer – and would remain so whether in Piccadilly or Pisa. That being said, he was in 1816 a man as rejected by his country as rejecting of it. Public opinion – and more particularly the opinion of the *haut monde* – was against him. He had violated their clear, if hypocritical, codes. Worse, he had had the temerity to act as if he were above their lionisation. So now he was forced back on his own spoiled-child mythology: if he thought he was greater than his kind and beyond its laws, then he could jolly well go back to his vaunted Continental paradises and flutter the dovecotes of London no longer.

This Byron did; but the natural homesickness in his heart was bound up in rage and remorse; for he knew, as he hadn't in 1809, that his excursion was not likely to stimulate love back home, nor could it reasonably be meant to. Now he was truly on his own. He had to find once and for all things in life worth living for. These had to be sufficient to replace lost home and family; and if he did not find them, the freedom which he had lauded and come to embody would be revealed as 'just another word for nothin' left to lose', as a 1960s rock-song put it. Crossing Europe Byron was, in the words of another song-lyric, 'goin' down the road feelin' bad'; and, as befits the existential traveller in such a frame of mind, he was forced to admit that his daring personae of previous flights had been false glorifications: that the 'wandering outlaw' of his dreams was little more than his sad self.[16] Travel, he admits, is on one level no more than a means of escape. Never again can Childe Harold pretend that by going away one can assure bright new morning forever. Creativity itself is revealed as a form of flight: a kind of narcotic taken to avoid thought which has become oppressive.

The new Childe Harold of the serious expatriation seeks his companionship in mountains and ocean. He watches the stars and wishes he were like 'the Chaldean', able to believe in their transcendental powers. Coming back to earth, he contemplates the battlefield of Waterloo where the hopes of liberal Europe have recently been crushed by the British and their allies of the *ancien régime*. In Napoleon's fall Byron characteristically sees his own destiny. Here is a testament to the futility of all heroism, whether political or poetic. Greatness is a lonely compulsion and martyrdom. Where does it lead but to overreaching and burn-out? And yet . . . and yet where would man be if it were not for those individuals 'extreme in all things' who were willing to commit *autos-da-fé*? Still revering the hero's aspiration to godhead while ruing this temporal evidence of its vanity, Byron distracts himself with a Rhine Journey. The Gothic castles, tumbledown and ghostly, chase phantoms of despair and replace them with renascent visions of outlaws – of land-bound corsairs – to give solace to the incorrigibly adolescent streak in his nature, as heroes out of Ossian did for Bonaparte during a low point in his early career.

But now, in adulthood, it must be acknowledged that such fantasising, like wandering, can become hopeless. In solitude and transcendental natural beauty, the Childe stops. He settles by Lake Geneva and considers the pantheistic spirit of the place, with its roving thunderstorms, louring mountains, clear waters and technicolour sunsets. The scholar side of his nature finds solace in contemplation of others who have expressed their souls nearby: Voltaire, Gibbon and above all that progenitor of the French Revolution and Romanticism at large, Rousseau. Monuments of unageing intellect for the first time make a dramatic appearance in Byron's values. Along with great Nature they provide some antidote to despair; and for attention to them he can thank the influence of another wanderer half-driven from England, Percy Bysshe Shelley, whom he meets for the first time by the Lake and whose pantheistic, transcendental and libertarian interests pervade the great poems he writes through summer there: 'Prometheus', *The Prisoner of Chillon* and the third canto of *Childe Harold*.

Via Shelley, Byron is also introduced to *Faust*. The drama re-awakens his own aspiration to write plays; and varying its themes, he pens his extraordinary evocation of existential despair, *Manfred*. This and an 'Alpine Journal' to the increasingly remote Augusta (she is being turned against him by the reforming zeal of Annabella) mark the bottom of his fall and beginning of his rebound. In the autumn he crosses the Alps to Italy. By midwinter, he is attending smart parties, listening to opera, even dabbling in the politics of liberating Italy from the Austrians. Settling in Venice, a city he has dreamed of since childhood, he embarks on a lighthearted regime of fornication which drives away the hurt over Annabella and even puts the loss of Augusta in the shade. Now he writes something new and entirely unexpected, a comedy as amusing as the melodrama of *Manfred* was bleak, a saga of adultory *à l'Italienne*, *Beppo*. Between these two works the character of his future production is staked out: the verse dramas *Cain*, *Heaven and Earth* and so forth; and the great picaresque, self-parodistic epic poem *Don Juan*.

But before future is reached, past must be put to bed. In the summer of 1817 Byron takes a journey through his new country (for Italy is quickly becoming the *patria* of his choice) with his old companion from the 1809 journey, the faithful and sober Hobhouse. In the course of this journey Byron writes the last and longest of his *Childe Harold* cantos, bidding farewell to youth and separating himself forever from the Childe's melancholy vision. The canto, though somewhat marred by Hobhouse's pedantic and interminable notes, is equal to its predecessor in innovation and achievement. Here more than in Switzerland Byron finds reason to live, and live well, among the monuments of unageing intellect. Stanzas pass extolling the great characters Italy has given to literature, from Shakespeare to her native writers, Petrarch, Dante, Tasso, Ariosto, Boccaccio and more. Nor is it just writers whom Byron glorifies. For the first time he is moved to praise great minds in other spheres: Michelangelo, Canova, Galileo, Machiavelli. Venice is celebrated as a city of festivity. Rome ('my country! city of the soul!') is praised for its statuary and architecture, its history and religion and gifts of culture to posterity.

In these places Byron declares himself happy for the first time. Both cities are in ruins, each retaining mere trappings of former glory. But Byron does not mock them. He sees in them the fate that his haughty homeland will realise some day and pities them even as he scorns her. He sees in them, too, his own self, 'a ruin among ruins', yet can be happy in this state. Man has a cyclic history: what was great once may be great once more. Italy will arise again as soon as her people throw off the cynicism begotten by slavery and degradation. Once they drive out the Austrians and reclaim the freedom Europe was promised by the French Revolution; once they regain the pride which is their birthright from the beauty of the land and splendour of her creations, all that now appears lost may be refound. Such is the sermon, partly inspired by Shelley and prefigured at Chillon: a sermon which Byron had rehearsed years before in Greece and would put into practice years hence with his covert aid to Italy's Carbonari and his overt championing of the Greeks against the Turks.

But here in *Childe Harold* the sermon is mainly for himself. Following *Manfred* and *Beppo*, this last canto represents the final poetic act in his self-rehabilitation. He has suffered great pain – greater than he had ever foreseen in the early cantos of the poem – but it has not been for nothing. He sees the time-transcending point of his efforts now: the unearthly force that will transport his spirit into a future his physical being will never reach:

> [For] there is that within me which shall tire
> Torture and Time, and breathe when I expire;
> Something unearthly, which they deem not of,
> Like the remember'd tone of a mute lyre,
> Shall on their soften'd spirits sink, and move
> In hearts all rocky now the late remorse of love.[17]

Knowing as much, Byron can release his hate for Annabella; slowly too he may get over the loss of Augusta and all it represents. Through the art of his words, perhaps even his actions, he will triumph over decay, like the stones of Venice. Thus he can now release a hero who was ever a product of adolescent lust for attention. He can release, too, his care for 'all-too-human' concerns, back to the element which has hurtled him forward and will carry him on:

> Roll on, thou deep and dark blue ocean – roll!
> Ten thousand fleets sweep over thee in vain;
> Man marks the earth with ruin – his control
> Stops with the shore; – upon the watery plain
> The wrecks are all thy deed, nor doth remain
> The shadow of man's ravage, save his own,

When, for a moment, like a drop of rain,
He sinks into thy depths with bubbling groan,
Without a grave, unknell'd, uncoffin'd, and unknown.[18]

Byron of course would not expire at sea himself:[19] it was left to his friend Shelley to do that. But from these lines we can see him readying himself philosophically to expire in whatever activity fate chooses for him. That it would be the fight for Greece is poetically proper. That he would be led to this via Shelley's acquaintance with the Greek leader, Prince Mavrocordato, and by Hobhouse's membership of the London Greek Committee nicely links the last act of his career to the presiding spirits over the last two cantos of his long poem: the expatriate's ultimate travelogue. But before he performs his own necessary *auto-da-fé*, Byron has something more worldly to accomplish. Defeated in London, he must now triumph in Italy over two elements which had fascinated yet eluded him there: woman and society. Thus back in Venice – and later in Ravenna, Pisa and Genoa – he pursues his 'last attachment', the most civilising affair of his career, the *cavaliere servente* relationship with Teresa Guiccioli, wife of one of Italy's grand insurgent nobles. Here Byron's expatriation anticipates the milieu of Stendhal or Henry James; and a great novel (for that is what *Don Juan* really is) proceeds from it.

Byron the adventurer and Byron the scholar continued to vie with and complement one another during these years of serious expatriation. The first took his pistol practice and riding every afternoon, swam from San Marco to the Lido, performed feats of prodigious love-making, and offered his authority to the nationalist cause with sufficient recklessness to attract the attention of the Austrian police. The second took up study of Armenian with the monks of San Lazzaro and later adapted local historical legends into his Venetian dramas, *Marino Faliero* and *I Due Foscari*. But the seriousness of this expatriation gradually brought a sea-change in Byron's temperament. What dropped away was the desperation for love, always part hostile, part self-protective. After the 'Alpine Journal' he was no longer writing with principal attention to women, or one woman, back home. He had either lost this audience or been betrayed by it, he believed; and when he turned to the subject of English women in *Don Juan* (as he had never directly before), it was a signal less of his nostalgia for them than of final detachment, thus some objectivity.

With the possible exception of the Countess of Blessington who sought out his company in Genoa, such women as he wished to impress now were Italian. English tourists enquired curiously about their exiled great poet; but apart from Shelley's circle who became his neighbours in Pisa, Byron avoided them. Nor did his correspondence with England extend much beyond his publisher and the old friends he had put in charge of his finances. All this must account in some part for the new, relaxed tone of his writings. Byron the adventurer and scholar is no longer a young man eager to impress with his energy and learning, but a man-of-the-world interested to find out the laws by which things work and wry in his reflections on them. Byron the lover is no longer obsessive or sentimental; he is chatty and lighthearted, regarding the matter principally as comedy of the bedchamber. Alienation in general gives way to philosophising. Bitterness is transformed into satire, about himself no less than everything that comes into his panoramic view.

Attitude is what makes *Don Juan* a great achievement. As acceptance has replaced hostility, so humour may drown out rage and tears. Sin is now taken as inevitable and universal, unlike in his Calvinist background; thus the author no longer has to waste spirit justifying his supposed criminality or 'evil'. Perhaps a notorious reputation was necessary to distinguish him as an outsider in England; but as a permanent expatriate he has become an outsider permanently. Moreover, one who has been known for 'sin', 'evil' and 'crime' in youth has more of a challenge, and perhaps more fun, in persuading society that he is really a hail-fellow-well-met. That being said, Byron's circumstances in Italy were also more secure than they had been in the north. Newstead was sold, relieving chronic debt; and when Lady Noel died there was further income, making him rich by the standards of time and place. Also, by 1817 Byron had three daughters, one legitimate whom he couldn't see, one incestuous whom he couldn't acknowledge and one illegitimate whom he sent to be brought up by nuns, only to have her die five years later.

These children may seem an ambiguous blessing. But having some blood attachment in the world must have eased the pain of forced separation from Augusta – which relationship itself may have been motivated in part by Byron's familial isolation after the death of his mother. More comforting still may have been his attachment to the Gamba family, parents and siblings of his mistress, which became quite intimate after she separated from her husband. Byron had never been part of a proper family: the Gambas were rich, aristo-

cratic intriguers with liberal sympathies, like himself; and he particularly liked Teresa's brother, Pietro, who went with him ultimately to Greece. In general, this attachment provided him with a
security that he may have been looking for subconsciously for years
in his adulterous affairs – with Caroline Lamb with her extended
Melbourne relations, or Lady Oxford with her many handsome children, the so-called Harleian Miscellany.[20] The purpose here is not to
psychoanalyse Byron nor to make out that his behaviour was always
a function of childhood loneliness, thus a quest for love. But some
reason must be given for some of his characteristic eccentricities; and
adultery, being a lifelong habit as well as principal subject of his later
poetry, is one of them.

In the sexual sphere adultery may be an equivalent – or at least an
analogue – to expatriation in the geographical. The expatriate wants
to free himself from the national attachment he was born with; at the
same time, he wants to sample other attachments he could have, if
free to choose; so he travels and perhaps settles for a time in this
country or that – until finally, if lucky, he creates a home in a place
which is sufficiently cosmopolitan or remote that he is able to fill it
with the properties, imaginative or otherwise, which will make it an
objective correlative for a better world. The adulterer likewise does
not want to be fully attached to or responsible for the woman he
sleeps with. He wants to create around her a universe not quite of
this world and its realities. Part of the game is for the woman to stay
married, so that her affair may remain laced constantly with idealism and fantasy. If the woman is suited to this sort of vicarious
existence, and is quite perfect in other ways, the lover may stay with
her. Otherwise, and more commonly especially in youth, he will
commit serial adulteries until, like the traveller, he may find that
exceptional situation which will allow him to imagine himself committed to no one or to many, free and secure at the same time.

Teresa Guiccioli provided Byron with a situation as close to this
ideal as he would get. But by the time he had formed his 'last
attachment' with her he had become sufficiently self-detected to
realise that the perfect attachment was a dream and that joy was in
the travelling. Thus the history of Don Juan, from his teenaged
adultery with Donna Julia, to his idyll with the Greek girl Haidée, to
his romp in the harem of the Sultan, to his calculating congress with
Catherine the Great. Finally, as Catherine's messenger and diplomat,
the young man travels to England where he has a liaison with
Aurora Raby, chaste it would seem, before disappearing from view

in a Gothic abbey, beckoned onward by a ghost. The amorous journey has no end, nor single Laura or Beatrice to guide it. For Byron,
experience is all; man is alone; there is no anagogical system of
grades to climb to the stars. But Juan does undergo an education, as
Byron himself has: experience is not hopeless; it is only mapless,
haphazard – a crooked path to a destiny unknown. So while the
story of Juan may be amusing, the chief interest of the poem is in its
author's remarks on the way. Without pattern, existence becomes at
best a narrative peppered with brilliant reactions.

Many of the concerns and prejudices of Byron's 'hot youth' are
still there. He still has no good word for Southey or Wordsworth,
Castlereagh or the British policy in Europe, Annabella, the British
climate or morals or critics or 'cant'. He still feels compelled to show
John Bull the world and by doing so show John Bull his own
philistinism and dullness. He still extols Mediterranean landscapes
and skies, food, languages, fashion, women, art, literature, libertine
and libertarian impulses, sex and sun and outlawry, noble primitivism and civilisation. He is in fact more outspoken about all these
now than ever; and when the poem was frowned on at home, even
by Hobhouse and Murray, he became truculent in defence of it.[21]
Byron *ex patria* finally becomes what the spoiled child wants to be:
an uninterrupted voice of opposition, with the vulgar, tyrannical
mother now entirely transformed into the only attachment on earth
the poet cannot escape: the origin of his language, his title, his
character and – if truth be told – success in the world. For Byron in
Don Juan finally discovers what an observer as acute as Goethe
already knew: that his was a quintessentially British mentality.[22]

There is no overt acknowledgement of this; but the fact that the
poem progresses to London, that treacherous 'Babylon' under soot
and fog, and stays in England for the last seven of its seventeen
cantos, may be an acknowledgement in itself. Nor does it dwell in
England only to afford the author opportunity to *épater* his own kind.
There is considerable affection under the satiric depictions of dinner
parties in town and weekends in country houses. There is also,
finally, an attempt to create the kind of comedy of manners which
the lionised Byron had avoided when he was living it himself, being
too awkward and serious. This comedy overshoots the mark at
times: a gaggle of bluestockings does not need to be named 'Miss
Reading /Miss Raw, Miss Flaw, Miss Showman, and Miss
Knowman':[23] the metaphysical verse-dramatist of *The Deformed
Transformed* was still no equal to his old friend Sheridan. What he

was, however, was an apostate trying at last to come to terms with the object of his apostasy: Britishness. And the fact that he actually has something complimentary to say about the English rose, seeking to explain her attractions in contrast to Continental counterparts, shows that he has now been away quite long enough to admit that the grass is not always greener elsewhere.

Indeed, he hints in the poem, as in contemporary letters, that he is growing weary of Italian 'operatics'.[24] A man cannot be a *cavaliere servente* forever – or at least he should not make it his sole profession. He should not, furthermore, rest the laurels of his career on scribbling either, however fine a poet he might know himself to be. A man, by the code Byron had grown up in – had been educated in and latterly made for himself – had to perform some action still: make some civic contribution at least, if not lead a Napoleonic cavalry charge. Thus among the Shelleyan expatriates in Pisa, Byron found himself underwriting *The Liberal*, a frankly political, oppositional magazine intended to upset Tory complacency at home. With the Gambas, he became involved in subversive activities, giving revolutionary advice and storing weapons in his *palazzo*. Finally, he accepted the offer of the London Greek Committee to be their representative on the spot in the land about which he had made his first, most impassioned declamations on Liberty. Having succeeded in the bedchamber, actually with Teresa and imaginatively with Juan, he now had his chance to prove himself among men: to perform a political act and perhaps affect history.

The Napoleon in Byron could not resist this. The Italians had muffed their revolution for the time being, and all indications were that the Greeks would do so as well. But where would he go now if not to some such adventure? And better Greece, the homeland of his revered classical education, than some alternative like Chile or Peru where he could only become the equivalent of an English gentleman-farmer and where there was no intellectual tradition. In Greece was a fight. The fight was for liberty. Liberty above all things was what Byron believed in and represented, unfree though he was in psychological respects and tied as he remained to his pedigree. Liberty, though, as he meant it, was a condition of the mind. The prisoner of Chillon had had it – he had had it indeed more than Childe Harold galloping across Estremadura or at sea. Liberty, Byron knew, was a spiritual condition – indeed, a metaphysical one. To have it in oneself was to be prepared for whatever destiny had in store. To have it with sufficient intensity to let it prevade all one's travels and works was to be prepared for transcendence. The admiration of posterity, where Time and Torture could not touch one, was thus the final destination and homeland. And for this expatriate the fight for Liberty, assuring his greatness, joined with literature to get him there.

3

Stendhal

Stendhal, whose real name was Henri Beyle, is the expatriate as dilettante. In France in his day, as in America and England in our own, this term carried opprobrium. Careerism characterised the Bonapartist era, class-consciousness the Bourbon Restoration, materialism the July monarchy. None of these suited Stendhal, though he wore different guises as readily as *noms de plume* and was a civil servant under Napoleon and Louis-Philippe. But *diletto* was always Henri Beyle's objective; thus Italy his chosen country. 'Rome, my country! city of the soul!' he would quote from Byron.[1] Florence and Naples also appealed to him; but above all he loved Milan. These Italian cities existed in both fact and imagination for him. Stendhal's Italy was the homeland of painting and opera, political intrigue and amorous passion: the Italy of Shakespeare's romances, of Ariosto and Tasso: the Italy which ravished Byron and became his home for seven years, giving birth to *Beppo*, *Childe Harold*, Canto IV and *Don Juan*. As Byron made his Italy an anti-England in order to show up the dullness of John Bull, so Stendhal made his into an anti-France, free of provincial viciousness and urban effeteness which he identified with his native Grenoble and Paris. Even more than Byron's, Stendhal's Italy is an ideal. Adapting his famous concept of 'crystallisation' from *De l'amour*, one might say that he crystallised on the country: that he literally created it out of a need to believe that such a land could exist and that he could inhabit it.

Stendhal was never thrown out of Paris as Byron imagined himself to have been out of London; but when he embarked on serious expatriation in 1814 he regarded it as unavoidable: 'I fell with Napoleon', he said.[2] Among other things, he was escaping massive debts and no prospect of a way to pay them off. Having reached a high level during the Empire, he was viewed, quite correctly, as too much of a Bonapartist to fill a position under the Bourbons. Milan, however, was not merely Beyle's Elba. While Napoleon returned to France for the Hundred Days, Beyle remained in his city pursuing a mistress. Nor was Milan Beyle's St Helena either, though his career there ended in the same year as Napoleon died on his last island. For Stendhal this magical city was a chosen destination: the better place he had kept in mind since first entering it with the French armies in 1800. There as a seventeen-year-old he had lost his aesthetic and sexual virginity, the first to an opera by Cimarosa, the second to the women welcoming the conquerors as their liberators from a despised *ancien régime*. To Milan Beyle returned whenever given leave during Napoleon's ascendance. His expatriation there thus never had the aura of an accident of wandering as Byron's to Venice sometimes did.

Measurement in terms of the two great NBs (Napoleon Bonaparte and Lord Noel-Byron) is implicit in Stendhal and useful to understanding his progress. Born the day after the latter, though five years earlier, he was swept up in Revolutionary fervour in youth. Spurning what he saw as the reactionary materialism of his father's house, he won a place to the *École polytechnique* in Paris to escape. Arriving in the metropolis a few days after the First Consul had himself declared dictator, young Beyle did not bother to pursue his studies but set himself up in a garret to win his own version of *gloire* as a great new classical playwright. Few teenagers (perhaps only Rimbaud) have ever achieved literary acclaim within months of putting pen to paper; thus, not surprisingly, the aspirant Racine found Paris impervious to his siege. Falling ill, he was rescued by maternal cousins, the Darus, whose eldest son, Pierre, was making a name for himself in the new bureaucracy of merit Napoleon was setting up. Always a realist as well as a dreamer, young Beyle conceded that a place of this kind might be a good thing for him too, providing experience, money and adventure while not preventing him from continuing his literary apprenticeship, as it were, at a pleasantly desultory pace.

Thus his life for the next fourteen years: a saga of travel across Europe with the troops, growing privilege as an Imperial commissar, continued attempts at playwrighting and notes toward an individual intellectual identity. As he came into the Emperor's service as an aspirant *literatus*, so he would depict the Napoleonic experience in writing as synonymous with the process of realising one's own destiny. Throughout his life Beyle worked on an unfinished *Vie de Napoléon*; he would dedicate his first important book to his fallen idol;[3] and he would make the dynamic example of the Corsican outsider a motive-force behind his greatest fictional character, the dark little meritocrat, Julien Sorel. To Beyle/Stendhal, Napoleon was a semi-divine, semi-demonic embodiment of tenacity, will, courage, self-determination – all the modern values which the Revolutionary age posed against the calcification and cynicism of the *ancien régime*. Napoleon was a force of Nature: an instinctive radical who could not be hemmed in by borders or laws: the quintessence of heroic restlessness, absurd when draped in Imperial regalia yet splendid above all when in his original persona of saviour of the Republic – the daring young general whose very image promised vigour, hope and beneficial change.

Beyle's important contact with Napoleon came on the road from Moscow: he served as quartermaster to the retreating French troops. The experience was a principal subject of his conversations with Byron when the two met in Milan in 1816. According to Hobhouse, with Byron at the time, 'M. de Beyle' reported that the Emperor had been so depressed and distracted that he would sign his despatches 'Pompey'.[4] Hobhouse had difficulty believing this and comments that 'M. de Beyle' (he had not yet become 'Stendhal' but styled himself with the bogus aristocratic preposition picked up when Imperial intendant in Brunswick) had 'a cruel way of talking'. This is perhaps a symptom of Beyle's own reduced state following Napoleon's demise. Like others who have found themselves on the wrong side in a war, the ex-quartermaster had to sing for his supper – indeed, for attention at all. This is not a condition from which Byron suffered, even at that fraught stage of his career. To impress the great poet no doubt struck Beyle as requiring more than pedestrian reminiscence. No doubt he embellished. No doubt, too, the gritty realism for which he would become famous, full as it was of drama and startling acts, arose in part from finding himself in this kind of position throughout his expatriate years.

The meeting with Byron came at the start of Beyle's new career as man-of-letters, and he had every reason to be in awe. Byron had all the things he wanted: acclaim as an author, success with women, a physiognomy as classically beautiful as his own was podgy and unprepossessing. Byron's character, on the other hand, struck Beyle as selfish: 'Byron thinks only of Byron', he would remark. This may, in fact, be less the sour grapes of an envious nature than disguised praise from the future creator of Julien Sorel. Quotations from favourite English authors would precede chapters in many of Beyle's books; and no author, not even the lauded Shakespeare, would appear more frequently than Byron. From Byron, Beyle quotes almost always from *Don Juan*, and this seems significant. Though he regarded Byron's hero as 'a mere Faublas' (insufficiently amoral

when compared to Francesco Cenci, for instance⁵), he doubtless found
in the poem's looseness of plot and exuberance of authorial comment
a model toward which to work. He would not achieve this in his first
novel, *Armance* (1827), which is nevertheless Byronic in a misanthropic, melancholic fashion (the hero commits suicide on his way to
fight for the Greeks). He would, however, reach something like it in
Le Rouge et le noir (1830) and yet more in his late masterpiece, *La
Chartreuse de Parme* (1839).

As Byron would realise his genius principally through *Don Juan*, so
Stendhal really became Stendhal finally through *La Chartreuse*, his
great book about an Italy of the imagination. Ironically, however,
this masterpiece, like Byron's, was written at a time when its author
was becoming disillusioned with Italy in fact – when love for the
chosen country had begun to give way to a tiring of 'Italian operatics', even to some longing for the salons of Paris which Beyle had
rejected years before. The watershed in his relationship with Italy
came at a similar date and for reasons similar to Byron's. Both men
were involved with women whose other associates were Carbonari;
thus both were harassed by the Austrian police. In contrast to Byron,
Stendhal was not a full *cavaliere servente*; and failure with his mistress
was an immediate cause of his departure, whereas satiety with Teresa
was only a contributing factor to the poet's. But both men's break
with Italy had to do with more than just politics and amour. Both
had attached themselves to the country out of a quest for happiness,
lightness, civilisation and the primitive in a combination not to be
found in the north. Both, however, were constitutionally restless;
and though travel, sex and writing were principally ways to subli-
mate traumatic experience, they were also always mere stratagems
to combat existential malaise.

Thus while Italy was the closest either could get to an earthly
paradise, even Italy's possibilities could become boring. Byron went
away to lead a political struggle in Greece; Stendhal's first idea on
returning to Paris was to dissipate his depression by assassinating
Louis XVIII.⁶ Neither left Italy expecting to find a better homeland;
both none the less had to leave. Nor was either departure simply to
gain new experience to stimulate inspiration, as might have been the
case with more single-mindedly ambitious writers. 'I write as one
smokes a cigar', Stendhal would claim, 'to pass the time.'⁷ His frequent abandonment of promising manuscripts, not least the volu-
minous unfinished novel *Lucien Leuwen* (1836), suggests that this was
more than just a dandy's quip. To a considerable degree Stendhal

shared Byron's contention that writing was not a proper profession, merely a way to 'conjugate the verb *ennuyer*' while waiting to lead a figurative cavalry charge. Neither writer was a self-conscious factory, like Balzac, that literary equivalent of the House of Rothschild. Both thought in terms of their full beings, their geniuses, before they thought of themselves as writers. Both, moreover, had the sense of being denied the place in worldly affairs to which genius entitled them.

This contributed to the waspish edge of much of what Stendhal, like Byron, produced. His barbs against flaccid romantic contemporaries – Chateaubriand and Lamartine, for example – were the equivalent of Byron's against 'the Lakers'. Each, as a liberal, was equally scornful of anything to do with the conservative order that Metternich and Castlereagh were imposing on Europe following 1815 (though neither was really a man of the people, both preferring the gay life of the dandy). In literature, both favoured eighteenth-century masters, in part as a way of putting themselves above the aesthetics of their times. Voltaire, Gibbon and Rousseau were great precursors for Stendhal as for Byron, though the romanticism of the latter he found dangerous and distorting. (In this connection, it seems doubtful that Byron would have found Rousseau so compelling were it not for the influence of Shelley, whose emotive nature Stendhal probably would have found tiresome.[8]) Both relied on scholarship, sometimes plagiarised in Stendhal's case, to give themselves authority early in their careers. Both furthermore never tired of the impulse to shock, Stendhal's bloody Italian tales written in Paris in the 1830s being in many ways an equivalent to Byron's Turkish tales in London in the 1810s.

Each displayed a manic need for literary fantasising when stuck in a fixed place, especially when that fixed place was the metropolis of his native country. For each, the most sustained bouts of creativity might be seen as imaginative compensation for feelings of being trapped. In antipathetic situations each sought to wrap himself in an aura of mystery, both personally and via fictive alter egos. Each also manufactured an atmosphere of sexual obsession, sometimes so extreme that it could only spill over into self-parody. All these things were symptoms of each author's need for expatriation, as well as causes of it. Neither could stand the idea of being tied to one place forever, any more than to one liaison. The perfect homeland, like the perfect woman, could only be found finally in the imagination. Somewhere far from the metropolitan *haut monde* – perhaps even beyond Mediterranean *dolce far niente* – stood some Olympus or Arcadian grove where dwelt what Lady Oxford had called 'the gods in Lucretius'[9] and Stendhal referred to as 'the happy few.'[10] Thus both authors bequeathed their memory to a non-parochial posterity, Byron's 'Time and Torture' finding its counterpart in the coterie Stendhal predicted would begin reading him around 1880 – as it in fact did, Nietzsche being among the first.

Both men were ever in pursuit of love and of belonging to some higher company. In this world, however, neither finally wanted to belong to anything but his destiny. That said, one should also point out that Stendhal, like Byron in *Childe Harold*, Canto IV (a work written following Byron's acquaintance with the Frenchman), identified closely with aesthetic and historical tradition. Most of his work other than fiction is concerned with music or painting; and monuments of unageing intellect had transcendent importance to him. It is almost as if being unbeautiful, unlike Byron, he had to find in the arts compensation for what he could never so easily find in life. In this respect his Italy is more artful and more fully created than that of the happy lover of La Guiccioli and tireless jokester of *Don Juan*. Stendhal's Italy is a land not only of the imagination but a place ever full of such intrigue and beauty that even a podgy, unprepossessing creature like himself might never lose touch with his sensual, passionate nature. As such, his Italy would remain the blessed country – but blessed principally because other lands had not yet learned what they ought: to aspire to its condition of epicurean perfection as well.

Why did Stendhal despise France? Was it mere anti-chauvinism? The lifelong petulance of a son seeking to distinguish himself from an odious father figure? There is something to this. Beyle's mother, who died in childbirth when he was seven, was always the favoured parent for him. He made much of an Italian strain in her ancestry – the source, he believed, for the *'espagnolisme'* of his own nature: his love for 'the land where the orange tree grows'. His father was matter-of-fact whereas his mother's family was by turns philosophical (his grandfather) or literate and dandified (his uncle). In a fragment of autobiography Stendhal tells us that as a boy he longed to possess his mother's body and cover it with kisses. Later he found an image of perfect happiness in a painting in his grandfather's house which showed three naked women bathing in a stream. Readings of semi-pornographic novels in his uncle's possession complete a picture of powerful, restless psychosexual urges, all relating in some way to his mother's sphere. In Freudian terms, we may recognise symptoms of a classic Oedipus complex.[11] In terms adapted from Freud by Herbert Marcuse, we might see the type of Orpheus-Narcissus: that personality which seeks always for pleasure and finds it only in sex, art, play, memory and death – elements of 'being' rather than 'becoming' such as found extreme expression in the drop-out cults of the 1960s.[12]

Throughout his life, the Orphic-Narcissistic impulse in Stendhal fought for dominance over the matter-of-fact professionalism he inherited from his father and found in the 'systems' of both the provinces and Paris. The struggle gave birth to a cult of the exceptional individual. Only such a person might have a chance to break out of social imperatives and get the *diletto* he wanted, or at least go in quest of it. Stendhal's digust with the provinces and later with Paris can be seen as an extension of teenaged rationalisations for leaving his father's house. Thus the essential deficiencies of these places are his father's writ large: excessive materialism and stunted imagination. Conversely, the virtues of the chosen place (*espagnolised* Italy) are the aestheticism and pleasure-seeking he projected on to the memory of his mother and her family. This said, we must not fall into the fallacy of some psychological criticism and imagine that because Stendhal's rejection of his *patria* had to do with elements of adolescent wish-fulfilment it was intellectually bogus. If the wish for something better were always interpreted in this way, no critical idealism would be allowed to grow up.

In fact, Stendhal's criticism of France was ameliorative in intent and no less vehement when a civil servant of 50 than a revolutionary fantasist of 15. The great novelistic treatments of it are *Le Rouge et le noir* and *Lucien Leuwen*, both written in middle age. The second cannot qualify as a great novel, being unfinished; the first, having been accepted in that category for a century, deserves our attention not so much as an expatriate book as an exposition of why its author should have become an expatriate. From the first chapters of the first volume, which essay the shortcomings of provincial life, to those of the second, which preview the shortcomings of Paris, the novel sets the reader up to believe that no man of merit can arise and exist in the France of 1830 in the way that Bonaparte had been able to do in 1800 and that therefore the only successful means to self-realisation must be flight, escape or retreat. The fact that Julien Sorel ends in the solitude of a prison cell is appropriate to a novel concentrated almost claustrophobically on one country and time. There is no scope here for consideration of foreign alternatives such as Stendhal took in his life. However, reading the novel against Stendhal's life, it is clear that the need for another country – a better culture – is implicit.

What is this France of *Le Rouge et le noir*? First, in the provinces, it is a culture driven by greed – greed expressed chiefly by obsession with property: speculation in real estate such as Stendhal's father went in for, squandering a small fortune, thus bequeathing his children a legacy principally of debt. Living on a soldier's small pension, Stendhal had counted on some inheritance to pay his way as a writer; and ten years after his father's death he was still irritated enough by not having received it that it colours his picture of Julien's single parent (the mother, as in Stendhal's own case, is dead). Papa Sorel's only interest in his son is how to make money out of him. The boy is bookish and frail, thus cannot be made into a useful workman like his brothers; so when the town mayor comes looking for a tutor for his children, Sorel jumps at the chance to sell Julien off. The mayor, Renal, is bourgeois where Sorel is only a peasant-made-good. But this does not mean that Julien's elevation is going to expose him to superior ethics. Renal is merely a higher-class example of provincial faults – a further characterisation of traits which Stendhal found repellent in his own father.

The mayor throws stones at a peasant girl who wanders on to his land. He rails against the poor and the Jacobins – anyone who does not thrive on the status quo which has raised him to privilege. Conventional and fastidious, he has a sense of show, but not of aesthetics. He complains of the cost of keeping the walnut grove which his wife, his children and Julien like to walk through. The cordon of his office constitutes his sense of fashion. Music and art have no place in his consciousness, always a deficiency *chez* Stendhal. He is too talkative – a characteristic which plagues all provincials. He discards old friends for being on the wrong side of political events (thus, ironically, leaving himself friendless when his rival Valenod collects 'the scum of all classes' against him). These are his outer faults. On the inside he is no better. He views women as childish, inferior creatures who make scenes and feign illnesses to get their way; and when confronted with the prospect of Julien making love to his wife, he is horrified, not because he is losing a beloved but because his routine may be upset – he may have to undertake the tedious task of breaking in a new wife, and he will lose the benefit of a legacy his wife will inherit from a rich aunt.

For Stendhal, love can only be understood by people of imagination and passion. In Renal, these qualities extend no further than paranoia over whether someone in the community might be doing better than he. Public opinion is what he fears: loss of face. This makes him a man who can have no real happiness in Stendhal's view. Still, Renal is more sympathetic than Valenod, Papa Sorel and others in the province, a fact which emphasises how really awful life in such places must be. What then of the alternatives – the great world and Paris? Do they provide better prospects? At first Julien thinks so. He leaves Renal's to enter a seminary, the Church having attracted him through the beauty of a ceremony he has seen. A young bishop has given him the idea that the higher the rank, the finer the sensibility. In fact, this is a stock set-up for disillusionment. In the seminary, Julien discovers that distinction is not wanted. Coming first in catechism is considered bad form, too much thinking a sin, knowledge suspect. Submission is everything, jealousy the reward for too much fluency, beauty or preferment. The church is no better than the society around it; and Julien's disquiet in it is a prelude to what he will find in the highest sphere he attains.

This is at the Hôtel de la Mole in Paris. On account of his prodigious memory displayed in the seminary, but which went unappreciated there, Julien is hired by a grand marquis to be his secretary. The hereditary aristocrat may give some value to the Bonapartist ideal of individual merit, but this does not mean that Julien will be accepted in his rarefied milieu. Class and birth take the place here of money and property in the provinces. A fixed order deriving from the Middle Ages is the ideal, urbanity and discretion its accoutrements. The Marquise de la Mole has a mind so fine that it cannot be violated by an idea.[13] The young men around her limit their attention to manners and dandyish quips. Derision, Julien finds, is their secret weapon – the equivalent of public opinion back home. All is posed against genius and expression of true feeling. Loud talk is *démodé*: people whisper and plot. Even the servants have disdain for the new man: is he not merely an unpedigreed *paysan*? In social gatherings, Julien's memory is shown off like the trick of a dancing dog. No one is interested in intellectual conversation; German mysticism is discussed only because it cannot be understood. Anything Jacobin or liberal is suspect. Meanwhile, a hail-fellow-well-met posing as a liberal in the street turns out to be a pickpocket.

The Hôtel de la Mole suffers from 'mental asphyxia', Julien concludes. This does not surprise him, however. By the time he has entered Paris he is no longer naïve. Like Byron's Don Juan entering

London, he finds the city from a distance unimpressive. Before settling in he already classifies it as the premier centre of hypocrisy. In
the Hôtel de la Mole, his initial pleasures are 'precautions': fencing
and pistol practice. Gradually, however, something more insidious
begins to take his attention: underneath politeness, ennui and reactionary posturing lurks a fundamental bad temper, a longing for
drama, a secret hankering after the unexpected. Though the system
ensures that no Napoleon may rise again to supplant it, it is far from
happy with itself. In its heart of hearts, this *haut monde* longs for
something or someone to surge up and act out its own latent urge for
self-destruction. We have entered an era in which 'joy has become a
subtle form of pain', as Arthur Symons would say in comparing
Wagner to Beethoven.[14] Stendhal's Paris of 1830 anticipates the era
which Stendhal predicted would be the first to appreciate him: that
of Wilde's *Salomé* and the fragmented music of Richard Strauss.

Chief representative of the decadent soul of this order is Mathilde
de la Mole, daughter of the house. Mathilde despises the age she
lives in and dreams of escaping into the epoch of Catherine de
Medici; then murder and elopement broke out in the de la Mole
family, and convention was shattered by passionate instinct. Mathilde
has no time for the mannered bitchery of the titled fops around her;
she longs for some ruthless plotter to carry her off in the manner of
a Renaissance *condottiere*. Machiavelli's is the philosophy behind her
actions; this is what attracts her to Julien, who alone shares in her
general contempt and is dedicated to his own advancement. The fact
of his strangeness in class and origin also contributes to fascinate the
young jade, and she works to make him love her. Mathilde's idea of
love is artificial, of course: copied from her fantasy of the mores of
her preferred *siècle*. She plays cat-and-mouse with her prey until
Julien has to resort to the absurd Korasoff's method to win her: a
programme for appearing to be in love with another woman. That
Julien falls in with Mathilde's game demonstrates two things: the
extent to which she is the most vital prospect Paris has to offer and
the extent to which life in such a milieu can only degrade a man,
alienating him from all sincere emotion and causing him to operate
cruelly.

Mathilde is fascinating; she is also capricious, destructive and
emotionally sado-masochistic. Stendhal does not blame her for this;
indeed, his identification of her with Renaissance Italian models
suggests some admiration; and when she defies her father's wrath
and proposes to elope with Julien to a part of the country 'as beau-

tiful as Italy', Stendhal surely means us to view her as taking a step toward positive self-realisation. But if Mathilde is more imaginative than the milieu she comes from, her behaviour is none the less appalling. That she is a Salomé is established by her expropriation of Julien's head after he is guillotined. Melodrama is her mode; the life she offers is not one a sensible, sensitive young man could take up. Thus as he contemplates death, Julien finds comfort not in her, but in the memory of Mme de Renal. The latter is like him: a victim in the first place of the materialism and lack of imagination of the provinces, embodied in an odious father/husband figure. Mme de Renal is the lost mother whose breasts and body Julien once possessed. His fixation on her as he awaits death underlines Stendhal's radical restriction in *Le Rouge* of pleasure to the maternal principle.

Mathilde intuits some of the power of her rival. Meanwhile, she uses her formidable imagination and connections to try to gain Julien's release. This is a measure of her development toward sincerity. But as Valenod and other hate-filled figures of the province prove more successful in assuring Julien's death than metropolitan friends do in saving his life, so the provincial wife triumphs in the end over the Parisian heiress. Mme de Renal has the power of genuineness, whereas Mathilde can never free herself entirely of the tendency to manipulate. Mme de Renal's great sole imaginative tool is her passion; her love is devoid of vanity; her sense of the material world only exists as a reflection of the tenderness and ecstasy in her soul. As the single mother-figure in the book, she inevitably becomes the landscape toward which Julien longs to travel in his mind. In an odious fatherland where no acceptable 'orange tree' alternative exists, this is the natural trajectory of Orpheus-Narcissus: toward some human correlative of *dolce far niente*, the womb-tomb which memory and solitude reveal as blessed finally. Death – the ultimate expatriation.

But one must not overdo this talk of 'easeful death'. Stendhal was not really half in love with it, as Byron in self-pitying phases. Nor was Stendhal's expatriation ever a quest for oblivion like Byron's, or a demand for love from back home. On the contrary, expatriation, travel and Italy provided him with reasons to live – they were the great prizes in this world – and the only suicidal period of his career came when he was forced to leave his chosen country and return in failure to Paris. We have established that Stendhal was too much of a realist to imagine that the perfect place could exist finally, even in the Milan he had loved. But Stendhal was not himself Julien Sorel; thus it was not for him to long to retreat to a prison, or even an ivory tower, willingly. He was committed to the world of vision, touch, song, taste – Hobhouse complained that he seemed ' a sensualist'; and if Byron's puritanical companion meant this to denote sin, then sinner Stendhal happily was. Given as much, his great land of the senses – Italy of both fact and imagination – could never be expelled from its high place in his *Weltanschauung*, no matter how cross he was at being thrown out of Milan or how bored he became during his last years as French consul at Civitavecchia.[15]

Italy remained the one reliable earthly correlative for where a satisfying life might be lived. But Italy as Stendhal wrote about it increasingly diverged from how he saw it in fact. This is crucial to understanding *The Charterhouse of Parma*,[16] whose plot was adapted from a history of the Farnese family in the sixteenth century and whose inception grew out of translations and adaptations of a number of gory tales of that time. In his final expatriation Stendhal became like Mathilde de la Mole: a yearner to inhabit some different century. As France after 1815 had come on evil days, so Italy seemed to be returning as well to the effeminate manners and institutions of the eighteenth century – indeed, to the effeteness which had afflicted it since Renaissance energy had been dissipated by the advent of the Spanish Habsburgs. Still, Stendhal believed that the Italian people retained in themselves the blood of heroic times and that conditions of climate and race meant that this could never die out entirely. He had seen evidence of this, or imagined he had, in the Milanese of 1800. Their underlying amoral exuberance was resuscitated for a time, he believed, by the arrival of the ultimate modern *condottiere*, the man whom threatened aristocrats liked to disparage with the Italianate pronunciation of his name: 'Buonaparte'.

It is for this reason that Stendhal begins his book with the entry of French troops into his favourite city; and this fact is a sure sign that the locus of the novel will be partly in nostalgia – in the ageing author's memory and desire. The opening is followed shortly by the famous tableau of Waterloo, making clear yet further that the Italy Stendhal sets out to reincarnate was generated in his mind in part by the best in contemporary French experience. In specific, Napoleon looms over the proceedings, as over the imaginings of Julien Sorel. The hero of *The Charterhouse*, Fabrizio del Dongo, is born of a liaison between an unhappily married Marchesa of the *ancien régime* and an officer of the liberating armies. At the age of 17 (the same age as Stendhal when he left his father's house), Fabrizio rushes off to join the Emperor for the Hundred Days, taking the appearance of an eagle in the sky as a sign of the destiny he must follow. For following it he is exiled from his home state, which like the rest of Italy reverts to the *ancien régime* on Napoleon's fall. Thus begin wanderings which will lead to Fabrizio's arrest and incarceration in the Farnese tower of the principality of Parma.

Fabrizio's arrest is ostensibly for the murder of a second-rate actor; actually it is political in intent. His problems are set in train in part by his titular father and elder brother, both adherents of the *ancien régime*. Thus we see his situation mirroring the problems of post-Napoleonic Italy as Stendhal interpreted them: a Bonapartist spirit is being snuffed out by the re-establishment of old father-authority figures. Good and bad in the novel are based on where characters stand in relation to this. The chief heroine, the Duchessa Sanseverina, is blessed symbolically by the fact that she was once married to an officer in Napoleon's army; and the wily Count Mosca, prime minister of Parma, is forgiven his support for despotism in part by his recognition that the court of Prince Eugene Beauharnais, Napoleon's regent in Milan, is the best recent example of good government. Stendhal's political prejudices are apparent throughout the novel, a main purpose of which is to satirise the restored *ancien régime* through the microcosm of the court of Parma, ruled by the Princes Ernesto-Ranuccio IV and V. That said, the novel is by no means predominantly a social critique, as we have argued of *Le Rouge et le Noir*.

Italy has fallen on bad times; yet what Stendhal presents is a recipe for how the Renaissance/Bonapartist spirit might live, even flourish, under inimical conditions. In contrast to the first part of *Le Rouge*, most of the characters here, even minor ones, are moved by passion, not greed. The poor are neither despised nor ignored, as in the milieu of M. de Renal. Convention does not rule the principals, nor does vanity or *amour propre*, so characteristic of Hôtel de la Mole. Fabrizio, the Duchessa, Mosca, Clelia Conti – all are motivated by love, often to the exclusion of all other considerations; and their relentless intrigues and manipulations are undertaken ever with this as object. The Duchessa throws away a fortune in diamonds to achieve the release of Fabrizio from prison. Mosca forswears position and material gain in order to be near the Duchessa in the end. Even the two Princes Ernesto-Ranuccio are touched by the atmosphere of obsession: both make fools of themselves for the Duchessa, whom both are imaginative enough to realise is the single magnetic and independently spirited creature in their otherwise conventional court.

The Duchessa is not a self-conscious actress like Mathilde de la Mole; she is heroic and decisive from the first – nor does it take a pistol-shot to make her so, as in the case of Mme de Renal. Count Mosca is never moved by empty fashion; music, art and *amour* are living pleasures for him, as for his alter ego Stendhal. Fear of slander does not paralyse these courtiers: unafflicted by the narcissism of *Le Rouge* each will sacrifice his reputation at a moment's notice, if it proves necessary. Only minor figures, like Rassi, the police chief, or General Conti, Fabrizio's gaoler, are touched significantly by ready-made ambitions, Rassi's to be a baron and Conti's to marry his daughter to the wealthiest noble in the land. Though class counts at court, none of the principals is finally moved by it, as the various love-interests show. The Duchessa is mad about Fabrizio, who is dishonoured; she also has a soft spot for the poet, Ferrante Palla, who lives like a savage for political reasons. Clelia Conti also loves Fabrizio, though she knows of him only as a murderer; nor does she have the slightest interest in the rich Marchese whom her father has selected for her.

Even the church here is different from *Le Rouge*: Fabrizio is defended by the Archbishop, and the people flock to his sermons because they are full of personal suffering. Knowledge – that materialism of the mind – is not a means to success here, as for Julien Sorel: Fabrizio is empty-headed but it does not matter – he has genuine passion, which is what counts. There is even less intellectual conversation at the court of Parma than at Hôtel de la Mole; but because it is so full of intrigue and desire there is no question of 'mental asphyxia'. Above all, the difference between this world and that of *Le Rouge* is that here love is real, not artificial or copied from some prior *siècle*. The quest of Fabrizio, driving force of his progress, is to find true love somewhere; and when he finally locates it – in prison of all places – it is a passion without the pathology that afflicts Julien to the end. Julien's turning to Mme de Renal is proof of his failure: reversion to a mother-principle cannot be real love – it is, as we have said, a function of desire to retreat from the world, into the womb and death. Fabrizio's turning to Clelia instead of the Duchessa is a testament to his success in finding, for a moment, a genuine equal and soul-mate.

What is the result of all this passion in *The Charterhouse*? Energy. Change. Everything is stirred up. Fabrizio escapes from prison. He has secret trysts with Clelia and fills her with child. The child is involved in a tug-of-war between real and apparent fathers, a return of the situation of Fabrizio's own parenting, ostensibly by an aristo-crat of the *ancien régime*, actually by a Napoleonic spirit. In part as a result of these continuing antagonisms, the child dies. Clelia follows soon after. Fabrizio retires to the Charterhouse of Parma where he himself will die within two years. The Duchessa, separated from the only man she has loved and saddened by his devotion to another, retires to Naples under the protection of Count Mosca, who still adores her and wants nothing more than to surround her with the delights of music art, conversation and fine cuisine. But the Duchessa is too much a creature of passion to be satisfied with the safe, civi-lised pleasures of dilettantism; thus she too expires before her time. The Count returns to Parma and his old job as prime minister; he opens the prisons and generally repeals the excesses of Rassi and Conti who have ruled in his absence. Thus it would seem that, in a political sense at least, Stendhal's microcosm of a real/ideal world can live 'happily ever after'.

The dénouement of the novel is sketched at the most breakneck of Stendhalian breakneck speeds. Owing to limitations imposed by the publisher, there was no space for further narrative or moral sum-mary; thus posterity has been left to debate whether the whole has been hopeful – whether, in short, there has been too much death and disappointment for the novel to stand as an adequate model for how life ought to be lived. About this it must be said that the plot does retain much from its Renaissance sources in the way of abduction, poisoning, Machiavellian plotting and duplicity. Added to these are the political tableaux of a potentially bloody revolt led by Ferrante Palla, the threat of suppression by Rassi's secret police and the assassination of Ernesto-Ranuccio IV for having defied the Duchessa. Stendhal's obvious taste for such material has led high-minded crit-ics to attack. Henry James, for instance, found *The Charterhouse* to be the opposite of a civilised ideal:

[Stendhal's] notion was that *passion*, the power to surrender oneself sincerely and consistently to the feeling of the hour, was the finest thing in the world, and it seemed to him that he had discovered a mine of it in the old Italian character. . . . It is easy to perceive that this doctrine held itself quite irresponsible to our old moralistic canons, for *naïveté* of sentiment in any direction, combined with great energy, was considered absolutely its own justification. In the *Chartreuse de Parme*, where everyone is grossly immoral, and the heroine is a kind of monster, there is so little attempt to offer any other, that through the magnificently sustained pauses of the narrative we feel at last the influence of the writer's cynicism, regard it as amiable, and enjoy serenely his clear vision of the mechanism of character, unclouded by the mists of prejudice. Among writers called immoral there is no doubt that he best deserves the charge; the others, beside him, are spotlessly innocent.[17]

Geoffrey Strickland suggests that this assessment ought to carry the qualification of Ezra Pound: when talking of French literature, Pound observed, James always tried to 'square all things to the ethical standards of a Salem mid-week Unitarian prayer meeting'.[18] Living through the First and Second World Wars, Pound rejected the lofty, moralistic detachment of cloistered Victorians; and the fact that he lived through the Revolution and Napoleonic period is a principal reason why Stendhal seems 'immoral' to them. But how could an author who had seen so much death and mayhem present a tidy, well-mannered world? The great achievement of *The Charterhouse* may be that, given Stendhal's experience, it is so comparatively unviolent. One assassination, after all, is the total of significant willed deaths. Moreover, the man assassinated has set in motion many autocratic acts of unfairness, not least the imprisonment of the hero, which would have led to his poisoning had not the Duchessa, Mosca and Clelia moved to prevent it. James's sensibility led him to leave undiscussed the autocracy and injustice from which Europe was still struggling to emerge. Nothing similar to the Revolutionary and Napoleonic excesses had occurred near him in his youth (though a less-detached writer might have been more affected by the American Civil War). Thus there was little instinct in him to glorify elemental passion and force such as Stendhal found essential for improvement in his world.

Stendhal's Italy is centuries and cultures remote from the touristic Romes and Tuscanies of James's grand excursions. Italy for James was in any case never an earthly paradise or exemplary better place; it was simply one of several great foreign cultures to which one might expatriate oneself for a time – 'foreign' here having the Anglo-Saxon connotation of perhaps finally somewhat inferior. James's search was for something different from Stendhal's anyway. He was looking for the ultimate in civilised behaviour whereas Stendhal still suspected that the 'best people' were partisans of the *ancien régime*. Stendhal was modern, even contemporary, in his desire for Truth over Form. 'He had the courage of his complications', said Paul Bourget;[19] and he would express them outright, whereas James would veil his under silken qualification. Stendhal's rawness, rebellion and resentment would have defined him as 'unbalanced' had he lived in some American suburb of the 1950s. In his happy indulgence of his status as misfit, he is a kind of cultivated, European James Dean – with whom, after all, he shares beliefs in energy, passion, partisanship to the individual's cause and hatred of fixed authority, hypocrisy, convention and cant; also the 'flip side' to all this, the lassitude of *diletto* and the blithe irresponsibility of Orpheus-Narcissus – Fabrizio in scornful retreat from the world, masturbatorily alone with memory and desire, or Count Mosca trying to narcotise himself with the sensuality of high art.

To defenders of the social norm such as Henry James it is not suprising that Stendhal should have seemed 'immoral'. But to less 'establishment' commentators like the French socialist critic and politician Léon Blum, he seemed ambiguous as well. Though admiring Stendhal for his championing of the individual versus the bureaucratic state, Blum regarded the philosophy of 'beylisme' as potentially 'toxic':

> A self-sufficient imagination, a distaste for everything which one considers beneath oneself, a lazy reverie, out of humour with real life . . . . The drug was heady, to say the least, and the future will judge, according to the results, if one must consider it as tonic or toxic.[20]

This has much truth, though one might well ask what writer of fiction is ever entirely in 'humour with real life' – if he were, why would he bother to create imaginary worlds? Henry James, for example, can hardly be seen as in humour with the 'real' if reality begins with proletarian conditions such as those that preoccupied Zola. It is doubtless true that, in *The Charterhouse* at least, Stendhal's version of the world is more poetic than 'real'; and if the poetic is always in some sense a dream, then he must have been 'out of touch'. But as to 'lazy reverie': in *The Charterhouse* this is confined mostly to moments of bobbing about in a boat on the northern Italian lakes – places of exquisite, transcendental beauty, where Fabrizio is allowed for a moment to get in touch with his individual soul. Are we meant to see in this something pernicious? Perhaps. Perhaps his reverie, followed by manic, passionate action, can be interpreted as an anticipation of the psychology of the German *Wandervögel* of the 1920s, who would allow himself to be swept up in the blond supermanism of the Nazis.

Such an interpretation would, however, require a pretty thorough reassessment of European literature at large. Moments in the perfect pastoral followed by passionate action are typical of most of Shakespeare's romantic comedies, for instance; but are we to see *As You Like It* and *The Tempest* as potentially 'toxic'? Some might believe so. (There is the argument about Prospero's mistreatment of Caliban as a kind of advance rationale for the white man's treatment of darker minions.) Stendhal would have dismissed such a view. He regarded these plays as among Western civilisation's 'monuments of unageing intellect', and he admired their morality inasmuch as it attempted to resolve the disparate impulses and demands inherent in microcosms of modern society. Something similar is the moral argument in favour of *The Charterhouse*. The impression it leaves is not of tragedy so much as of attempted resolution of terribly competing impulses. It is a 'great' novel precisely because it is so 'real' in its sprawling cast of characters, it complexity of ethical conflict, its un-small, unrestricted, unrefined and mannered scope. This too is what distinguishes it from so many novels of the Victorian period, reaching their apogee in James, which – like the plays of French classicism – deal parochially in problems of a *haut monde*.[21]

Whereas James undertook his expatriation in part to escape the largeness and squalor of Whitman's America, Stendhal undertook his in part because he knew that poetic truth could not be defined by the narrow values of post-Napoleonic France. Having said as much, one must also point out that the happiest moments of his expatriation involved a majestic calm similar to that which his American successor would aspire to. Consider, for instance, the opening of his autobiographical fragment, *La Vie de Henry Brûlard*:

> The sunshine was magnificent. A hardly perceptible sirocco wind caused a few small white clouds to rise above Mount Albaro, a delightful warmth was in the air, I felt happy to be alive. . . . The whole of ancient and modern Rome, from the Appian Way with the ruins of tombs and aqueducts to the magnificent garden of the Pincia built by the French, spreads out before me . . . .[22]

The pursuit of such moments – a condition of Jamesian repose – was a motive force of Stendhal's lifelong quest:

> I have searched for beautiful landscapes, with an exquisite sensibility; it is for that reason alone that I have travelled. . . . [A lovely landscape] has the same effect on my soul as a skilfully handled bow on a resonant violin; . . . it enchances my delight and makes misfortune more tolerable.[23]

The difference is that Stendhal was too in touch with the real world of men, war, politics, failed affairs and the rest for such a condition to be adequate for him all the time, or even desirable. His expatriation was also in pursuit of a fuller integration and acceptance of all kinds of experience.

> It was only when he discovered Italy [biographer Gita May goes on] that he became esthetically reconciled with the underprivileged inhabitants of the slums. In the ragged Roman urchins roaming the streets of the city, he sensed that irrepressible passion and psychic energy, albeit in raw form, that he admired in Italian opera, art and mores.[24]

The ex-soldier of the armies of the Revolution was too much of a believer in '*liberté, egalité, fraternité*' to retreat entirely to the Jamesian tower, or even his own version of it – some palace of music and Art. (The American master, curiously philistine in aspects of culture not tied to social behaviour, would show less appreciation for such a 'dilettantish' paradise.) Stendhal felt compelled to incorporate into his fictive world experience like that of the soldiers he had seen dismembered and dying on the road from Moscow; thus Fabrizio's reactions at Waterloo are no less important in his work than the mannered intrigues of Prince Ernesto's court. Thus the dispossessed Ferrante Pallas and class-excluded Julien Sorels are his heroes, not the more privileged alter egos of his kind – Mosca in hedonistic pursuit of art, love and pleasure. This is his morality. To some it might seem that, in its sympathy for society's victims, it is more 'moral' than what can be found in James. At the same time, because they are never mere victims, crushed and despairing over their condition, Stendhal's characters might be said to show more moral fibre than the pathetic masses for whom sentimental socialists would seek to provide paternalistic answers – the tradition of Hugo, Zola and Léon Blum.

Stendhal's work has given rise to charges of self-indulgence – wish-fulfilment as we have said. On inspection, however, it provides its own implicit critique of himself as dilettante; nor was that persona finally more than one of several masks he held up against a difficult world. But even as dilettante it was not enough for him to aspire to a condition of pure civility, as for James. The condition he sought to realise in his art was an opera by Mozart or a painting by Correggio. But Mozart portrays the horrific end of Don Giovanni, the 'immorality' of Count Almaviva, the chiaroscuro of Sarsastro's mystery rites; and Correggio is a master of the fleshly and sensual – not atmospheres toward which James would aspire, any more than some tableau of revolt by Delacroix, also favoured by Stendhal. The artistic ideal toward which the so-called dilettante worked is complex, ambiguous and more in tune with the turbulent Italianate tradition than what would come after, at least in a high, moralistic, Anglo-Saxon sphere. Even more than Stendhal's French contemporaries, James would eschew 'the primitive energy of the Roman populace and of which the Italian brigands offered spectacular examples'.[25]

Stendhal's love for these is the ultimate reason why 'moral' critics must find him suspect, while a 'transvaluer' like Nietzsche would have such respect for him. Supreme emphasis on energy and passion almost inevitably leads to celebration of crime. Julien Sorel's shooting of Mme de Renal is the famous instance of this: Stendhal actually created his hero out of a newspaper report of a petty murder in the Dauphiné. In *The Charterhouse*, the Duchessa's commission of the assassination of Ernesto IV is the most important incident – the one which offers evidence for James's description of her as 'a kind of monster'. But these crimes are small in the scheme of the worlds in which they are undertaken. Furthermore, they are morally purposeful and instructive in their effects – one could even say ameliorative. Thus while they might be cited in evidence against Stendhal, they also underline his belief that the world can only be made right by a renaissance of more unrestricted self-expression, more appetite in the human, more bestiality of a kind even, certainly more animal sensuality and basic passionate reactivity, such as he found in Italy.

Regarding the cultures of the north, he shared with Nietzsche a hearty contempt for what he saw as their boringness, hypocrisy and coercive self-righteousness. The linkage may make it tempting to see him as a precursor of fascist enthusiasms – even to see in Julien Sorel a prediction of Hitler, or in Count Mosca a preview of the Cianos and Ribbentrops of twentieth-century neo-Bonapartist states. This is unfair, I think. What Stendhal loved best, what drew him out of the cold and control of the north, was a vision of creative anarchy. Nor must this anarchy be seen as bloodthirsty. The Waterloo chapter of *The Charterhouse* is one of many tableaux which show how Stendhal was revolted by the real blood and suffering he had seen first-hand in organised war. His anarchism is that of the long tradition of Utopian libertarians. He went to Italy to achieve his own version of 'the long summer's afternoon of freedom' which goes back to myths of Arcadian Greece.[26] His legacy is a plea for the northern races to look south to the 'lands where the orange tree grows', where there is sun and fine art, passionate love and intrigue unfettered by false vanity, and to achieve liberation thereby. The alternative is to be damned to the condition of Mme de Renal before Julien Sorel wounds her: a life of quiet desperation.

4
James

Henry James is the unavoidable, monumental, perhaps even arche-typal expatriate writer. However, far more than Byron or Stendhal, he will always seem somewhat parochial in his concerns. Though he had 'the productivity of genius'[1] in greater supply than either, though he dedicated himself to his art with more single-mindedness than even his revered Balzac, his scope was radically restricted. He him-self would complain of his deficient knowledge of 'Downtown':[2] of business, which by the end of the nineteenth century was replacing war and politics as the arena of Napoleonic endeavour. He had little knowledge, either, or care (as stated) for the condition of the great mass of mankind which did not inhabit the upper-middle or upper classes. Can a novelist be 'great' whose focus is limited to these, in only three or four countries, and predominantly to the concerns of one sex within them? Perhaps not. James was a miniaturist inside the ego and energy of an epic-painter. He was, as H. G. Wells would charge,[3] a Leviathan trying to pick up a pebble. No Balzac or Zola in social scope, no Thomas Mann even in intellectual or historical frame-of-reference, he was a precursor of the narrow spheres of Proust and Joyce – a great writer by virtue of his persistence in trying to find a universe in a detail: a harbinger of the specialisation of the early twentieth century, which would reduce literature from romantic dimensions into exploration of the inner, the psychological and the linguistic, to the point of breakdown of language itself.

This is not the place to argue whether such modernist 'greatness' will stand the test of time. In any case, James, like his exhausting successors, has long been accepted as one of those masters who drove development of the novel to its apogee (or nadir); and for the sake of historical continuity at least, let's take his status as given. In this study, he deserves a central position because his narrow subject, theme of his most famous novels, was specifically the 'international' one: the condition of expatriates – in particular (though not always) of upper-middle-class Americans in flight from the material abun-dance of their puritan, pioneer country to Europe, where they expected to find real civilisation. James's own life was about this. Barred from sex by either injury or disposition,[4] and from manly enterprise by 'sensibility', he lived almost entirely for his art – so much so that, in contrast to Byron and Stendhal, the life may seem an irrelevance. But life determines art even when restricted to country-house conversations and the urban round of dinner and tea. James focused on these with the intensity that his predecessors had placed on *amour* and war. His career may seem grey beside theirs. Yet is is perhaps typical of an era in which Pax Britannica had ended the ructions of the early century and was holding off those of the next; when bourgeois ascendance was established over the *ancien régime* and the immense new democratic power of America was making its international début.

The great decision of James's life, to expatriate, was predicated on youthful experience between New and Old Worlds. His first memory, recorded in *A Small Boy and Others*, was of the Place Vendôme in Paris – an image which prefigures perhaps the taste for Napoleonic *gloire* which rather surprisingly recurs in his works.[5] His father had taken the family to Europe in a periodic fit of belief that the finest education could not yet be found at home, at least not in Albany, New York. Henry James senior was a philosopher, writer and be-liever in transcendental religion; he had a spectacular 'vastation' in London the year after Henry junior was born and thereafter became a disciple of Swedenborg. Of independent means (his father had been the second richest man in New York), James senior had access to almost any circle; thus his children grew up familiar with the comings and goings of Emerson, Longfellow, Carlyle, Dickens, Thackeray and similar lights. Henry senior led his brood from London to Switzerland and back to New York; from Germany, Italy and other European places back to Newport, Rhode Island. Finally be established them on Quincy Street in Cambridge, Massachusetts, a provincial town which then as now regarded itself as the centre of intellectual life in America and which came to provide the family with a standard of reference, not least because the eldest child, William, became a professor at nearby Harvard, writing *Varieties of Religious Experience* and *Principles of Psychology* – books which in some ways formed a compendium of Henry senior's mystical thinking and theoretical counterpoint to what would develop as Henry jun-ior's 'inwardly romantic' art.

Henry junior was aesthetic where William was scientific: this was a distinction established early on. In dividing the spoils of their father's mind, as it were, the one took Europe and high civilisation while the other took America and the academy. Both were interested in – obsessed with – the two properties in which a Swedenborgian or theosophical type of thought abounds: individual psychology and spiritual transcendence. This must be remembered in Henry's case as much as William's and belies to some extent Ezra Pound's charge that the novelist squared all moral judgements by the standard of a Salem mid-week Unitarian prayer-meeting. That James was ever aware of such standards is apparent. That he was ever in some rebellion against them is even more obvious. Nor did such rebellion begin with his expatriation and gradual assimilation of European mores; it was implicit in Henry senior's long-established quarrel with provincial American thought, even that of Transcendentalist friends like Thoreau.[6] Henry senior wrote theoretical books which nobody read; he was 'a prophet without honor in his own country', Van Wyck Brooks tells us[7] – thus his view that even the most developed of American cities, New York, was 'a half-way house' and 'den of Philistines' in which he could 'not permit his children to take root'. Henry junior accepted these prejudices. His career may have begun from knowledge of the rock-hard puritan morality and philosophical idealism of an early American home, but it would not end there. Like his father, he was bound to quest further; and like his father, he never believed that home truths could provide a standard to measure up to the requirements of ultimate civility.

James's attitudes were reinforced by early reading of English, German and especially French classics. What had America produced to stand beside these? The novels of Irving and Hawthorne? But didn't these authors need to go away to Europe to find fertilising spirit for their art? Yes, there was a great young new land to have tales told to; yes, there was the manly westward push to have myths made of. But there was also, once cities had taken root, civilisation to build in place, a way of life to refine. The Declaration of Independence had established America for the purpose of Life, Liberty and the Pursuit of Happiness – Stendhal's cherished *'chasse au bonheur'*. Yet where was the pursuit of happiness in mere conquest of soil and machine? in mere wresting of new fortunes from the land and erection of what Jack London would call 'the wonder cities of the Iron Heel'?[8] Bookish, contemplative, unathletic, well-bred, James was by background and character ill-suited to exuberant exploration of the American scene, certainly with the zest of a Whitman or wry acceptance of Mark Twain. To him, America was a magnificent chaos: a sort of Frankenstein's monster, full of charm, innocence, strength and pathos, yet absolutely unschooled when it came to sophisticated life, thus potentially dangerous. The country had little place yet for a class of easy means and refinement. For it the European dream beckoned. Such amenity as existed in Washington Square or Newport had to be imported or imitated. And when it came to literature, what educated American writer could avoid looking nostalgically to Europe as 'the Great Good Place'?

Of his principal native precursor, James would write:

It takes so many things, as Hawthorne must have felt later in life, when he made the acquaintance of the denser, richer, warmer European spectacle – it takes such an accumulation of history and custom, such a complexity of manners and types, to form a fund of suggestion for a novelist. . . . The negative side of the spectacle on which Hawthorne looked out, in his contemplative saunterings and reveries, might, indeed, with a little ingenuity, be made almost ludicrous; one might enumerate the items of high civilization, as it exists in other countries, which are absent from the texture of American life, until it should become a wonder to know what was left. No State, in the European sense of the word, and indeed barely a specific national name. No sovereign, no court, no personal loyalty, no aristocracy, no church, no clergy, no army, no diplomatic service, no country gentlemen, no palaces, no castles, nor manors, nor old country-houses, no parsonages, nor thatched cottages, nor ivied ruins; no cathedrals, nor abbeys, nor little Norman churches, nor great universities, nor public schools – no Oxford, nor Eton, nor Harrow; no literature, no novels, no museums, no pictures, no political society, no sporting class – nor Epsom nor Ascot! Some such list as that might be drawn up of the absent things in American life – especially in the American life of forty years ago, the effect of which, upon an English or a French imagination, would probably, as a general thing, be appalling. The natural remark, in the almost lurid light of such an indictment, would be that if these things are left out, everything is left out. The American knows that a good deal remains; what it is that remains – that is his secret, his joke, as one may say.[9]

It was a secret, a joke that James was largely content to keep to himself. His earliest writings are mostly critical and demonstrate his unease with native voice and subject: they adopt an affected, somewhat English tone. No real fiction would come until he went to Europe on his own; from that period dates his first important novel, *Roderick Hudson* (1874), which is about artistic exile and reflects his fear that to leave one's country might be a dangerous course, leading to demoralised idleness. The young man returned to Boston in the early 1870s, but he felt even less at home there now – *The Europeans* (1878) comes as close as he would get to evoking New England sympathetically; but already his focus was on the 'international' theme, and the Americans he depicts in their provincial habitat can hardly be called attractive, however virtuous they may appear compared with Europeanised cousins. At length, James made his 'momentous decision' and went back to Europe to settle for good, first in Paris, then a year later in London. There he stayed for most of the rest of his life, making frequent trips to the Continent and two extended sojourns back to the States, taking up residence as a sexagenarian on the south coast of England. The decision to expatriate gave him a burst of artistic confidence. Its initial result was to allow him to 'discover' his countrymen in a way he had been unable to at home. Rather than moulding himself to antipathetic native personae, he would more or less reinvent the American after his own type. Establishing where he was 'coming from' in this way, he could achieve a distinctive voice.

The path was not always smooth. In this early phase, James I (as he's been called)[10] had two principal subjects: Americans seeing Europe for the first time and American life as if it had European attributes. In the first instance, he would send his travellers off uncertain of what they were looking for, only knowing that it was something they did not have at home and which culture and tradition proclaimed as desirable. They would arrive in a toy world that seemed unreal to them – something they could pick up and play with for a time, but continue to play with only at their peril. Childishly entranced, they would not be prepared for the depth that this kind of play required; and when they misunderstood the rules of the game they would recoil, imagining it vicious. That James himself had this turn of mind is apparent from *The American* (1875), whose depiction of venal French aristocrats is unbalanced to the point of music-hall melodrama.[11] Nor were his attempts to present American institutions as equal to their European counterparts wholly successful. English audiences were nonplussed by *An International Episode* (1879), in which James sought to satirise them as knowingly as his compatriots. Why should this foreigner think he knew enough of English country-house life to imply that it was no better than Newport? And wasn't it a form of chauvinist special pleading to make his heroine, a mere daughter of American commerce after all, turn down marriage to an English peer chiefly on the grounds that – despite his member-ship of the House of Lords – he had no political enthusiasm?

James I shared with the new rich of his country a desire to be accepted among the 'best people' of Europe. Though pleased to escape the 'philistine' monster of home, he takes in his carpet-bag its democratic principles and its assumption that no nation has ever achieved such idealism. At the first sign of Old World closedness, snobbishness or non-admiration, native pride is aroused. Drawing on ancestral roots – the puritanism and transcendentalism never fully discarded – pride produces an arch moral tone. Thus the primness, fastidiousness – censoriousness even – which stands be hind James's mannered tableaux. Thus too the faint whiff of evil that seems to lurk behind them. 'Her sense will have to open', it is said of the heroine of his last novel, *The Golden Bowl* (1904), 'to the wrong. . . . To what's called Evil – with a very big E: for the first time in her life. To the discovery of it, to the knowledge of it, to the crude experience of it.'[12] The 'evil' James means here is adultery and the duplicities that sustain it. To a European growing up in the traditions that we have seen producing Byron and Stendhal, this may seem 'evil' with less than 'a very big E'. But to the American of James's times, with such underdeveloped social arrangements – and cer-tainly no romantic traditions of *cavalieres servente* or troubadour-lovers stretching back to Eleanor of Aquitaine's courts of love – such matters posed great moral obstacles: greater indeed, ironically, than the impoverishment of the South following the Civil War or the pogroms of Chinese workers in San Francisco by the Irish who had lately been their fellow-builders of the transcontinental railroad.

These were the *données* of American growth. Social nuances were relatively unknown; and the unknown, especially if foreign and complex, perhaps always appears in a mask of 'evil' when first faced by the innocent. 'When America begins to consent in the existence of evil is when she will come of age', Walter Rathenau would say in a political context in a later era.[13] To some extent James's development, beginning with his father's wariness of his own country and leading on to different fears provoked by Europe, shows this progress at work. Doesn't initiation into the Old World, even at the highest level, always threaten a fall from grace for the 'best type' of Ameri-can? And in this connection isn't it significant that, while James at home regarded his countrymen as having the antipathetic qualities his father ascribed to them, once abroad he began to depict them as radiant in their native guilelessness, freedom of choice and simple delight in the *good*? This may appear anomalous but it should not surprise. In the first place, homesickness was at work: that nostalgia natural to all *émigrés*, no matter how relieved to have broken loose. In the second, separation often causes memory of the bad to diminish in an idealistic consciousness. In the third, it is inevitable that James should have seen the American abroad as the best of his type: he was after all doing just what James had done; and by his act of travelling, he was probably not only admitting the limitations of his culture to date but also showing its best qualities – its outward-lookingness and desire to learn, thus to improve in the ways of civilisation.

So we have Christopher Newman of *The American* and Isabel Archer of *The Portrait of a Lady* (1881), characters in whom James's most natural confidence resides. But take it a stage further, from travelling to expatriation, and the American abroad undergoes a sea-change. James I is quite wary – even afraid – of the types who settle in the Old World, submerging their brightness and naïveté into its ancient, unfathomable codes. Thus the Tristrams of *The American*, Winterbourne of *Daisy Miller* (1878), Madame Merle and Osmond of *Portrait* – all are examples of those who have perhaps 'stayed too long': who have lost their moral bearings through imperfect acculturation and thus become trivial, indifferent, parasitical or cruel. How to expatriate is the great problem James I finally encounters. Within five years of his 'momentous decision', he has achieved sufficient mastery to write one of the most finely balanced novels in the language, a book entirely about expatriation, whose heroine bridges the two worlds of narrow Yankees (Caspar Goodwood and Henrietta Stackpole) and American *déracinés* (Madame Merle and Osmond). Evolution into the latter is a dangerous fate; and in making his heroine marry Osmond, James takes the bright morning glow off her native innocence forever. But in allowing her to fall from grace in this way he forces her to a level of stoicism and honour that she might never have had the chance to achieve at home, unchallenged by real civilisation. Thus Isabel Archer becomes the still-point in James's universe: the great example of how the best sort of American might encounter European complexity, gaining deeper knowledge of himself thereby, as well as offering to it his own peculiar insight and perhaps higher spiritual refinement.

What developed after *Portrait*, the phase of James II, was for many years a brilliant, partly unsuccessful jostling for position, for real power and perspective as a writer. Though he went back to America for an extended stay in the early 1880s, James had already 'beat out his exile'[14] in moral terms; and the prospect of home seemed even more limiting and discomforting than before. One element in this was the deaths of his parents and a younger brother in quick succession. Another may have been the pressure, real or imagined, represented in his elder brother William, who had had a nervous breakdown shortly before Henry first went away and whose proximity almost always caused Henry a migraine.[15] Sibling rivalry as well as love seems to have been a constant between these brothers: as late as the turn of the century William would refer to Henry as 'superficial'; and though he would never say so publicly, Henry no doubt found the Harvard don by turns provincial, humourless and unsophisticated in ways he had learned in Tuscan *palazzi* and London drawing-rooms. With the deaths of his parents and brother, and in the early 1890s of his beloved sister Alice, Henry's principal blood mooring became the William James family. He would return to it for an extended period during his American tour of 1904. But the divergence between brothers remains a motif to the end. A look at the double portrait of the two in their sixties underlines this: Henry is round, Roman, sharp-eyed, patrician, mobile and dressed with the dark elegance and formalism of international fashion. William on the other hand is bony, dry, angular of feature, with veins and lines of stress around eyes that stare forward pale and immobile, as if in the presence of transcendental light; his beard has the aspect of America, politician or pioneer, and his suit is of a tweedy, light, coarsish material, appropriate to the academic suburb.[16]

The contrast is telling. Had he stayed home Henry might have developed into an even more problematic 'case' than he was destined to abroad. F. W. Dupee tells us:

In Osmond James portrayed, ironically of course, a good many of the possibilities of the eternal American reactionary: his personal dandyism, his exaggerated devotion to refined pleasures, his proud connoisseurship, his social and aesthetic snobbishness which cannot afford to temper itself with the European *noblesse oblige*, his ancestor-worship, his rage for the static, his luxurious joy in the possession of a general theory – pessimistic of course – of human nature.[17]

Superficially, as he lives in Italy, Osmond appears the face of what James feared by spending too long away: what William's voice inside him chided was likely to be his fate as 'man without a country'. At a deeper level Osmond may in fact represent what James suspected he would become if he stayed home. Osmond was, after all, the last important persona he created before returning after five years; as such, he might be seen as a defensive mask the author was subconsciously preparing against the possibility that he might not receive the welcome he expected in view of his success abroad. In the event, this was partly what happened. But in general terms, the Osmond attitude – the aestheticism, traditionalism and cosmopolitan manner adopted to the point of self-parody – may have been the only identity young Henry had ever had available to him to distinguish himself from the other lights of his race. William, after all, had the intellectual, quasi-religious sphere; James's youthful friends William Dean Howells and Charles Eliot Norton held the indigenous realist and critical literary spheres; Whitman, Twain and others knew the basic America better than he ever could, even had he wanted to.

Had he stayed home, Henry would probably have set up shop in New York, not Cambridge — everything in his work suggests it as a more congenial, cosmopolitan place, from his nostalgic depiction of it in *Washington Square* (1880) to his location in it of the narrative character of *The Bostonians* (1885), Basil Ransome, a transplanted southerner whose somewhat reactionary, male-chauvinist views suggest more of Europe than of the northern city of the book's title. Isabel Archer is from New York, as is Milly Theale of *The Wings of the Dove* (1902), James's other most-developed and sympathetic American heroine; so too is Fanny Assingham, the exotic internationalist of *The Golden Bowl*. Caspar Goodwood, the Newsomes of *The Ambassadors* (1903) – indeed, most of the dogmatically virtuous, narrowly American characters of James's fiction – come from Boston, or Massachusetts: a fact which underlines Henry's permanent need to distance himself from the environment of brother William and his family. Had he set up in New York one imagines development of a sort of Victorian Gore Vidal. No doubt his early career as critic would have continued. No doubt he would have taken on American art and mores with a tongue ever more lashing as the spirit intuited that it was not going to find incarnation in a proper fertilising element. Would he have written novels? Could he have achieved the positivity and lyrical attachment necessary for great art? By his own standards, *Portrait* and *The Ambassadors* are his masterpieces, repositories among other things of the finest architectural balance. But these books are the single productions entirely about those partly imaginary creatures of his own kind: upper-middle-class Americans abroad. Could he have written about Americans at home? Can we see promise in his grand attempt at it: the first of his three novels of the later 1880s, his most extensive work after *Portrait* and the apparent result of his long return 'home'?

This is *The Bostonians*. Of it, James himself said that it suffered from too cumbersome development[18] – all that verbose 'expatiation' in the middle: a sign perhaps of an author uncertain of his subject, or at least of his commitment to it. And what are we to make of this story of an attempted 'Boston marriage' between a wealthy blue-stocking spinster and the verbally gifted, yet emotionally malleable daughter of a religio-psychic charlatan? Does the scenario adequately embrace the society implied by the book's title? Where are the businessmen and financiers of State Street; the merchant princes, inheritors of John Hancock and other founders; the new immigrant Irish and Italians; even the legitimate intellectuals of Cambridge? The counterforce to the protagonists is a southern male chauvinist. This is novel, but is it 'Bostonian'? Does the indigenous culture have no counterforces of its own, or is this James's very point: that it is hopelessly dominated by strident, self-righteous feminists and other ideologues, with traditional male order substantially removed (almost wholly replaced by impresario types) and the only really attractive alternatives, the cultivated Burrages, coming like Ransome from New York? Clearly, few Bostonians could accept this as accurate. The book's ending in particular strikes an imbalanced note: the lecturess is just saved from the gaping maw of a crowd at Symphony Hall – a lion's pit of public consumption into which all Bostonians who supposedly love her have thrown her, to have her exceptional gift swallowed up by the all-engorging American publicity machine.

Perhaps there is some metaphoric truth to this finis. More obviously, it seems evidence of James's own fear of being pushed into a Roman circus if he stays home: of having his genius torn apart while those closest to him look on with scientific objectivity. Some psychological block of the sort inhibits his powers. He cannot 'see' Boston judiciously; and the novel, for all its appeal as social criticism – even as subtle anti-American polemic – partly fails as work-of-art.[19] Indeed, the most relevant question it raises may be why James bothered to attempt it in the first place? Why, having discovered his literary 'true Penelope'[20] across the sea, did he return to throw himself into what he already knew would strike him as a lion's pit? Fundamentally, of course, he had to come back because of illness and death in the family which inhibited his work and perhaps contributed to a jaundiced tone. More significantly, however, there was always this pressure: a pressure such as Henrietta Stackpole applies to Isabel Archer and Mrs Newsome of Woollett applies to her son Chad through successive 'ambassadors': to be, finally, a true American. James belonged to too prominent a family for him to cast off the national attachment lightly. At the same time, his love for the fixed order of Europe – the reactionary quality, if you will, developing in him – had the ironic effect of driving him back to his roots: of trying to find evidence of a fine, perhaps superior, natural nobility there, or – in its absence – at least to instruct his own kind in where it was going wrong (*à la* young Byron). But to be 'a prophet in his own country' was to risk becoming marginalised like his father. Unlike *Portrait*, *The Bostonians* did not sell; and James's American public from this time became suspicious of a native son who preferred to live among 'decadent' pleasures elsewhere.

James II, as I've said, appears in any case to have been jostling for subject matter in the 1880s. Having succeeded so supremely with *Portrait*, where did one go? Back from the 'international theme' to *scènes de province*? *The Bostonians* also emerges out of a desire to do with his origins what Balzac had done with his native Tours, dressed up as Orléans or Angoulême. But essential conditions are not in place here. James could not connect his provincial city extensively to the great capital of his culture because he did not really know New York as an adult, as Balzac had known Paris; and London, which he did know, had no relation to Boston in the way Paris did to Tours or any lesser city within the French language's imperial sphere. James's province and his chosen metropolis were cut off from one another: Bostonians did not and would not accept the cultural supremacy of London for them; Londoners might regard Boston as interesting in a foreign sort of way, but it was not an integral part of their empire in the manner of Dublin or even Cape Town. Whereas a Tourian would naturally become a Parisian when ascending the ladder of sophistication, a Bostonian would not become a Londoner: Boston was an end in itself; and Bostonians were not eager to laugh at themselves from the point of view of a Londoner any more than the English had been eager to do the reverse when satirised by the outsider-author of *An International Episode*.

Outsiders, to be accepted, must be polite: must in any case hide their witty barbs behind deference and cultivation. James by the mid-1880s had become an outsider in his own country. Where could he turn then to have the insider's view that is traditionally the basis of a novelist's art? The province hadn't worked, therefore it was back to the metropolis. He followed *The Bostonians* with *The Princess Casamassima* (1886), most extensive and researched of the books he would set in London, most direct stab too which he would make at Naturalism, complete with the grit of social abjection and resentment; and the attempt was an even more signal failure. For if James was no Balzac, able to pose province against metropolis, he was no Zola either, able to feel in the nerves the life of modern city streets. In his preface to *The Princess* he would admit that many knew the subject-matter better than he; but he goes on to contend that it was sufficient to present the 'luminous halo'[21] of these things - the vague awareness combined with wariness of subterranean evil that the journalism-reading mass would have of, say, anarchist cells. Can this be acceptable? Critics and public have thought not. A work based on impressions rather than facts may be art, but if so it has more to do with the artist's own consciousness than with the mimetic function. It is moving in the direction of abstraction rather than representation. It is beginning to propose that fatal modernist notion that the mind of the creator may be more interesting than the world he depicts; and that, by extension, the reader's function is not to recognise an outer world so much as to dream up an inner one of his own.

In James of this period we can see art for art's sake and the obsession with interior labyrinths beginning to be born out of insufficient attachment to the external world; and we can place that insufficiency largely at the feet of his decision to expatriate. *The Princess* fails. So what does he do next? He tries a third gambit, this perhaps closer to the reality (or ideality) he now knows best, but far afield from traditions of the novel *à la* Balzac. This is the novel about art itself, the novel of ideas: a step in the direction of, say, the discussion plays of G. B. Shaw, or even (though flowing from a more physically dammed-up source) the compendium of realist fiction and philosophy developed by D. H. Lawrence. Thus *The Tragic Muse* (1890), in which James turns to 'one of the most salient London "social" passions, the unappeasable curiosity for the things of the theatre; for every one of them, that is, except the drama itself, and for the "personality" of the performer (almost any performer quite sufficiently serving) in particular'.[22] Can this be promising material for the son of the Swedenborgian philosopher and brother of the Harvard professor? One has the sense that in throwing himself into the trivia of London, James was supremely ill-equipped. He was too earnest, too ponderous, too slow, no matter how perspicacious – too much, in short, an American of his times to be anything but a Gulliver among Lilliputians, a Bottom lampooned by fairies.

How could a man who had once described Shakespeare as 'that lout from Stratford'[23] have imagined that he could depict the life of London theatre successfully, or at least sympathetically? How could he, to take it a step further, have imagined that he could achieve success in that world himself? For in the 1890s, following the failure of the last of his middle-period novels, James began his attempt to write plays. Much has been said about this five-year interlude ending in the débâcle of *Guy Domville*. For our purposes it may be sufficient to add that an expatriate of the type essayed in this study is bound to come a cropper if he attempts an art which – even more than successful fiction – requires intimacy with the language, thinking and prejudices of a specific time and place. Byron writing historical or biblical verse tragedies in Venice had no hope of popular success in London of the kind achieved by, say, his friend Sheridan: a Scotsman by birth, he had always been too remote from its sensibility. Stendhal, Grenoblois and traveller, was similarly not familiar enough with Paris to succeed as a playwright there, even had its audiences still been eager for classical drama *à la* Racine. Like these predecessors, James failed to perceive the peculiar connection between author and audience necessary for success in theatre in the capital of his language in his day; and in believing that he could turn to drama at this stage, he was showing another symptom of how he was becoming detached from reality and beginning to indulge in aesthetic adventures that had to do chiefly with himself.

The extent of his self-delusion may be seen in his surprise that one of Wilde's comedies could have greater success than his eighteenth-century melodrama about a young man torn between love and the church, with which it ran contemporaneously. James excoriates Wilde for a ' "cheeky" paradoxical wit of dialogue' designed to appeal to the gallery.[24] One is reminded of W. B. Yeats, whose contemporary taste for unpopular verse drama led him to deride London audiences as 'those quite excellent people who . . . want only to be left at peace to enjoy the works so many clever men have made especially to suit them';[25] and James joins Yeats in the category of *fin-de-siècle* aesthete (ironically, Wilde was its standard-bearer) who felt increasing need for a more symbolical art to explore man's spiritual potentialities. James's plays appealed to some of the best minds of the times: Shaw praised *Guy Domville*; but this practical man-of-the-theatre also knew what James either did not want to acknowledge or (more probably) could not get the hang of – that to be popular, one had to throw a hostage or two to the low. And James did want to be popular, unlike Yeats and Co. He had not yet 'turned his back to the wall', as he would do after the rejection for serialisation of *The Wings of the Dove*.[26] He had not yet announced that 'the best and finest ingenuities' might only come when a writer did not have to put up with the 'compromises' and 'momentary properties' imposed by theatre managers and magazine editors. He simply and self-consciously was trying to break loose from the solitary enclosure of expatriate prose and become a working part of a life with give and take in a milieu to which he could belong.

In spite of his increasing detachment from the *prima materie* of the outer world, James of the middle years had grown more and more deft in the alchemical processes of his art. *The Aspern Papers* (1888), however much about moral degradation, is a virtuoso performance for narrative roundness, consistency of voice, economy and symmetry. Much the same might be said of many 'blest nouvelles'[27] of the period, several of which – *The Siege of London* and *The Reverberator*, for instance – return to the 'international theme'. Through such works, so often experiments in form, James exceeded the bounds of narrative possibility achieved by previous writers, even his masters Balzac and Flaubert. It was a great accomplishment – arguably his most important bequest; and ironically, he may have realised it chiefly because he had become deficient or jaundiced in 'real' life. The novels of the 1880s had already shown exceptional variety in structure, from the 'perfect arch' of *Portrait* to the 'processional' of *The Princess*, to the dramatic, or conversational, of *The Tragic Muse*. But now armed with the concentration on dialogue and 'blocking' of theatre – also perhaps made devil-may-care by his failures – James performed what many consider his most breathtaking stylistic feats. In *What Maisie Knew* (1897) he surveys contemporary London's morals from inside the consciousness of a child: a child who by her nature will never be censorious, only quietly hurt, endangered in her pristine innocence by the self-indulgence of her elders. In *The Turn of the Screw* (1898) he extends and partly reverses this approach by ventriloquising

the voice of a young governess alarmed and shocked by the apparent behaviour of children brought up in ways foreign to her. In *The
Awkward Age* (1899) he disappears into the unrestrained talk of adults:
talk which is suggestive, compromised and elliptical, yet bound
willy-nilly to become the mode of a young girl who ought to be
shielded from it.

These books show the author's disillusionment with the milieu
which had rejected his plays, also a growing fascination with spiritual
darkness – the hints and shadows of evil which had always lurked at
the bottom of his soul, both as American and European *déraciné*.
England is his home now: the one place he can present with a
modicum of first-hand knowledge; and so he 'renders' it. But how?
At first glance, it seems that he blows a raspberry at it like the one he
blew at his homeland with *The Bostonians*. But James had mellowed
in these years – that too can be a product of disillusionment – and as
social critic he was more polite. What are his narrative tricks but
devices to allow him to appear removed as author, objective, non-
judgemental? This of course is in part self-serving deception, but it
also may show the extent to which James's attitude toward his
chosen city was different than toward the native province. The satire
here is subtle; the purpose on second glance seems ameliorative
rather than rejecting. London in any case is ancient, established,
virtually unending; thus it can afford to ignore or absorb his barbs
without ostracism. And why should it ignore him entirely? What
does he represent but a rather charming outside point of view and
amusingly mannered eccentricity? Perhaps he does carp at the edges
of native life, but isn't he still acknowledging its pre-eminence by his
attention and continuance there? And what is the bone he has to pick
anyway but the same bone that English middle-class moralists had
to pick with the sexual loucheness of London in an epoch of scandal
around the Prince of Wales, the fall of politicians through adultery or
syphilis, and not least the furore around Wilde?

In taking up the moral primness of a little old (or young) lady,
James was of course revealing his own easily mocked fussiness; and
to criticise London from such a perspective was far less hurtful than
to satirise Boston head-on for its self-righteousness and sexual inversion. Following his disappointments there was no doubt an element
of sour grapes in what James wrote; but London could stand this. It
could be amused, even awed, by the tact and skill with which this
frustrated genius delivered himself of his little jets of bad temper.
Wasn't he finally, in terms of the new age that was coming – the

explosive century of liberation – one of the most extreme and in-triguing symptoms, even one of the most tragic examples, of what Victorian/Yankee-puritan inhibition could produce? Poor, lonely, middle-aged old maid that he now came close to appearing (was it a fate he feared even more than Osmond?) – how could anyone begrudge him his exquisite whinges? In face of the hardly disguised self-pity of 'The Lessons of the Master', 'The Altar of the Dead' and 'The Beast in the Jungle', how could anyone deny that at some level he was telling tales against himself more than anything else? warning not to do as he had done: not to give oneself up to a caged solipsism; not to cut oneself off from one's origins, one's *prima materie*, the prevailing spirit and morals of the times? Look, he seemed to be trying to caution, at the terrible price one pays in attempting the moralist's variant of the Faustian pursuit. Wasn't it sheer, self damning fantasy to try to create a more ideal new world, where transcendent goodness and spiritual beauty might reign in pristine detachment from the rutting and resenting, duplicity and deviation, earthy and 'evil' of the old?

The spectacle of James in late middle years is of a man becoming more wound up in private doubts and 'what-ifs'; in the spectre of his attachment to nothing concrete, thus in elaboration and rationalisa-tion. To work through the books of this period is to put oneself in a position analogous to that of a professional reader trying to make sense of an amateur who has not yet gone beyond the thrill of reading his own words as he writes them, trying to find the 'figure on the carpet' from them and thus learn where he is going. Where, we might ask (as James seems to be asking), do his loyalties finally lie? Who does he actually love and hate, admire or despise? Or has the world at last become morally opaque: a tableau no longer of distinct colours, or even of discrete blacks and whites, but of muted, impressionistic shades of grey – rather like the canvases of his con-temporary fellow-expatriate, James MacNeill Whistler? What would emerge in the end, in the three great novels of James III (the 'Old Pretender'), would have an element of triumph in it; but this would be principally because of the author's realisation that he had to get back to that still point in his universe once again. In the great works of the middle period, from *The Bostonians* to *The Awkward Age* – all these books which do not reflect the international theme directly but seek to 'render' America or England on its own – we see an author who, lacking his most reliable external contrast, has to create irony and critique through narrative arrangement and trick; and the result,

almost inevitably, is to make him seem manipulative, snootily superior and perhaps unreliable.

Through works of the late middle years the sensitive reader is
thrown back on the question raised by English audiences over *An
International Episode*: what does this precious mandarin know finally
that is sufficient to justify his lofty dismissiveness? When one reads
James's successor Thomas Mann, another mannered spirit created
by the *fin-de-siècle* and driven by a 'productivity of genius', one always finds along with witty social satire a depth of political, historical and even metaphysical documentation. To re-read *The Magic
Mountain* or *Dr Faustus* is to comprehend the transformation of
contemporary Western civilisation on all sorts of levels.[28] To re-read
James as he approaches his so-called 'major phase'[29] is to recognise
increasingly that what passed for profundity at first glance may in
fact be massive evasion. William James sought hard knowledge;
aesthete Henry eschewed it. He was a great observer, a titan of
psychological detail perhaps. But in the end his admitted deficiency
in all other matters makes us begin to wonder if his preoccupation
with social velleities may mask essential emptiness. We encounter in
James at his most disillusioned an author who looks more and more
like the dreaded Osmond who snatched promise from the lady. The
unmoored dilettante collects a bit here, entertains a bit there; mostly,
however, he creates bubbles of private resentment against the societies to which he has struggled to prove himself superior. Confronted
with James of, say, *The Awkward Age*, we are tempted to ask if he did
not write out of the same spirit in which Osmond gave parties: not
for who to invite so much as who to exclude. To exclude is to snub.
To snub is the weapon of the snob. The snob is a person who has
decided that he does not wish to know more about life, or real
people: who seeks to close his door on empathy with their condition
and consider alone the narcissistic image on a coin of a long-ago
dispossessed prince.

In *Portrait* James depicts Osmond as a man full of envy, yet finally
deriving power from resignation: from a pride which refuses to
stoop to compete against easier, if somewhat more superficial,
Europeans, such as Lord Warburton. Is this not James himself versus
Wilde in the era of plays, or versus Wells in the later dispute over
Boon?[30] Faced with ostracism at home and with the status of oddity
in England, James ascends the steps of his private tower, up the
winding stair of his increasingly unstoppable obsessions with form
and the inner life. He will not stoop to modernise himself with

anything so vulgar as knowledge of science *à la* Wells or political economy like Shaw. Genius must not stoop; it must simply realise itself, ascending toward its transcendental possibilities while boring down toward its natural core. Thus James devotes his great powers to overdone metaphors, locutions which take in every possible expression, narratives which dally so long with alternative options that the reader loses track of who and what. The themes of *The Ambassadors*, *The Wings of the Dove* and *The Golden Bowl* are merely grand recapitulations of the great themes discovered by James I and worked over many times before. The plots are reduced to bare bones while development is fleshed out rotundly. What are these novels but 'blest nouvelles' expanded: 'rendered' to the point of such bewildering, stultifying complication that the reader is forced again and again to wake himself out of reveries drifted into on his own? Mallarmé wrote while the Wagnerian orchestra dictated: so the French described the process of the symbolical literary art of the 1890s.[31] The last three great James novels come from a decade even more given over to abstraction; and the Old Pretender might be characterised as performing the literary equivalent of, say, a Mahler symphony, which extends the still-programmatic Wagner into truly 'unending melody'.

One recalls Shaw's remark on reading George Moore's *The Brook Kerith*: 'I read about thirty pages [and] it began to dawn on me that there was no mortal reason why Moore should not keep going on like this for fifty thousand pages, or fifty million for that matter.'[32] To be caught in the very long, entirely unbroken paragraphs of the beginning of *The Wings of the Dove*, or almost all of *The Golden Bowl*, is not to be pleased or entertained but to be forced to walk through rooms and rooms of a gallery before seeing the one really great painting that is the reason for visiting the exhibition in the first place. Once got through, these long novels have majestic conclusions. They are all healing books: books in which the author partly casts off the Osmond persona and becomes more like Ralph Touchett, the humane if idle observer of *Portrait*, an American expatriate too, but one who is securely based in an English country house and surrounded by family, rather than in a Roman villa populated mostly by guests he does not even like. And perhaps the allusion to *Portrait* is telling; because, for pleasure of form *and* content, what reader wouldn't be happier to turn back to it than to these difficult late masterworks? In *Portrait* James was discovering his great cast of expatriate and European characters for the first time; still delighting in the outer world, he was content to let his representatives of it explain it in their own

words and thought-patterns rather than in projected ponderings of
his own. It may be true that *The Ambassadors* has the most fully realised architecture of James's books: even more of a 'perfect arch'
than *Portrait*.[33] But for personality, can any reader remember Maria
Gostrey as well as Henrietta Stackpole? Jim Pocock better than Caspar
Goodwood? Madame de Vionnet as vividly as Madame Merle?

   Lambert Strether may be a still point in James's universe even
more than Isabel Archer, but does he finally absorb our attention
half so well? Chad Newsome may be an ironic reincarnation of
Christopher Newman;[34] but if so, isn't he a preview of the 'ugly'
American compared to James's youthful representative of the type?
These last books are sinuous but hardly seductive. When he came to
write them James was far adrift from his early moorings in realism;
and to admire their content we must read them principally as moral
revaluations. In Strether versus Isabel, Kate Croy versus the
Bellegardes, Prince Amerigo versus Osmond and so on, James is
making amends for the failings of earlier personae. In showing
motives in far greater detail than before, he underlines his refined
message: that in all questions of good and evil, there are too many
nuances for one to proceed with anything less than humane pragmatism. 'Everything's terrible, cara, in the heart of man', says the
Prince;[35] but out of this terror, as Milly Theale shows, great spiritual
beauty may emerge. Here is James's principal defence of the rightness of his method: of his endless shades of grey and delicate ironies.
There can be no certainties, no fixed *données* anywhere, anytime: not
at home, not abroad, not even in some rarefied third place combin-
ing the two. James turns on the judgemental strain in his nature and
shows that such Old World vices as adultery may make of a Chad
Newsome a healthier, more rounded spirit than could otherwise
have been produced by virtuous Woollett; yet conversely, that such
a narrow moral universe as Woollett's might, by its simple emphasis
on virtue, be more likely than elsewhere to produce a spirit like
Strether's, which sympathises with the fallen woman and wishes to
educate itself in why she has done what she has done.

One admires James professionally for these qualities: immense psychological sensitivity, unrivalled attention to novelistic form, critical
progress against native tendencies to self-righteousness, puritanism,
censoriousness. One admires him personally for his courage in going away, in creating a unique subject-matter out of an unpromisingly

narrow field of real knowledge, above all in persisting along his path beyond rejection and apparent failure. He remained high-minded, dedicated, exemplary to the point that one might begin to see him as a kind of secular saint. In many ways, too, he is an expatriate American version of contemporary European aesthetes: thus his relation to Proust. With his aristocratic airs, he also has elements of a dispossessed prince of the *ancien régime* or perhaps even a fallen Bonapartist, keeping up old standards in the face of a world quickly sliding into new, strange ways. In the end, James's fascination with the *passé* may be the predominant strain in his type of maleness. We can track this from Roderick Hudson to Osmond, painting his water-colours of antique coins, to Adam Verver of *The Golden Bowl*, who parlays an American fortune into collecting European *objets*, not least of which is his daughter's husband, the Roman prince whose family has fallen on hard times. Add to this the aura of mystic quest inherited from his father and one might even begin to see James decay into a kind of prosy, New World cousin to, say, Count Villiers de l'Isle-Adam, with his fantasy of Axël shutting himself in a remote chateau to pursue occult studies and contemplate possibilities for transcendence.

James is the last phase thus circles back toward what the William James voice in him had called him back from when young; what Caspar Goodwood and Henrietta Stackpole try to keep Isabel Archer from becoming: a servant to the Osmond in himself; an apologist for an antisocial international élite which imagined it could breathe more rarefied air. Thus *The Golden Bowl*. There are, of course, counter-tendencies to this: Lambert Strether finds common humanity with the people of Paris in the office of *Postes et Telegraphes* , and Milly Theale identifies with the poor women in Regent's Park once she discovers she is terminally ill. Elements in the stories, too, show that James was not entirely absorbed in precursors of the *Dallas/Dynasty* rich, notably his depiction of low Londoners in 'The Real Thing' and 'In the Cage'. But James's affection for Cockneys seems little more than an extension of a humane aristocrat's decency to his serving-people or of a lifelong, semi-touristic fascination with the Dickensian aspects of his chosen city. Nor are these nods to the common folk of Europe matched by a similar attraction to low Americans, especially in the last phase. Strether prefers Mme de Vionnet to the Maria Gostreys and Jim Pococks. Milly chooses a Venetian *palazzo* to die in rather than go back home to New York. James himself returned to America for an extended visit: he admired its energy and ingenuity and even allowed himself to be caught up in its publicity machine at last, that business of the future which Chad Newsome goes home to take up. But two of the most significant homegoings of his fiction, those of Madame Merle in *Portrait* and of Charlotte Verver in *The Golden Bowl*, are cast as penances for bad behaviour in Europe; and James's last important word on his country, *The American Scene* (1907), testifies to his continued and deepening feeling of alienation from it.

He preferred to retire to Lamb House in Rye: a locale where he could wile away his senescence dictating to two secretaries, being waited on by butler, cook and maid, and entertaining for all the world like an English country squire, in sight of the Continent he loved. A small cult of admirers gathered around him. In Edwardian fashion he identified with that new *ancien régime*, the *haut bourgeoisie* of Europe, soon to be threatened by a class war the reasons for which he never appears to have understood. James III was arguably both reactionary and ignorant. He had arrived at that apogee (or nadir) of Anglo-Saxon sophistication which T. S. Eliot would sum up in the half-mocking phrase: 'He had a mind so fine that it could not be violated by an idea'.[36] Ideas were for facile writers like Wells or 'talking sewing-machines' like Shaw. They were for intellectuals; and behind the grand manner of James, as to some exent of Eliot later, lurks anti-intellectualism. This is ironic, but should not be surprising in expatriates who came from the hyperintellectual atmosphere of Cambridge, Massachusetts, and were concerned to define civilisation beyond it. In Eliot's case, the fruits of Harvard study would be partly ineradicable and the grand manner would come to be defined clearly by attachment to the church. In James's, on the other hand, one begins to wonder if the intellect ever existed far outside of itself (he had dropped out of Harvard Law School after less than a year and never took up academic study again) and if the manner finally amounts to much more than so much rhetoric about taste – the moral/aesthetic equivalent of the joke about the Episcopalian whose only idea of sin is using his dessert fork to eat his salad.

The rational pragmatism and secular mysticism of the James family prevented him from turning toward the church in the end, as so many contemporaries did; and his major preoccupation of later years was to revise his works and attach ornate explanations to them, an activity which was not intellectual or spiritual so much as an example of authorial playing with one's food. The egregious instance of this is the prefaces to the New York edition of his collected works, which note the time and place of conception of each, the difficulties and joys of cooking them up, the hopes and frustrations of serving them to the world and viewing their ingestion. Other instances include the travel pieces he had written throughout his life, many of which were now collected in sumptuous limited editions. An example of these is the piece on Siena written originally in 1873 and reworked, or added to, for *Italian Hours* (1909). The early impressions are 'charming', if somewhat surprising for their already circumlocutory, old-mannish tone; but they abound in attitudes detached from real knowledge. The Siennese school of painting is dismissed without discussion of its historical significance, and the façade of the cathedral described with no identification of the statues or inscriptions which cover it. We are told only what a refined 'sensibility' might see for itself; the point of view is of a tourist reasonably well-off and pleasant but hardly ardent in pursuit of culture. One is reminded of the slow tempoed, verbally showy 'Letters from . . . ' that appear in the *New Yorker* to this day, not what an educated European contemporary of James's might have noted, or even an intellectual compatriot like Henry Adams.

Both would have tried to penetrate the spiritual and artistic motives of those essential others involved: the men of the high-Gothic centuries who had actually built the place. Ezra Pound would make this process into an artistic and moral method. James, by contrast, does not even seem to see what he lacks: that as critical guide he was in fact bluffing. From the perspective of 36 years, he comments merely that his 'young friend' may have missed much but that the first impressions of people are always interesting in themselves, so he will leave his words in their pristine form. James in this vein strikes the nonplussed reader as having something in common with beatniks who believed in 'spontaneous writing': in the sanctity of one's original feelings caught in the instant of most intense experience. The difference between him and Kerouac on this score may not be in how they cherish the impression, but in how James would prefer to recollect it in the comfort of a well-appointed hotel room rather than in the back seat of a '49 Ford. Could James then be characterised as a kind of mandarin, anal-retentive Henry Miller? Was it only because he lived in an age of *l'art pour l'art* that he forced his *aperçus* into conventional forms, thus hanging his last novels on skeletons of plots rather than hurtling them forward in the style of *Tropic of Cancer*? I make fun here. Still, there are traits in common between this American on the road, alienated from 'the air-conditioned nightmare' of home, and his successors of the 1920s and 1950s.

Like them, he really finds his new *patria* not in England or Europe but in art – in writing: *scribo ergo sum*. For unlike Byron or Stendhal, European men of action, James did not take up the pen as a way to pass time not spent in more manly pursuits. As an American he belonged to a culture which seems, at least since his day, often to misapprehend or perhaps wilfully disregard the traditional relation of art to life as a whole. Art has, finally, only a place. It may be a great place, as Shelley indicated with his 'poet as legislator of mankind'; it may be a sacerdotal place even, as Wagner, Mallarmé and even Wilde fantasised. But it is a place only: not one to supersede politics, war, sex, food, children, horse-riding or any number of other cultural *données*. Mozart, who gave his life to his art, would have understood this – did indeed see himself as part of the larger fraternal entity of European civilisation. Balzac even, hurtling across the Continent in pursuit of Mme Hanska, knew that life went further than a monk's robe, black coffee and the pen. But in these cases we have genius which did not feel compelled to decipher its own genius, any more than Christ felt obliged to discuss his chastity.[37] In James of the revisions, the James who came at last to analyse endlessly the creatures of his own mind, we begin to see a kind of hapless monster on the verge of swallowing itself tail-first. We see a sensibility showing, like Joyce's and Stein's decades on, that one can go only so far in indulging the products of a self-enclosed, deracinated consciousness before the whole process veers toward private madness.

James's career on his own terms (Balzac remained the standard) was in part a failure, if an honourable one. The failure led toward intensification of an already present tendency to inversion. Pride prevented the failure from being acknowledged fully; more typical was denial, rationalisation, even self-congratulation – and here enter the prefaces. Are they not symptoms of a kind of megalomania? Is it not possible to see in them the beginnings of the delusions which led the stroke-ridden James on his death-bed to dictate letters to members of his family as if they were the Bonapartes and sign them 'Napoleone'?[38] Perhaps this seems a shock. Posterity, after all, regards James as a landmark in the civilised attitude – in sanity, if you will – and this to an extent he may be. But if so, he is also a demonstration of the extent to which the pressure to attain and maintain a civilised state may imply severe doubts and discontents, suppressions and schizophrenias – conditions, in short, leading almost inevitably to the psychoanalyst's couch or one's personal version of it. The tensions in James's case are obvious. They increase as he goes on and are partly summed up, especially in regard to the prefaces, by Max

Beerbohm's cartoon of the clean-shaven Old Master confronting his bearded younger self and saying: 'How badly you wrote!', while at the same time his younger self is saying out of the same phrase-bubble, 'How badly you write!'[39]

And how sadly, too, on occasion. For many times in the prefaces we are confronted with indications that he no longer realises how what he is saying may sound. Frequently he mentions the value he puts on 'economy' when neither the phrase he is using nor the work he is referring to has a whit of economy about it. And then he remarks that the chief problem with *The Wings of the Dove* is that the second half is too short in relation to the first, whereas the common complaint is that the first half is endless while the second is almost satisfyingly direct. James of the prefaces is an erratic critic; but perhaps his main purpose now is advertisements for himself. We suspect as much when he talks of his 'supersubtleties' and 'arch-refinements'; of touches which 'on reperusal, [he finds] striking, charming and curious'; of characters who still stimulate their 'painter's tenderness of imagination'. What has happened at last to the vaunted 'good taste'? Modesty has fled the place. The muse stands in her chamber, encircled in mirrors, and the mirrors reflect back her slim, lovely form. But as she undresses she is somehow transvested into a waistcoated shadow of her portly invoker. The veil of the temple is rent and the transcendent secret revealed. But on inspection it is not God or history or political faith or artistic and cultural tradition even, so much as James, James and more James.

The prefaces are a disappearing dervish. Beyond them, one's most enduring impression of James may be from his last novel, *The Golden Bowl*, which projects his attachment in posterity to a new age of jet-setting 'beautiful people'. The Prince and Maggie on their exclusive international stage become Windsor and Wallis, Rainier and Grace Kelly, Onassis and Jackie Kennedy. Sentimentally, one might prefer to remember James for his last good American travellers, the inno-cents Strether and Milly, who take their charm from their author's nostalgia for a type of Good American he had realised in Isabel Archer. But James's experience of America in 1904 proved even to him that such types hardly existed in fact; and without his anagogical 'heiress to the ages' he was not able to complete another novel.[40] The pristine creature he had created circa 1880 had in any case been a necessary fiction in part: a semi-conscious exercise in patriotic PR designed to show that the American experiment had produced something worthy of being included in the best of civilisation. The act might have the beneficial side-effect of proving that his 'momentous decision' was not a national betrayal so much as a high 'ambassadorial' mission. But the exemplary virgin James peddled abroad was always a projection of his anima more than a truth: of his semi-religious desire for a still point in the universe. And finally we must ask: had she really existed at home, would he have condemned himself to a life of expatriation to capture and recapture her in his mind?

5
Maugham

Somerset Maugham may seem unworthy of this study: the expatriate as mediocrity. To many *literati*, particularly academic, he is distinctly not 'great'. A Yeats scholar, when I told her I was going to include Maugham, responded by paraphrasing the poem I cite in my epigraph: 'An ageing Maugham is but a paltry thing'. Turning to Maugham after James, one has an idea of what the scholar meant. Apart from anything else, there is a steep drop in the level of difficulty. Both writers were great travellers and instinctive Europeans; both set out self-consciously on versions of Byron's grand tour; both were entranced by Byron's myth, the examples of Stendhal and Balzac,[1] French form and style, Germanic metaphysics and Italianate modes of living, including traditional adultery; both were consummate observers and note-takers, desiring to find out how men really worked; both were fascinated with theatre and steeped in conventions of nineteenth-century melodrama; both became citizens-of-the-world, mannered, social yet single, repressed and to greater or lesser degrees 'inverts'; both were preoccupied by the proper balance between private contemplation and public relation; and, despite theosophical speculations, both were essential agnostics and pragmatists. Each wrote his greatest novels about expatriation, in Maugham's case *The Moon and Sixpence* (1919) and *The Razor's Edge* (1944), as well as parts of *Of Human Bondage* (1915). Meanwhile, the great novels each wrote that were set in a fixed place – in Maugham's case, *Cakes and Ale* (1930) and again parts of *Of Human Bondage* – betray characteristic marks of an instinct to move, to entertain a foreign point of view and discover a brighter, more insightful ethos outside of the restricted sphere. Beyond this, however, the similarities largely stop. For if Maugham admired James's formal bequest and saw himself as working in its tradition, he also saw James's stylistic shortcomings and was in quest of a different achievement.[2] He conceived of himself as a professional rather than a 'master' and wished to be judged accordingly.

By the standards of Leavis, cited at the beginning of this study,

James was the archetypal 'great' writer. He 'changed the possibilities of the art for practitioners and readers' and was 'significant in terms of the human awareness [he] promoted';[3] he had 'rich matter to organize', 'subtle interests', 'strength of analysis of emotional and moral states'; like Jane Austen, he viewed 'with unprecedented subtlety and refinement the personal relations of sophisticated characters exhibiting the "civilization" of the "best society" '; like George Eliot, he brought to his subjects 'a radically reverent attitude' and 'a profound seriousness of the kind that is a first condition of any real intelligence'; like Joseph Conrad, he could be seen as 'one of those creative geniuses whose distinction is manifested in being peculiarly alive in their time – peculiarly alive *to* it; not "in the vanguard" in the manner of Shaw and Wells and Aldous Huxley, but sensitive to the stresses of the changing spiritual climate as they begin to be registered by the most conscious'. Above all, he exhibited the 'deep and sincere' attitude to his art that Leavis glorifies with an epigraph from D. H. Lawrence: 'One ought to be able to pray before one works. . . . One has to be so terribly religious, to be an artist.' Now Maugham may have exhibited a religious discipline in his work but he would have been embarrassed to make such a statement. For all his criticism of English middle-class values, he remained drenched in its undemonstrativeness and would have found such earnestness as Leavis lauds and James typified discomforting if not pretentious. Though he rendered the manners of 'the best society', he often delighted in mocking or rebelling against them, a course neither Austen nor James would have dared (though Lawrence, more like Maugham, as we shall see, would have). Maugham was suspicious of relentless high-mindedness and diffident about being didactic; he was out to entertain his readers, or at least to engage them. Finally, except in the picaresque *Of Human Bondage*, he would studiously avoid a vice which Leavis might have used to dismiss James as he did Joyce and Proust: 'The demand [they] make on the reader's time is . . . prohibitive.'[4]

Leavis did criticise the later James: 'This inveterate indirectness', he noted, 'this aim of presenting, of leaving presented, the essential thing by working round and behind so that it shapes itself in the space left amidst a context of hints and apprehensions, is undoubtedly a vice.'[5] Elsewhere (in relation to Conrad), Leavis criticises the tendency of authors to 'make a virtue out of not knowing what [they] mean', thus raising 'the vague and unrecognizable' to the status of 'the profoundly and tremendously significant'.[6] In such commonsensical values Leavis might be making a case for the unemotive realism which characterised much of Maugham. At another point (when reassessing Dickens in the light of *Hard Times*), he might be talking about the approach which the successful playwright (as Maugham was) naturally took: 'The genius of the writer may fairly be described as that of a poetic dramatist, and . . . in our preconceptions about "the novel", we may miss, within the field of fictional prose, possibilities of concentration and flexibility in the interpretation of life such as we associate with Shakespearean drama.'[7] But earlier and more memorably, Leavis has dismissed Dickens for being principally an entertainer and for relying too heavily on stereotypes;[8] and notwithstanding Maugham's own criticism of Dickens on these bases,[9] Leavis might have complained of the same vices in him. I say 'might have'. Generally the position of critics like Leavis was that Maugham was beneath consideration. Edmund Wilson spoke for them when he turned a review of one of Maugham's Renaissance Italian romances into a famous attack: 'Maugham is a half-trashy novelist, who writes badly, but is patronized by half-serious readers, who do not care much about writing.'[10] Such condemnation strikes one as a matter of temperament as much as of aesthetic judgement. Like Leavis, Wilson came from a puritan moral tradition and might be described as a critical Roundhead. Maugham was an instinctive cavalier: he preferred Continental, Catholic traditions to Anglo-Saxon, Protestant ones; and when it came to writing, the great value for him was to communicate. To be a fine story-teller was more important finally than to be a stylistic or contentual innovator.

Defenders of Maugham have always found something unfair about the Leavis/Wilson attitude. The latters' dismissals sound the élitist Modernist note that in literature James prefigured and Pound became chief propagandist for. To be popular was to be low-brow *ipso facto*. To write the well-made play or story was to contravene the requirement to 'MAKE IT NEW'.[11] To digest wholly one's psychology before writing was to create character by contrivance, not in its living, breathing roughness. To be 'a natural', as Maugham claimed he was,[12] was to eschew the sacred duty of the artist to explore the inner reaches of consciousness to the point of pain, even madness: to take on the asceticism or perform the *auto-da-fé* of the mediaeval saint. To lampoon 'high brow' culture, as Maugham did in 'The Creative Impulse', for example, was to expose oneself as an aesthetic reactionary. To favour common-or-garden variety taste was to show one's lack of courage to break with the norm and one's essential philistinism. How could a 'great' writer pursue money and ease with the assiduity of a stockbroker, as Maugham did? Weren't penury and suffering his inevitable due, even by his own standards, as in the case of his artist-hero Charles Strickland? How could a serious writer of the early twentieth century display not a jot of messianic purpose? In the face of terrible class ructions and wars wasn't it his obligation to adopt socialist, fascist or at least partisanly conventional sociopolitical views?[13] And how could an expatriate writer travel, live abroad and at the same time delight in coming home twice yearly? How could he on the one hand laud a primitivist, Gauguin-style life in the South Seas and on the other be a dedicated exemplar of high civilisation, a version of his own Jamesian persona, Elliott Templeton, living the life of a Windsor or a Grimaldi on the Côte d'Azur? What significance did any of his acts have when they all seemed adapted to increase pleasure: the pleasure of the reader; the pleasure of his own lifestyle? Wasn't the man finally simply a wanderer along the path of least resistance? a rather selfish *homme moyen sensuel*, without any moral purpose of consequence nor with sufficient fibre to take unpopular positions – not even on his own 'three-quarters' homosexuality — or experience an instructive meltdown?

To all this a cynical, sophisticated realist (which is what Maugham was generally seen to be) might be tempted to respond with the literary equivalent of Senator Hruska's comment when President Nixon was accused of appointing a mediocrity to the Supreme Court: 'Most of the American people are mediocre and they deserve to be represented too.' A less frivolous post-romantic might simply ask why in literature we must always praise the rarefied, the extreme, the inaccessible and uncompromising. Is it necessary finally to pay obeisance to neurosis, to the *wrongness* in character of a Byron or a Pound which results in the peculiarly fascinating spectacles of their careers, if not of their art? Such a position must have positive virtue at the end of the twentieth century as we look back at the chaos wreaked by modernist messianism in all spheres, political as well as artistic, behavioural as well as literary. Tradition having been deranged, turned upside-down or stamped on altogether, might we not now long for a few simple standards of what constitutes the well-crafted thing? In political life, totalitarians of all stripes are clambering for sane, liberal, democratic government. In post-modernist aesthetics, anti-ideological eclecticists are calling for more representation and less abstraction. In the post-psychoanalytical be-

havioural environment, the general will is in favour of simple decency over the mollycoddling of lunatics. Given as much, would it
not stand to reason that in literature we should find it more rare and
pleasing to pick up a book that has a straightforward narrative and
comprehensible tale to tell than to wade through pages of expres-
sionistic/exhibitionist 'genius'? So a writer like Maugham might
now begin to sneak back into our notion of the 'great'. Isn't he after
all, at this remove, a better exemplar stylistically than Joyce? a more
satisfying dramatist than the self-important Shaw? a more deft story-
teller than contemporary practitioners of that genre like, say, Lawrence or Hemingway?

I raise these points more to provoke than to proclaim. The com-
parisons illuminate Maugham's failings as well as his accomplish-
ments. One may never experience in his work a sense of the original
as ravishing as in Joyce; of sociological insight as in Shaw; of passion
as in Lawrence; of economy as in Hemingway. There is in contrast to
all of these a softness and lack of astringency; above all a lurking
indifference to absolute truth. Swinburne, it is said, often sacrificed
comprehensibility to the euphony of a line; Maugham, it is charged,
often sacrificed the integrity of a situation to the pleasingness of a
sentiment. He himself complained of the strictures of popular writing
and claims that he gave up plays for the novel because it could be
more truthful, less confining.[14] But even in novels which begin bril-
liantly he 'peters out', as Humphrey Carpenter puts it, 'into banality
or melodrama'.[15] Thus the hero of his most naturalistic book, *Of
Human Bondage*, ends by preparing to marry a maternal lower-class
girl rather than 'coming out', as the psychology suggests; and the
initially offensive Jewish protagonist of 'Mr Know-All' turns out to
be sweetly unselfish in the end, an irony which – as John Symonds
says [16] – is more ingratiating than credible. Repeatedly Maugham
justified the improbable in his writing by stating that man is various;
fact is stranger than fiction; and in his long life and wide travels, he
has come upon volte-faces that make the changes in his characters
seem commonplace. Well, maybe. On the other hand, the meta-
morphosis of Charles Strickland from a comfortable, quiet, family
man and stockbroker into an amoral, chaotic, Nietzschean artist
does strain belief, especially when it is meant to happen without any
material or interpersonal catalyst, and at the age of 40. Maugham's
work is studded with such transitions. The truth may be that in his
success in the broad psychology of popular theatre (something which
eluded Byron, Stendhal and James, as we've seen), he learned tricks

that he could not have discarded fully even if he had wished to. Thus in his most sensitive novels we still find elements of the sensational. Frankly, he always preferred dramatic action in a glamourous *beau monde* to the humdrum activities and nuances of response in, say, a Leopold Bloom.

Of Human Bondage comes closest to being an exception to this rule. Longer than *Portrait of a Lady* and *The Charterhouse of Parma*, it is the 'greatest' effort to be covered in this study in terms of size. Written in the mode of Mann, the classical *Bildungsroman*, it lays claim to importance in the fulness of its rendering of a *Zeitgeist* and explo-ration of the education of an individual. This is done on a European rather than a provincial stage, like Joyce's contemporary *Portrait of an Artist* or Lawrence's *Sons and Lovers*, and places it in a genre which Leavis particularly derided and James would never have dared: the European novel-of-ideas. The hero, Philip Carey, studies philosophy in Heidelberg and painting in Paris; he thrives on metaphysical discussion and café polemic about all the new 'isms' of the day. In general, he goes 'to encounter the reality of experience'; but instead of forging the uncreated conscience of his race, he forges that of his individual being. Thus the typical Maugham hero: as elsewhere, he is chiefly in pursuit of self-realisation, of geographical, emotional, spiritual and perhaps even temporal liberty – thus the compulsion to free himself of every sort of 'bondage'; to travel, observe, think, pick up and discard philosophies and personae, almost as if he were a reincarnating soul of Hindu myth, making his progress through successive stages of karma until all possible identities have been exhausted, whereupon (and only then) he may reach the ultimate nirvana. Maugham's greatness, if accepted, consists in this, to which Leavis and his kind have given scant value: the achievement of personal wholeness *à la*, say, the Siddhartha of his contemporary, Hermann Hesse; the declaring of independence from mores of con-vention and tribe, which in Maugham (ironically for such a social lion) are always under suspicion. Add to this the 'productivity of genius', which he had almost to the clockwork degree of a Mozart, and mastery of craft – in play, novel, memoir, story and travel-piece – which he had to a similar degree as Mozart had over opera, symphony, concerto, sonanta and serenade – and one has a basis on which to make the case for his inclusion in this study.

He was not 'great' in the Leavisite sense; but he had a virtuoso ability to give pleasure, even to instruct; and this, as Anthony Burgess points out,[17] must count for a great deal. Having said as much, we must now turn to the question of whether he deserves to be considered an 'expatriate' proper. The common assumption is that he was a tireless traveller with affinities to the British colonial mentality as it approached the end of Empire, but that his residence in France was established for reasons of his homosexuality and tax and had little more to do with idealistic expatriation than did the retirement there of so many rich Anglo-Saxons. This may be refuted by the facts and by Maugham's intentions as revealed in his writing. Meanwhile, by the definition of expatriation set out at the beginning of this study, we can say categorically that Maugham was not an exile, banned from his country like Wagner or Marx, Mann or Solzhenitzyn, except during the period of the Second World War when he was blacklisted by Dr Goebbels and forced to leave his elected *patria*, France, to spend five years in the United States. By the same token, he was never, except arguably in this phase, an *émigré*, in flight from his country because of stated political or sociological distaste for some regime there, as were contemporary White Russians. He was not the type who traded one *patria* for another; for though his home was in France for nearly 40 years, his intention was never to write in French or become a naturalised Frenchman in the manner of Conrad and Eliot becoming 'Brits'. Nor was his living away from home meant to enable him to render that homeland better, as in the case of Joyce with Ireland or some of the Americans in Paris of the 1920s with their native Midwest. He had tendencies always to the 'retrograde' form of expatriation I spoke of in my introduction: the impulse, often related to seafaring, to bury oneself and one's over-civilised northerness in some dark, distant spot of a more southern world. But this was not dominant in him finally, as is shown by his ageing persona as *grand seigneur* of the Villa Mauresque at Cap Ferrat.

Compared with the other writers concentrated on in this study, we see that Maugham sought greater freedom in his travels whereas James sought superior order. This may be a fundamental difference between classic European and American forms of expatriation, especially in this pivotal period around the turn of the twentieth century. James, as we've seen, was in flight from what he imagined to be a 'half savage' country, to use Pound's phrase;[18] nor, in spite of the Osmonds and adults Maisie knew, did he ever give up his idea that a more congenial life might be found in Europe, even if only by an American élite there. Maugham, brought up in England by pillars of Victorian rectitude – the vicar of Whitstable and masters of the

King's School, Canterbury – had no fear of savagery in his past to expunge; on the contrary, the deficiencies he perceived in his nature and environment came from excessive inhibition. He needed to 'come out' in the largest sense: to develop a more multi-faceted moral outlook; to let in fertilising chaos. This is the last thing James, or Eliot following him, would have wanted. The Americans, like their nation, were in pursuit of some new moral purity to impose on a world they were inheriting. The British of Maugham's generation and ilk were weary of Empire, or at least of the moral certainties they had had to impose to maintain it, and were avid to discover new, more natural ways to *live*. We can see this in Lawrence and Forster, among other contemporaries; and Lawrence in particular might be a rival to Maugham as the representative 'great expatriate' of the period. In my introduction I dismissed Lawrence as a traveller with essentially British or universalist concerns; much the same might be said of Maugham as well – indeed, has been. The difference, I think, is chiefly of degree. Both men were driven by *Wanderlust*; and as Maugham in his prime never settled anywhere out of England for long, so Lawrence, had he lived, might have opted Maughamishly for a semi-detached expatriation among like-minded compatriots in Tuscany or the South of France.[19]

In both we see a pattern of flight which had become *de rigueur* for a kind of British writer, at least since Shelley perched in Pisa and collected a 'nest of singing birds' around him. In his efforts to get Aldous Huxley and others to set up a kind of commune with him, Lawrence might have been imitating self-consciously the anti-establishment, yet essentially English, impulse in Shelley which attracted Leigh Hunt and Trelawny and even the misanthropic Byron to his side. Political and sexual radicalism, mixed with a lively curiosity for old and new elements in great European (or world) culture, were leitmotifs in both. As for Maugham: though he stood aloof from the communal enthusiasms of Shelleyan contemporaries (which included beyond Lawrence many of the cosmopolitan Americans and British expatriates in Paris), he was definitely one of them in the desire to transcend narrow, middle-class national consciousness and find a more inquisitive, eclectic lifestyle elsewhere. Though he avoided trendy political aspirations (and affectations), he resembles most among Romantic precursors Byron, whose club foot he borrowed to stand in for his own stutter in Philip Carey. Like Byron, Maugham dashed out of England at the first moment of adulthood, to revel in a more colourful and natural Mediterranean realm; also to develop sexually as he pleased, homoerotically in his case no doubt, away from tricky laws and prying eyes. In first travels he went to so many of the same places as Byron – notably Seville – that one suspects he at times fantasised himself to be a modern Childe Harold. But most striking of his similarities to Byron is his preoccupation with maintaining his reputation as a well-bred Englishman, dedicated to the best in the public-school code and – however eccentric – loyal to class and nation when the chips were down. Byron's ultimate service to the London Greek Committee, making his death in effect a martyrdom to his own nation's interest as much as to Greek liberty, has its counterpart in the intelligence and propaganda work Maugham did in both World Wars, especially the mission to revolutionary Russia which contributed to the most critical illness of his prime, a collapse with tuberculosis.

The fact that Maugham's preference for the Continent dates from Byronic 'hot youth' belies the argument that he only expatriated to France in the 1920s for the negative purposes of escaping British tax and homosexuality laws. Born in Paris, he spent the first nine years of his life in France, before the death of both parents led to the break-up of the only steady family he would ever have. The period was perhaps the happiest of his career. Not only was French his first language, it was the literature he was first exposed to and the one he would always prefer. All this was compelling. Though he had not a drop of non-English blood in him, Maugham grew up, like James, feeling nostalgic for scenes of youth amid foreign grandeur. As the wanderings of James senior made young Henry an instinctive expatriate from birth, so the residence of Maugham's parents in and around Paris made him an instinctive European. Maugham's treatment of his adolescent years in Whitstable and Canterbury (all except in *Cakes and Ale*, a wistful farewell to the best of his English past written upon moving into the Villa Mauresque) shows that he viewed them as a purgatory. Rather than go to Cambridge in the steps of his estranged brothers, he prevailed on the German background of his guardian's wife in order to get back to the Continent at the first chance. A year in Heidelberg proved just as thrilling for him as for Philip Carey: a release for the pent-up curiosity in his soul, also a verbal liberation for a shy boy who stuttered. (To exist in another language was always a relief for Maugham: in periods of malaise in later life he went so far as to take up Arabic and Russian – a version perhaps of Byron's eccentric attempt to learn Armenian when recovering from emotional wounds in Venice.) Returning to England from

Germany was anticlimactic, even given his swift move to the relative liberty and excitement of London. Fixed residence at home was as constricting as fixed profession would soon feel. At the first sign of hopes for success as a novelist, he gave up his intention to be a doctor and went off again to lands 'where the orange tree grows'.

This was the pattern of his first decade of adulthood, before unexpected success as a playwright forced him to keep to the fixed base of London. But even gaining theatrical acclaim in the metropolis of his language failed to keep Maugham settled happily. First and foremost of the things financial liberation could buy him was the ability to travel wherever and whenever he chose. The wherever was easy: he went to New York, Switzerland, back to Capri and so on, writing most of his new plays while away. The whenever, though, was restricted by exigencies of the theatre; and the frustration this caused no doubt contributed to the greatest feeling of malaise of his adult life – the brooding on adolescent unhappiness which led him to write his most grey and melancholy work, whose title exposes the 'bondage' he felt. One might argue that Maugham's *Bildungsroman* would not have been written, or anyway written at such length or with such raw naturalism, had he not been tied to a desk in London; the original of it, drafted years before in Spain, was a relatively brief, aesthetic effort as experimental as it was soul-baring. The marriage implied at the end of the book found its counterpart in the liaison that Maugham had embarked on with Syrie Barnardo Wellcome, under the influence of the social/theatrical milieu and perhaps in part to disguise his true sexual nature. This led to Syrie's pregnancy, divorce from an estranged husband and marriage to Maugham just at the time when he was beginning the love-affair of his life with Gerald Haxton, a complex of events not dissimilar to those surrounding Byron's disastrous marriage following his incest with and probable impregnation of his half-sister. Though Maugham rarely played out his dramas so overtly as Byron (he confined to theatre what the poet could only stage in life), the effect of these events was equally traumatic to him and certainly contributed to his mania for escape to the South Seas. Beginning in 1916, exactly one hundred years after Byron's second and serious expatriation, Maugham's flight instantly produced a work which has few rivals for the feeling it gives of claustrophobia and the need to kick down the doors.

This is *The Moon and Sixpence*, and it is the crucial document in support of the argument that Maugham was an instinctive expatriate all along. It reads like a description of an archetypal condition: a case study of what we are after in its pathological form, though the hypercivilised muddle which immediately inspired it makes it appear that Maugham was after a more retrograde form of expatriation than was ever true on balance. The story romanticises his determination to leave the 'safe' atmosphere of London, which he depicts as suffering from 'mental asphyxia' as much as Julien Sorel's Paris. In glorification of the bohemian haunts of his past and present, Maugham sends his hero, Strickland, to Montparnasse to be a painter and then finally to Tahiti, where he goes thoroughly native. Maugham claimed that his model was Paul Gauguin; but Gauguin's art and life provide material only for the last part of the book, which from a stylistic point of view is the least successful, petering out as it does into double and even triple first-person narration and betraying the change of mood Maugham felt on returning to the novel after interruptions caused by the War. The idea for writing about Gauguin came to Maugham through an artist friend he had known in Paris in 1904. The other extensive treatment of that period, besides *Of Human Bondage*, had come in *The Magician* (1908), a work inspired by the notorious Aleister Crowley, a 'gentleman of Cambridge' who had eloped with the sister of Maugham's lifelong friend, the painter Gerald Kelly, and ended up travelling around the world performing black magic according to his self-styled 'Law of Thelema': DO WHAT THOU WILT SHALL BE THE WHOLE OF THE LAW. Maugham would not like to have admitted that he had Crowley in mind again when writing a second expatriate book set largely in Paris; but the ruthlessness and authenticity which had fascinated him in 'the Great Beast' (Crowley's 'magickal' nickname) are Strickland's chief characteristics; and it is striking to know that at the time Maugham was writing his book, Crowley had begun to devote himself to painting in an outrageously expressionistic and colourful style which might be described as a grotesquification of Gauguin.

Without dwelling on the point, it seems plausible that Maugham once again found inspiration in this initially reputable but ultimately revolting Englishman who had abandoned and ruined Kelly's sister (as Strickland does the wife of his one faithful friend, an artist) and his subsequent wanderings to exotic places to practice his 'beastly' arts. Strickland's flight and work are described several times in terms of 'demonic possession'. Moreover, Maugham makes him end up in a wet-hot environment with a woman whom he exploits in order to create diabolical masterpieces; he then makes him die of a horrible, putrescent rotting, which is just what he had done to the

Crowley character in *The Magician*, though in that case the disease was heart failure rather than leprosy and the creation was grotesque homunculi rather than massive primitive tableaux. In both cases, dying men and shocking works are discovered by good doctors whose services are not wanted; and in both, an aura of extreme antinomianism, even evil, pervades the scene. As Maugham writes of the finis of Strickland:

> The beastly stench almost made [the doctor] faint. His eyes grew accustomed to the darkness, and now he was seized by an over-whelming sensation as he stared at the painted walls. . . . From floor to ceiling the walls were covered with a strange and elabo-rate composition. It was indescribably wonderful and mysterious. It took his breath away. It filled him with an emotion which he could not understand or analyse. He felt the awe and delight which a man might feel who watched the beginning of a world. It was tremendous, sensual, passionate; yet there was something horrible there too, something which made him afraid. It was the work of a man who had delved into the hidden depths of nature and had discovered secrets which were beautiful and fearful too. It was the work of a man who knew things which it is unholy for men to know. There was something primeval there and terrible. It was not human. It brought to his mind vague recollections of black magic. It was beautiful and obscene.[20]

This is the retrograde part of what the overcivilised Maugham wan-dered to find: a 'heart of darkness' where his northern morality might dissolve as surely as the Victorian world's depicted in Eliot's contemporary *The Waste Land* or Yeats's 'The Second Coming'. The narration continues:

> The colours were so strange that words can hardly tell what a troubling emotion they gave . . . purples, horrible like raw and putrid flesh, and yet – with a glowing, sensual passion that called up vague memories of the Roman Empire of Heliogabalus . . . deep yellows that died with an unnatural passion . . . . Who can tell what anguished fancy made these fruits? . . . There was something strangely alive in them, as though they were created in a stage of the earth's dark history when things were not irrevocably fixed to their forms. . . . It was enchanted fruit, to taste which might open the gateway to God knows what secrets of the soul and to mysterious palaces of the imagination. They were sullen

with unawaited dangers, and to eat them might turn a man to beast or god. All that was healthy and natural, all that clung to happy relationships and the simple joys of simple men, shrunk from them in dismay; and yet a fearful attraction was in them, and, like the fruit on the Tree of the Knowledge of Good and Evil, they were terrible with the possibilities of the Unknown.

In *Somerset Maugham and the Quest for Freedom*,[21] Robert Calder made the case that Maugham's pattern of life and great theme was a perpetual, even manic, drive toward liberation on all levels; sexual, financial, artistic and the others already stated. This is so plain that it hardly needs a book to argue it. At his worst, Maugham was a classic case of escapist pathology: the 'fight or flight' syndrome. We can see his wanderings of the 1920s as a direct reaction against the implicit fights he had to face in London, in the ill-advised marriage to Syrie and with the critics and competitors who are always lying in wait for a successful writer in his prime. This explains *The Moon and Sixpence* on a psychological basis: in this phase Maugham's 'quest for freedom' requires the carelessness, even cruelty, of a Strickland towards domesticating females, tedious and trivial urban society, conventional ideas of fine art and so on. By necessity, to break loose Maugham had to evoke a 'beast'; nor is it coincidental that this was the exact moment in his career when he had to admit to himself finally that he was not 'three-quarters' heterosexual and ran off with the wicked, witty, brave yet partly worthless Haxton. Even so, Maugham remained unliberated. So conventional was he, and so afraid of what they might say back in London (again like Byron), that he sought to keep his homosexuality a secret. This too might be a factor in the sneering guiltlessness he embodies in Strickland: the great amoral escaper is a compensation for the timidity of his creator, as well as rationalisation for his temerity. But finally Strickland is not Maugham, nor even a programme for how Maugham wished he could behave. The novel is told in the first person, by an author/traveller/observer who keeps full balance between urban European civilisation and the lure of Tahiti, which after all is the most Gallic and civilised of 'primitive' spots. Maugham's depiction of Strickland is of a tragic drop-out whose genius he admires but whose life he finds loathsome and whose exploitative behaviour to others is contemptible. *The Moon and Sixpence* is thus a critique of the primitivist strain in the expatriate urge as much as a glorification of it.

Maugham was not a Crowley or a Gauguin. He was not even

finally an expatriate in the style of Malcolm Lowry of *Under the Volcano* or Lawrence of *The Plumed Serpent*. Frieda Lawrence saw this when she and her husband met Maugham and Haxton in Mexico, a locale Maugham found disappointing and from which he could not wrest a novel:

> An unhappy and acid man [Frau Lawrence observed], who got no fun out of living. He seemed to me to have fallen between two stools as so many writers do. He wanted to have his cake and eat it. He could not accept the narrow social world and yet he didn't believe in a wider human one. Commentator and critic of life and nothing more.[22]

This is of course an unfair assessment; it arose from what is reported to have been a bad-tempered meeting on all sides. Maugham could get fun out of living, as he would in the 1930s at Villa Mauresque; and he was much more than a mere critic of life, as the philosophical sections of *The Summing Up* (1938) and *The Razor's Edge* would show. But D. H.'s wife was right in her perception that he embodied conflicting impulses and that he would not often burst loose with Lawrentian paeans to dark phallic energy or a chthonic Life Force such as he comes close to in descriptions of Strickland. There was a limit to the apocalypticism of Maugham's vision, just as there was to his taste for wandering the South Seas. It was a wide limit: he would return to Oceania, Southeast Asia, China and various exotic 'hearts of darkness' compulsively with Haxton throughout the 1920s; he would get many of his most famous stories from travels there, as well as two novels on expatriate (or at least colonial) themes, *The Painted Veil* (1925) and *The Narrow Corner* (1932). But he could not end his life there, any more than he could hone the message of his art into sustained propaganda for some emblematic 'woman who rode away'. His own ideal of primitivism seems to have settled with 'the beachcomber', who 'like the artist and gentleman perhaps belongs to no class' and who is 'easy of approach and affable of conversation' whether in Polynesia or Paris and has all the best tales to tell.[23]

But even this was not enough. There remained in Maugham a serious moralist who, like the heroine of his Chinese novel, longed for duty in the end; who admired *goodness* and needed always to return to Western civilisation. This Maugham revelled in his Alroy Kears and Elliott Templetons and 'three fat women of Antibes': that exquisitely-heeled class of beachcomber we call 'beautiful people' or 'jet set'. But most of all he yearned for a mediating third type of person: a kind of godly, all-seeing, all-tolerating hero to stand between the necessary social order of the West and the vagrant primitivism of more equatorial zones. Something of this sort he instinctively perceived to be the true, successful and necessary type of the citizen-of-the-world of his times. For the world had moved on from the upper-middle-class *données* of Pax Britannica just as it would move on from the jackbooted, primitivist, working-class movements that were now being instrumental in transforming it. A third way had to emerge — indeed had been emerging for some time, in the novels of Hesse, for instance, as already mentioned, the psychology of Jung and the theosophical activities of ascendant gurus such as Jiddu Krishnamurti: a new type of individuality which could travel freely between both worlds and on further, to higher landscapes beyond. And so we come to what many regard as Maugham's most appealing achievement: the great 'free spirits' of his fiction: the pliable, pleasing Rosie Driffield of *Cakes and Ale*, who lives entirely for love and must leave narrow Blackstable as a result; and much more significantly in the expatriate context, Larry Darrell of *The Razor's Edge*. I have written about Darrell in my book, *Art, Messianism and Crime*, and have shown how he prefigures the Orphic-Narcissistic 'flower child' of the drop-out cults of the essentially American 1960s. I have also suggested that his type might be a 'white magical' refinement of the 'black magical' Oliver Haddo whom Maugham had essayed in his earliest expatriate novel; and this still strikes me as credible. In fact, I would suggest to the reader that *The Magician*, *The Moon and Sixpence* and *The Razor's Edge* together provide a trilogy of Maugham's essential soul-development, spread across the 40 most important years of his working life.

All are set principally in what Anthony Curtis calls 'self-releasing Paris';[24] each is about psychologically breaking loose. In the first, the 'free' character, Haddo, is portrayed as pure evil, while Maugham's narrative persona is not yet ready to leave the bourgeois world, its professions, expectations of conventional sex and marriage and code of morality. In the second, the 'free' character, Strickland, is more attractive: he at least creates fine art to compensate for his amorality; and Maugham's narrative persona is now willing to travel around the world to at least contemplate, if not imitate, him. In the third, the 'free' character, Darrell, is now nearly pure good: by leaving the bourgeois world and its expectations, he acquires 'powers' that en-able him to heal those who stay behind; and though his good intentions may lead to some disasters among the unsteady – the self-destruction of Sophie Macdonald notably – he is by no means directly responsible for this; and Maugham's narrative persona is content to sit back and contemplate him in his humble, humane splendour as if he were a new breed of Western 'white Christ'. Maugham has been accused of choosing his subjects to coincide with the appeal being generated by more original contemporary works and impulses in the *Zeitgeist*. Thus with *The Magician*, he was trying to 'cash in' on the enthusiasm for 'magic' around the *fin de siècle*; with *Of Human Bondage*, for the development-of-the-young-man spate of novels coinciding with the First World War; with *The Razor's Edge*, for Eastern and mystical ideas taken up by wandering young writers of the 1930s, including, among Englishmen, Huxley and Isherwood.[25] There is no doubt something in this. On the other hand, a fundamental path through excess and error toward the 'palace of wisdom' of Buddhistic quiescence seems to have been prefigured in Maugham's career ever since he heard Kuno Fischer lecture on Schopenhauer at Heidelberg in the first moment of his intellectual and geographical breaking-loose in the 1890s; and Darrell with his picaresque education and growing enlightenment strikes one as an idealisation of Maugham's own intellectual self more than a character designed cynically to 'cash in' on a trend, as some of his youthful creations might have been.

Corroboration for this comes in the non-fiction Maugham wrote in the 1930s, particularly his great semi-memoir, semi-aesthetic and philosophical tract, *The Summing Up*. Maugham had been moving for years, steadily, inexorably, toward the broadest, most tolerant, most inclusive yet still useful kind of moral position. He was after clear spiritual ideas in an age which had lost religion. This is at the core of his wandering in all senses: through the many genres and traditions of literature as through the countries of the world. He was a seeker – what great expatriate, finally, in the best sense isn't? Eliot, for instance, only put an end to his wanderings and status as expatriate at the moment he became sure of his faith as an 'Anglo-Catholic'. Scepticism, agnosticism and pragmatism are part of the givens for any complete citizen of the world. These don't have to become a cause for despair, as for Byron in black phases; they might equally open the doors toward brotherhood with 'the happy few' as envisioned by Stendhal and sometimes perhaps lived by James. But they have to be combined by something: a cohering force – not mere order, which in eras of breakdown of certainty can only lead to some brand of fascism (which Maugham hated), [26] but some principle of spiritual sweetness and sympathy. Here we come back to a word mentioned before, and which Maugham himself struck on finally: Goodness. In the last part of *The Summing Up*, Maugham identifies this as the greatest of the three transcendental values, the other two being Beauty and Truth.[27] Beauty, like passionate love, is transitory and ends by losing its force. Truth is undefinable except as a pattern; thus the purpose of Art, which, Maugham implies, is for him as it was for Goethe an attempt to harmonise the 'bundle of mutually contradictory selves' that comprise the individual personality. The pattern of life Maugham defines as 'self-realization tempered by a lively sense of irony, making the best of a bad job'. The 'value of art' finally is 'right action'. Right action is Goodness. Goodness is 'the retort that humour makes to the tragic absurdity of fate'. It is the quality of observation and humility that asks for little and sympathises with much; that in the end encourages each man to be content to 'act in conformity with his nature and his business'.

The message finally is a version of 'man know thyself'. Indeed, knowledge is a large part of what Maugham was after: education from life rather than from academia, which he had avoided since youth. The many non-fiction works of his career attest to this, not least the ones written in his seventies and eighties. The quest for freedom becomes on the one hand a quest for wisdom; the trajectory of Larry Darrell. On another it remains, as it always has been, a quest for worldly repute and success: that of Elliott Templeton. The two are two faces of the American expatriate of the age – indeed, of civilised expatriates at large, certainly of Maugham's own kind. Larry is the new type: the 'lonesome traveller' who rejects materialism, imperialism, class and duty and in the mildest possible manner fights for a new age of thoughtfulness, tolerance and love. He finds his 'knowledge', his *gnosis* 'on the road' in Europe and in India. Elliott is the old type: an Osmond with humour; a collector of people and *objets*; a snob and dilletante who nevertheless has strong familial concerns – whom his neice should marry and so on. He has become a Catholic for reasons of connections and tradition; in contrast to Larry, he entertains no metaphysical doubt and imagines that anyone who does is either ill-brought-up and beneath consideration or in need of rapid instruction. Where Larry goes to Paris and ultimately India as a drop-out, Elliott has gone to Paris and ends on the Côte d'Azur as a drop-in. Where Larry leaves America to find Truth, Elliott has gone to admire Beauty. Where Larry searches for Self, Elliott has sought Society. Cosmopolitanism for each achieves opposite ends. Elliott has rejected America because it lacks taste and glamour: he regards its conventions as under- or mis-developed and has adopted, like James, what he thinks is a superior conventionality. Larry abdicates from the America of bourgeois expectations, in money, manners, business and family responsibilities. It is in a sense too civilised for him: he needs to be a free man and build his life from scratch. Thus the last thing he is willing to do is trade American upper middle-class *données* for supposedly superior European ones.

We have the nice irony then of the anti-snob snubbing the snob – something Maugham ever delighted in, indicating that his own wanderings may have been in part a quest for the individual authority to allow him to reject any rejector. Larry as drop-out, like Strickland before him, is a way for Maugham to circumnavigate the treacherous careerism and status-seeking that he encountered in his urban social persona, whether in Europe or in America. Elliott triumphs in this sphere, but only up to a point: at the end of his life, he is reduced to pathetic concern over whether a certain hostess (an American expatriate too) is going to invite him to a party or not. Here is Maugham the host to Churchill and the Windsors at the Villa Mauresque: the Maugham who cared who came to visit and was hurt when he didn't receive an OBE like Hugh Walpole and only got a CH in the end, unlike Henry James who got an OM.[28] In reaction there is Maugham the partly self-protective, partly genuinely indifferent 'Departer', to use Anthony Curtis's word:[29] the Maugham who was never in doubt that he was better than the Walpoles or Jameses because he also embodied a type of free spirit who went beyond their narrow, upper-middle-class, urban First World milieux. The aesthetic, order-loving citizen of a higher realm of 1880–1930 is now a mere ornament, inadequate to the age – this Maugham instructs us in *The Razor's Edge* as elsewhere. But what about the metaphysical beachcomber he erects in its place, the Larry Darrell persona? Is this finally much more adequate? Doesn't Maugham himself express scepticism in his argument with Larry over the sense of giving up his inheritance in order to be truly free, even of material possessions? In the decades following *The Razor's Edge*'s publication, large numbers in the West went through Huxley's 'doors of perception' and sought Isherwood's or even Kerouac's form of '*satori*'.[30] But now haven't we come to a point in the *Zeitgeist* where the successor has to be succeeded: where

Larry's type has gone to seed, driving its taxis in New York, and Elliott's type may have set out again to discover the higher *données* – an Ishiguro come from Japan to ventriloquise the civilised voice of an observant butler in a 1930s English country-house?

Larry and Elliott are opposite yet equal forces in a more timeless expatriate urge: a kind of ever-oscillating yin-yang of the type in its most life-enhancing manifestation. Thus Elliott must be seen as part of the triumph of *The Razor's Edge* too. For all his preposterousness and despite Larry's contrasting (yet subtly irritating) perfection, he emerges as sympathetic. In his hypersocial, conventional way, he is another example of Goodness. He is *serviable*, in Maugham's word; but this is not just a matter of making himself available at short notice for luncheon when a hostess has come up with an odd number; it is an acute watchfulness, a sensitivity to the condition of others which provokes him to go to Chicago to sort out the affairs of his sister when he would rather stay in Paris, or to make over his Paris flat to his neice and her family when they have come on hard times. No doubt there is a self-seeking element in some of his charitable acts: he is very pleased to receive a bogus title from the pope in return for endowing a new church in the Pontine marshes. On the other hand, there is real selflessness in the way he attempts to advance the careers of other young expatriates following in his footsteps: Paul Barton, who uses Elliott's contacts yet laughs at this refinement and adopts the brash manner of a Scott Fitzgerald era; and Larry, who turns down all overtures Elliott makes to introduce him to the 'best' people. Elliott is not only an Osmond and a maiden-aunt caricature out of James, he is also a Strether. That Maugham had James in mind is indicated by a reference to him in the first chapter of the book – an apology for attempting American characters with the same presumption that 'the Master' had attempted English ones. In fact, *The Razor's Edge* is in many ways a full-blown American-abroad novel *à la* James. Not only in Elliott is this apparent but in his sister, Mrs Bradley of Chicago, whose steady imperviousness to the more trivial graces of the Old World makes her seem a cross between Mrs Newsome and Mrs Touchett.[31] Maugham admires this and implicitly contrasts it to the transformation that later overtakes her daughter in Europe, a girl who, like James's most famous 'heiress to the ages', happens to be named Isabel.

This is no accident; for *The Razor's Edge* revolves around Isabel Bradley Maturin's bad marriage and expatriation just as *The Portrait of a Lady* does around Isabel Archer Osmond's. Maugham had been

in America three years when he began the book; he had had a
principal relationship with an American for a quarter of a century;
he had become the highest-paid author in the world largely on
account of American readership; his financial affairs were arranged
by an American; he was living in his American publisher's house;
his only principal associates were American; and his principal attachment to Britain at the time was a brief to help the War effort by
emphasising the ties between British and American cultures. If at
times before and after he expressed jaundiced attitudes toward 'God's
Own Country' as cultured Europeans are wont,[32] in this period he
was grateful for American support and genuinely fascinated by its
society. The most striking accomplishment of *The Razor's Edge* may
be its evocation of the American at home and abroad. Indeed,
Maugham's apology, though polite, seems partly unnecessary: his
understanding of America, at least in the elements he focuses on, is
acute; and to an American – this American at any rate – the book
seems one of the few which has really seen into the forces of class
and conformity at work in that culture and noted the obstacles
placed in the way of true freedom among its upper-middle classes.
To a reader of the 1960s the book must have seemed uncannily
contemporary, unlike the novels of James which had long since
become ornamental artefacts. There are false notes – in the use of
language, for instance, the lacuna the foreign author most apologises
for yet covers nicely by using first-person narration and setting most
of the action in the past and in Europe. But then there are very sound
notes too, not least of which is the dilemma of Isabel, especially in its
early phase. What is a girl of her expectations to do? Marry the free
spirit Larry whom she loves but who will always put self-realisation
before her; or marry Gray Maturin, football player and stockbroker,
who adores her and will do everything the good American husband
ought to in the way of supporting wife and family and making them
the imaginative centre of his life?

   The plot thus turns on a simplified, updated version of Isabel
Archer's vacillation between Lord Warburton, Caspar Goodwood
and Osmond; and as for *that* Isabel, any decision must be half-bad,
because it will close off options which have real attractions, thus
limiting what we have seen to be the highest value for Maugham –
the contemplation of unlimited possibilities. 'I'm on the threshold',
says Larry when Isabel asks him why he can't come back to Chicago,
settle into a job and support her in the conventional manner; 'I see
vast lands of the spirit stretching out before me, beckoning, and I'm

eager to travel them.'[33] Isabel calls this 'sophomoric'. She says that the ultimate questions Larry wants answered are not answered already because they are unanswerable and ought, by a practical person, to be left that way. She makes an eloquent plea for America and its future ('Europe's finished. We're the greatest, most powerful people in the world') and for its citizens' duty to contribute to it. This is dramatic, but it's not mere invention: it is the way American women from Isabel's class and era would have talked; and the fact that it falls on ears that hear a different drumbeat is galling to her not just as a woman but as a proponent of American material progress. Swallowing her pride, Isabel accepts loss of love and marries Gray. All is well until years later Gray loses his fortune in the Great Crash, and the ordered American life – the 'doing the done thing' – for which Isabel sacrificed her inner desire is shown to be less durable than Larry's non-material quest. Maugham says in *Of Human Bondage* that nine out of ten suicides are committed over money, not love.[34] In *The Razor's Edge*, it seems implied that if Gray had not been ruined and Larry had not walked away from the Crash unscathed because his small capital was left neglected in bonds, things might have turned out differently. Isabel might not have become so overtaken by possessiveness of Larry that she precipitates the demise of her childhood friend Sophie, who has become an expatriate of the new wild, decadent type and whom Larry wishes to marry in a vain attempt to save her from a preview of the 1960s free-spirit's *auto-da-fé* via sex, drugs and rock-n roll.

Something more is at work in Isabel than merely having made a half-bad decision in marriage herself years before. Some deep-seated pride is threatened, some competitive streak that has made her determined to be taken as an 'heiress to the ages' always and to do what is necessary to maintain her status in that guise. This goes well beyond having power over Larry. In Paris she has become a kind of less-obvious female equivalent to her Uncle Elliott. Mimicking the ways of a native *femme du monde*, she makes herself beautiful by art and regime. Having rid herself of the bloom and tendency to plumpness of American teenage, she now paints her nails and marcels her hair as if in this way to expunge the last traces of naïveté and provincialism. She becomes manipulative, underhanded, more determined than ever. In short, her trajectory is to become the American female as, finally, matriarchal monster. Some may take this as evidence of Maugham's misogyny: the same readers perhaps who see Larry Darrell as 'a compassionate homosexual', in Anthony Curtis's phrase.[35] But as there is the textual evidence of Larry's liaison with Suzanne Rouvier to counter the latter, so there are sympathetic female characters – Rouvier, Sophie and Mrs Bradley – to combat any blanket charge of the first. Moreover, before dismissing Isabel's type as imbalanced, one has to ask whether it is believable; and there is plenty in American literature and culture of the time to prove that the materialistic, manipulative, maternal monster exists. Furthermore, what Maugham does with Isabel, however disturbing, has logic; and to the end he (the narrator) has understanding, if not sympathy, for her motives. Throughout, Isabel retains the same native assurance that rang out in her early speech trying to dissuade Larry from throwing his life away 'in a backwater' (expatriation).[36] She is a kind of youthful Volumnia figure who sticks by her homeland in the end and believes Coriolanus should do so as well. Hers is the voice of reason over romance: the voice, ironically, of Henrietta Stackpole and Caspar Goodwood against Isabel Archer's vagaries; of William James calling back Henry or Mrs Newsome sending Strether to bring back her son Chad.

It is a voice, too, of many characters in Maugham's early novels and plays warning against thralldom to the wayfaring 'magic' preached in its ugliest form by Oliver Haddo but even in more *raffiné*, housebroken guise carrying substantial risks. One may be put in mind of the speeches of Lady Kitty to Elizabeth at a crucial moment in *The Circle* (1921), finest and most expatriate-focused of Maugham's many plays (which, like his wealth of expatriate stories, there is unfortunately no space to go into here). Elizabeth is about to leave England for love, a course Kitty took years before and has lived out in all its consequences, rather like Maugham would with Haxton or – more prophetically still – Edward VIII would with Maugham's friend Wallis Simpson:

'Look at me, Elizabeth, [Kitty says,] and look at Hughie [Lord Porteus, with whom she eloped]. Do you think it's been a success? If I had my time over again do you think I'd do it again? Do you think he would? . . . Of course in the beginning, it was heavenly. We felt so brave and adventurous and we were so much in love. The first two years were wonderful. People cut me, you know, but I didn't mind. . . . We settled in Florence. And because we couldn't get the society we'd been used to, we became used to the society we could get. Loose women and vicious men. Snobs who liked to patronize people with a handle to their names [cf. Uncle Elliott].

Vague Italian princes who were glad to borrow a few francs from Hughie [cf. James's Prince Amerigo] and seedy countesses who liked to drive with me in the Cascine [*the femmes du monde* whom Isabel Maturin apes]. And then Hughie began to hanker after his old life [as does Gray Maturin in Paris]. . . . Are you shocked? One sacrifices one's life for love and then finds that love doesn't last [as Isabel feared would have been the outcome with Larry]. . . . Oh, Elizabeth, my dear child, don't go. It's not worth it. It's not worth it. I tell you that, and I've sacrificed everything to love.'[37]

Elizabeth, the romantic, listens yet still goes. Isabel, the realist, holds back and becomes evil, or at least vengeful, as a result. Elliott, Larry and Maugham himself – all three Great Departers – left and, if not finding full happiness (and surely not constant love) thereby, at least achieved conformity with their true natures and business.

6

Pound

In her memoir of Paris in the 1920s Gertrude Stein remarked that Ezra Pound reminded her of a village explainer: 'excellent if you were a village if not, not'.[1] Pound regarded himself as an itinerant wise man: an aesthetic-intellectual incarnation of the Yankee pioneer, made sage by travels through time as well as space. Confucius was the precursor he most aspired to be like, making cryptic pronouncements *ex cathedra* to guide kindred spirits on future quests. Though he lived in Europe for more than a half-century, he never became an essential European, like his friend Eliot or James. Whereas Eliot hardly ever spoke of America and when he did, did so with subtle Anglicised disparagement, Pound never tired of talking about *'patria mia'* and saw himself as a potential saviour of its founding ideals. Within a few months of arrival in England Eliot's accent had lost all traces of its midwestern and Bostonian antecedents; Pound's by contrast reverted increasingly to stage 'Amerikin'. At the same time his manner became increasingly American in the ruminative tradition of Whitman, whom he admired (unlike Eliot and James), or even some seller of nostrums out of Mark Twain. 'In England', Eliot would observe, 'one keeps one's platitudes to oneself, but in America one shares them with one's neighbours.'[2] Pound did plenty of such 'sharing', even while living far from America. Curiously generous, especially among fellow writers, he never ceased to spread his big ideas; nor in the spirit of Jeffersonian democracy did he think it amiss to have ideas on every subject, even ones he knew little about, even when the ideas partook of rage, race hatred or Nietzschean cruelty. Pound rated authenticity over goodness. In his metamorphosed pioneer vein he felt instinctively that only the fittest survived: that the world belonged to genius and the strong. He himself was by all accounts shy and sensitive. Perhaps it was to counteract this that he became exhibitionistic and belligerent. As his career progressed he gave himself over to what his friend Yeats might have called an antithetical mask. He was the expatriate as knight errant, *errant* being the crucial word.

Like James, Pound had been introduced to Europe early in his life. While on his father's side he derived from a frontier congressman, a Western firebrand who had built a company town, on his mother's he found a congenial spirit in a maiden aunt who took him to Spain and Italy in teenage. 'Monuments of unageing intellect' glimpsed there combined with traditions of the Republic inculcated back home in suburban Philadelphia to make him as a student peculiarly attached to the past. Like Byron, he was an only child in a family which seemed to have come down somewhat in the world. Pound's father (unlike his father's father) was a mere civil servant: an assayer at the Philadelphia mint. The environment, moreover, was not the great, masculine, open frontier, but that eastern seaboard America which the expatriate Henrys (Adams as well as James) saw as being stolen from its original promise by an influx of immigrants from the ruck of Europe.[3] How to sustain distinction in the homogenising (and perhaps degenerating) melting-pot must have been a topic around the Pound table (Pound's mother was descended from the Wadsworths, a good old Yankee puritan clan). It is in this context that the boy escaped into the dead language and courtly traditions of mediaeval Provence. Poetry was his passion, especially that of the troubadours. At university his articulateness on the subject attracted the attention of other poetry-minded students, notably two whose career he would help, William Carlos Williams and Hilda Doolittle (H.D.). The latter became his first conquest, as he was hers. With her he made calf-love in the radiant light of North American spring; simultaneously, both would read from and write in imitation of the classics. Such experience constituted a medallion for Pound: an Eleusinian moment of aesthetic-sexual intensity which he would try to replicate throughout his career and to isolate from the demands of the 'real' world: financial, careerist, combative. Meanwhile, in the spirit of romance *à la trouvère*, Pound learned that it was necessary to be a warrior as well as a lover: a crusader dedicated to protecting precious romance – and indeed his own poet persona – from glib, materialistic, philistine sensibilities: a Bertans de Born, as adept at wielding a broadsword against adversaries as at wooing and winning fair ladies through song.

We can see here that even before embarking to Europe, Pound was an expatriate from his epoch. It may seem an irony in a writer who would come to embody the modernist NEW; but Pound was always in some ways 'out of step with his time', as he would put it in reference to his *manqué* persona in *Hugh Selwyn Mauberley* (1920). In specific, he was out of step with whatever presented itself as the acceptable norm. At school, according to Carlos Williams,[4] he had been a misfit among easy-going, democratically-minded peers; at university he wrote:

> I am homesick after mine own kind
> Oh I know that there are folk about me,
> Friendly faces,
> But I am homesick after mine own kind . . .[5]

His 'own kind' he defined as 'those that know, and feel / And have some breath for beauty and the arts'. Apart from disciples like H.D. and the aspirant painter to whom he would dedicate his first book of lyrics, this 'own kind' could not be found in what he would call 'a half-savage country'. His view of America already partook of the prejudice of James by the time he was dismissed from his first job, teaching at a college in Indiana, for having the temerity to wear dandyish clothes and to allow a burlesque dancer to spend the night in his rooms. This incident released an animosity against the American academic and intellectual establishment which would rival young Byron's against the literati of his day in *English Bards and Scotch Reviewers*. It was 1908 and Pound was 22. With 50 dollars and a rucksack of book-knowledge he set out for Europe and 'the reality of experience'. Travelling on a cattle-boat, he nevertheless had high hopes that he was sailing to 'the holy city of Byzantium', as Yeats would write a quarter of a century later when visiting him in Italy. Pound settled first in Venice, which 64 years later would become the last resting-place of his expatriate career. He came to be instructed, to invoke the gods and heroes of legends he had read as a boy, to become a voice in the present through which the great poets of the past might once again speak. 'The living give life to the imaginings of the dead', he could also have said in anticipation of Yeats,[6] the only living poet he rated as among the great company. Within a year he had moved to London and attached himself to the Celtic bard, soon more as guru than as disciple.

He came armed with a slim volume he had printed at his own expense in Venice. Soon after arrival he induced a publisher to bring out a survey of Provençal poetry based on his unfinished doctoral thesis. Rather like the young Byron, he felt he needed scholarly as well as poetic attainments to be taken seriously in the metropolis of his language. Nor was his procedure in 'the siege of London' entirely unlike Byron's in other respects. Still a dandy, he diguised native shyness under purple trousers, mauve jackets and pink cravats.[7] At a mannerly literary luncheon he ate flowers from the bowl in the middle of the table. Among women he developed some cachet as a lover. Among fellow writers he adopted a tone of radical proponency for things foreign, vigourous and perhaps revolutionary. Like Byron, he used poets of the past to elbow his way around the establishment of the present, in this case the 'Georgians', not the 'Lakers'. But whereas Byron had bashed in favour of recent Augustan tradition, Pound deplored the recent Victorians (except Browning) and bashed for traditions so old and foreign as to seem new: the troubadours, obviously, and later the poets of ancient China and Noh playwrights of Japan. As he was not British and only 'European' in interests, Pound was of course less clubbable than Byron. He was also much poorer and, being no lord, less readily forgivable for bad behaviour. Perhaps these factors are part of why he adopted such an arch posture as literary arbiter. In any case, Pound would prove, in Wyndham Lewis's word, 'unassimilable' in England.[8] He did not want to be, as Eliot would be and to a large degree James had been. Though attached to Europe aesthetically, particularly its Mediterranean traditions, Pound shared with Byron an ineradicable feeling of *oblige* to his own country: a blood attachment to its legislative processes (derivation from early settlers and frontier congressmen was apparently his notional equivalent to hereditary peerage) and therefore responsibility to teach it how better to behave in a world which did not always view it with the same complacent admiration with which it viewed itself. Taken in this spirit, Pound's career, with its disastrous finis in political adventure, might be seen as a distorted modernist version of the Romantic's progress to Missolonghi.

What was Pound's 'quarrel with America'? Before returning home for a period in 1910 he wrote: 'America presents itself to my mind as rather a horrible nightmare, a jaw of Tartarus effect ready to devour me if I lose grip on things present.'[9] The image echoes James's characterisations of America during his early, reluctant trips home. It also has an Oedipal ring; and Pound's trepidation might be linked partly to a subconscious fear of being engulfed by a domesticating maternal principle. Literary and academic America seemed to him suffused with an unadventurous, middle-brow, pseudo-English gentility; publishers and editors of magazines earned his contempt as 'old maids' – not least James's friend William Dean Howells (model perhaps for Strether in *The Ambassadors*), though not, ironically, James himself. Running away from these was escaping the neutering influence of mummy – an uncharismatic person in Pound's case, who fussed too much over her only child, rather like Lady Byron over hers. Taking up the warrior-lover code of a de Born or the outlaw persona of François Villon was not only rejecting a stultifying American present but also identifying with a 'wild west' European male tradition, even a kind of 'men's lib'.[10] Such a tendency in Pound would grow with the years. In his affairs with women, as with Byron's, there is evidence of a compulsion to prove a superior manhood. In his eventual descent into economic theory he may have been trying to work out some vindication of his father, the assayer, a never-quite-successful or satisfied man who, like many American males of his type, was probably overshadowed by his wife in the home. Here is not the place to analyse the Freudian 'figure on the carpet' which propelled Pound to some of his most bizarre and self-damaging acts. But it seems likely that he shared with his friend Hemingway a latent preference for his father over his mother and determination that he was not going to be overshadowed by a female in a similar way. This might explain why he felt compelled to take on exaggerated male opinion, daring and 'genius'; why he had to try out a plethora of male 'personae' before finding a suitable identity for himself; why, meanwhile, he left woman in the periphery of his work, lest she – like the mother-country – become a 'devouring jaw of Tartarus'.

While his poetic production began with troubadour paeans to the goddess Amor, it was the troubadour, not the goddess, he was concerned with. This is a stand-in for an uncertain self. The goddess must of course exist in the background: she is the audience without which young-mannish antics of rhetorical derring-do would fall on deaf ears – as essential as dazzled young ladies back home were for the Childe Harolding Byron. But she must be kept back home, at arm's length, in ideal. The reality of woman is ever scantly depicted in Pound and when it is depicted – as in 'Portrait d'une femme', for instance[11] – it is not overwhelmingly positive. Woman as ideal, *patria mia* as ideal — these impelled him; and not finding them in fact, he created poetic substitutes for them – the Cytherean goddess of the Eleusinian rites, an apparition which would reappear in the most sublime moments of *The Cantos*; and the 'City of Dioce, whose terraces are the colour of stars', a shadowy utopia which would transfigure his most disreputable rantings into contrapuntal laments for the unattainability of perfection on this earth. Pound's quarrel with America was his mother's secret quarrel with his father: he was not a great man. It was his father's secret quarrel with his mother: she was not a dazzling goddess. It was the quarrels of both of them with themselves: they did not live up to their own, let alone others', expectations. It was finally their quarrel with their environment: it did not grant them the status they imagined they should have had as birthright. In suburban America, toeing a conventional line, they had seen their dreams wither to next to nothing; and Pound instinctively was not going to let the same happen to himself or his kind. Thus we see him from early in his expatriation collecting American artists around him – Williams, H. D., Robert Frost, later Eliot, later still Hemingway and the composer George Anthiel – and becoming the protector as well as promoter of their aspirations. To build a new age for them and himself in a more insightful locale – this would be the leitmotif of much of his career; and not just for them, but also for European *déracinés* whom he saw as his 'kind' – Yeats, as mentioned, Joyce, Ford Madox Ford, the novelist and painter Wyndham Lewis, the sculptor Gaudier-Brzeska and more.

Pound spent his early years in London gathering the scattered limbs, as it were, of a composite identity as great poet. At first he suppressed American tones. Only Whistler and James of his countrymen did he rate, aspiring to the barbed wit of the former and mastery of multiple points of view of the latter. Of Whistler, he wrote:

> You also, our first great,
> Had tried all ways;
> Tested and pried and worked in many fashions,
> And this gives me heart to play the game . . .
>
> You had your searches, your uncertainties,
> And this is good know – for us, I mean,
> Who bear the brunt of our America
> And try to wrench her impulse into art.[12]

Of James and other favoured precursors, he would write Byronically:

> From these he learnt. Poe, Whitman, Whistler,
>   men, their recognition
> Was got abroad, what better luck do you wish 'em,
> When writing well has not yet been forgiven

In Boston, to Henry James, the greatest whom we've
seen living.[13]

With Whitman he would elsewhere make a famous 'pact', acknowledging that the exuberant vagabond had been the seminal voice of
authentically American (as opposed to Americanly English) poetry:
the progenitor of a largeness and looseness in which Pound would
ultimately share – *The Cantos* would be Whitmanesque in these
qualities, as in their visionary atmosphere and almost spontaneous
style, all of which would make Pound a (perhaps *the*) essential link
between Whitman and the Beat poets of the 1950s and 1960s. But in
London of the 1910s such proto-hippy impulses were not yet in the
open. Though he wore polka-dot hat-bands and spoke in learned
riddles, Pound was producing poems in a 1890s-ish manner, with
Arthurian elements, Pre-Raphaelite damosels and much of the vague,
mystical paraphernalia which he would encourage Yeats to get rid of
in favour of the hard and the clear. Yet amid Symbolist niceties he
was already deploying a number of motifs which would become
characteristic of his mature work: the cult of travel, on the road or at
sea; the *poésie des départs* and element of homesickness not unlike
that which pervades *Childe Harold*; paeans to the beauty of the
Languedoc and other storied spots of Mediterranean Europe; a tendency to linger in *dolce far niente* counterpointed by sudden calls to
battle or to a madness of inspiration.

   Some of these motifs were borrowed from old Anglo-Saxon ('The
Sea-farer', for instance). Most, however, came from Provence; and in
identifying with the culture which had produced Eleanor of Aquitaine's courts of love, the Grail epics and to some extent even Dante,
Pound was attaching himself subliminally to the heretical traditions
which had led to the crushing of the Albigensians and Cathars by the
combined forces of the pope and the king of France. What these
heretical sects actually believed in had to do in Pound's mind with
sex and fertility rites derived from the ancients – the shadowy
mysteries of Eleusis, as we have already mentioned, and cults of
Tammuz, Adonis and Osiris made fashionable in the period through
Sir James Frazer's studies in *The Golden Bough*. Also impressive to
Pound was the valorous code of the Crusades, which in his meta-
morphosis was stripped of its Christian trappings and revealed as a
neo-pagan doctrine of strength – a kind of Nietzschean 'master
morality'. Like the German existentialist philosopher (favourite
reading for Yeats when Pound was intimate with him), Pound made

a point of despising the church, which he saw as hypocritical, coercive and hostile to true individualism. His personal vision of Christ, offered in the 'Ballad of the Goodly Fere', is a brave 'lover of brawny men, / O' ships and the open sea': a proponent of '*la gaya scienza*' and exuberant action, doomed, almost before he has begun, to martyrdom at the hands of a bureaucratic establishment.[14] Pound's Christ might have been the leader of a secret grail order. Pound himself was instinctively assuming a Parsifalian role in his London literary quest, drawing F. S. Flint, Richard Aldington and even D. H. Lawrence among young writers around him – 'goodly feres' in a movement for new excellence in poetry, this in reaction against what all of them considered the complacent taste of a comfortable establishment. Pound's quarrel with America thus expanded at this time to encompass a quarrel with England, with what he viewed as the similarly unadventurous 'old maids' who ran its publishing houses and magazines and who were supported by a closed class and economic system. In *Ripostes* (1912), and more remarkably *Lustra* (1915), we find the voice of the poet becoming that of the social critic, the castigator of all those forces which he sees as arrayed against the art, and thus the free spiritual expression of his kind.

Not least among these forces is the middle-class London woman. This Jamesian type Pound sees as having a mind not so much 'so fine that it could not be violated by an idea' but so full of 'ideas, old gossip, oddments of all things / Strange spars of knowledge and dimmed wares of price' that she is made up of 'nothing quite [her] own'.[15] Keeper of '*moeurs contemporaine*', she is 'dying piece-meal / of a sort of emotional anaemia'.[16] An exemplar of an 'end of breeding', she affects a boredom 'exquisite and excessive'. She is a debased goddess of culture, Eleanor of Aquitaine decayed into Lady Ottoline Morrell, presiding over a 'generation of the thoroughly smug / and thoroughly uncomfortable'. She might have taken up Pound when fresh from America, unfledged and writing about 'the picturesque' with a promise of young Byron's 'vertigo of emotions'; but now that he has 'lost his illusions' and become combative, she regards him as 'shameless', 'impertinent', 'indecorous'. She is a sufferer from 'unconscious oppression', 'the tyranny of the unimaginative', suburban 'ennui', marital misalliance, concealed failure, thwarted desires and received opinion – a spiritual cousin to 'The Rest': the 'helpless few' of Pound's own country ('O remnant enslaved!') who have been 'thwarted by systems' and had their 'finer sense' 'broken against false knowledge'.[17] The latter Pound counsels to 'take thought' from him who has 'weathered the storm' and 'beat out [his] exile'. To all these sufferers, he sends his songs, in an effort half to liberate, half to *épater*. Adopting an increasingly élitist bohemianism, he enjoins the songs to 'express . . . baser passions', go forth naked and 'half cracked', seek 'praise from the young / and from the intolerant' and move 'among the lovers of perfection alone'.[18] 'Let us resurrect the very excellent term *Rusticus*', he declares; let us 'mate with [our] free kind upon the crags'; let us imitate 'the gilded phalloi of the cro- cuses' and admire 'the pale wet leaves of the lily-of-the-valley' as we lie beside our lovers at dawn; let us be like gypsies and walk the roads of the past and see the gods return 'with fear, as half-wakened'; let us 'bathe [ourselves] in strangeness' and take 'the plunge' into other worlds, whether mediaeval Perigord or even more remote Cathay, Pound's furthest favoured land of exile in both time and space, where river-merchants dream of travelling homeward to their wives and a 'lone sail' seems ever to 'blot the far sky' and sunset inevitably puts one in mind of 'the parting of old acquaintances'.[19]

Cathay, the first of Pound's Chinese translations, appeared also in the middle of his London period; and from the Oriental example, among other influences, he was developing an ideogrammic approach to writing which would turn out to be one of the chief stylistic achievements of literary modernism. Thus we have the *image*, which Pound would elaborate into the *vortex* through which a wealth of connotations and associations might flow. Later, in *The Cantos*, he would develop this into the *paideuma*, a term derived from the German historical philosopher Frobenius, who believed that each epoch was characterised by a cluster of ideas and events which might be reduced to a vortical image, as it were: a series of ideogrammic representations of the *Zeitgeist*, such as Pound would use with stunning effect in the gong-like homilectics of 'Section Rock-Drill'. That Pound was adapting his most important techniques from foreign ideas (perhaps partly misunderstood) no doubt con- tributed to his alienation from the English mainstream in this period, also his growing obscurity. It had to do, too, with an impulse he shared with many of his contemporaries to gather out of the great sweep of tradition certain ineradicable truths. One thinks of Yeats, trying to plot historical cycles according to quasi-astrological laws in *A Vision*, or of Joyce, trying to devise a universal 'nightspeak' out of all Indo-European languages in *Finnegans Wake*. The drive to unity is the great theme of *The Education of Henry Adams*, a classic of the American self-critical tradition, which Pound read and admired when it came out in 1918; and finding some new single principle to explain history began to obsess Pound from this stage. For most, such an impulse was provoked by the continuing decline of the Christian consensus; for Pound in particular it was given urgency by the collapse of nineteenth-century bourgeois order into the chaos of the First World War. Thus while Adams sought his quasi-religious answer in science and Yeats in neo-hermetic ideas, Pound became fascinated with economics: specifically, the Social Credit theories of Major C. H. Douglas, which Pound believed could eradicate maldistribution of wealth and thus remove the chief cause of war. This may have been prescient considering the dominance of economics over politics and religion in the later part of the twentieth century. But among writers and artists of the time it was viewed as eccentric: the Pound they admired (if they did) was the innovator of imagist-vorticist technique, not the half-baked monetarist.[20]

Pound's later London years were overshadowed by the War and its consequences. It was a time of pain and anger for him as for many. His friend Gaudier-Brzeska had been killed in a trench in France; other friends had been wounded or had their careers disrupted. Meanwhile, the battle for renovation of the arts had been impeded in London by patriotic afflatus or sheer prejudice; and Pound's persona as social critic became more marked as a result. Just before the War he had collaborated with Wyndham Lewis on the radical arts-and-politics magazine *BLAST!*, which was inspired in part by the Italian futurist, F. H. Marinetti. Hemingway would sum up Lewis's character by saying that he had 'the eyes of an unsuccessful rapist'; and though Hemingway may have had special motives for his assessment,[21] his conclusion that Lewis was not a good influence on Pound probably has something in it. With the wild Marinetti he certainly encouraged Pound to new bellicosity in print. That this was in part a false mask is indicated by the fact that at the same time Pound was wooing and winning the daughter of a prominent solicitor and of Yeats's former mistress. Dorothy Shakespear was demure, submissive and possessed of a comfortable annuity in blue chip securities. On the surface she was an embodiment of everything Pound railed against – the English rose *par excellence* – and while one part of him was evidently attracted to this (the precious only child of his genteel mother), another part (the macho expressionist) must have felt rather like Byron on attaching himself to the strait-laced Annabella Milbanke. We have seen how Maugham's ill-advised marriage, undertaken at about the same time as Pound's (and both exactly one hundred years after Byron's) impelled him to escape England and embark on his most characteristic (and bad-tempered) expatriate work; we know also that Pound eventually found Dorothy a disappointment[22] and spent much of his later career with Olga Rudge, an American bohemian by whom he had a daughter (whom like Byron he farmed out in the northern Italian countryside to be brought up). Given as much, it seems fair to suspect that Pound's increasingly vocal contempt for middle-class England was the result not only of objective cultural disgust and the example of Lewis and Marinetti, but also of feelings of being entrapped in a wrong marriage.

This theory gains credence when one considers that until well after the Second World War Pound was dependent on Dorothy for economic support and that simultaneously economic injustice grew to be the monomaniacal theme of his work. The poverty of the true artist was the greatest impediment to the NEW in the arts, he believed. Writers and painters who pandered to safe, popular taste could always earn a living; but writers and artists bent on revolutionising perception had to scrape and beg, relying on patrons like Yeats's father's friend John Quinn, whom Pound cultivated, or the dilettante editresses of little magazines, for whom Pound wrote and procured material tirelessly. *The Egoist, The Dial, Poetry, The Little Review* and later in Paris *the transatlantic review* and *The Exile* – through essentially expatriate publications like these, Pound continued to promote Joyce, Eliot, Hemingway and others whom he regarded as the pathfinders of the literature of the future. Meanwhile, in a magazine called *The New Age* and later *The New English Weekly*, he developed his economic and general cultural theories. All these activities led him beyond the safe precincts of literary London – such journals as *The Spectator* and *The Quarterly Review*, where he had been *persona non grata* since at least his association with *BLAST!*. Once a lionised newcomer, he was now an outcast. This hurt him financially, if not in sensibility. But Pound's reaction was gritty: he castigated his rejectors the more, declaring that England was irrelevant to the NEW, travelling to Paris and Provence and making more extensive connections with Continental *déracinés*. In 1920 he bade farewell to London in his last lucid and easily accessible work, *Hugh Selwyn Mauberley*. A summation of what he saw as the situation of the artist in England after the War, *Mauberley* states that for a poet to succeed there he must wallow in shallow imagination or sentimental confession. He must not dare to offend his 'betters', must deal in 'mildness', must wear his coat in proper fashion, must cultivate the right hostesses and reviewers and tolerate the 'mendacities' of politicians and the press. He must, in short, become a tepid rerun of James: a literary diplomatist like Eliot eventually would be: a canny shinner-upper of the greasy pole – something hardbitten Ezra, scion of Western pioneers, could not, like his Bostonian compatriots, ever come to do . . . not even to please his in-laws.

Pound was a rebel. He was 'born for opposition' in ways James and Eliot were not. Even more than Byron he saw his role as being literature, even government, in exile. It was a messianic self-image and, as all messianism, partly deluded. The delusion was inevitably exacerbated by isolation from the centres of his language and culture. This was not immediately apparent in Paris, where Pound went to live in 1920; for Paris at that time was, as we have said, an international capital of art and culture – indeed, the only place where an expatriate avant-gardiste like Pound could ever be quite in his proper element. But this must be qualified too. The drinking and nightclubbing which Hemingway would depict in *The Sun Also Rises* were characteristic of Parisian bohemia of this time; and though Pound participated in them, the lifestyle was not congenial to him, as it was to fellow expatriates and literary pioneers such as Robert McAlmon and Harry Crosby. If Pound was self-destructive, he was unconsciously so. Never did he douse himself in wine like his friend Joyce, drugs like his pet poet Ralph Cheever Dunning, or even spiritual despair like Eliot before writing *The Waste Land*. Pound would not dare his death through physical danger like Hemingway, or shoot himself like Crosby, or disappear back into American obscurity like McAlmon; and this is important in viewing his character and career. He was in for the long haul, for better or worse. Had he quit his efforts with *Mauberley*, or perhaps *Homage to Sextus Propertius* (also 1920), and retired by the age of 40, he might have been remembered as an interesting innovator and advocate of the great. Had he died young he might have come down to us as a kid of American expatriate Shelley of his time. But Pound forged on, determined not to be just a prophet and promoter of others but also a producer himself of the Great Work. Because of this he descended into the confusion of *The Cantos*, the rag-bag of theoretical pronouncements surrounding and supporting them and ultimately the most self-damaging pursuit of his errant career: the taking-on of European anti-Semitism and fascism and their promotion with the same tireless energy that he had always devoted to the NEW in the arts.

Descent into these delusions began in earnest in Paris. In *A

Moveable Feast Hemingway suggests that Pound was always in some ways a naif;[23] and certainly there is a basis to argue that among the Cocteaus, Picabias and other avant-gardistes he mixed with, Pound picked up ideas and manners which did not always serve him well. He became enthused at turns by Dada and early Surrealism, by some Cubist painting and other abstract art, by the music of Anthiel to such an extent that he took up playing the bassoon and composed an opera (*Villon*, 1925); and of course he was also profoundly impressed by the great modernist works of literature he coaxed to completion, *Ulysses* and *The Waste Land*. All of this forms a background to *The Cantos*, especially their difficult, disjunctive, challenging style. As young Pound in 1910 wrote 1890s-ish poems *à la* Yeats and in 1914 began *BLAST*ing in the style of Lewis and Marinetti, so as he embarked on his great poem in the 1920s he adopted what he thought was the most advanced mode of that time – a mode not only created by himself but dictated by the *Zeitgeist* as he saw it. This may have worked for some cantos – the first XVI, perhaps, published in sumptuous limited edition by expatriate William Bird's Three Mountains Press. But one of the difficulties inherent in such 'a cryselephantine work of immeasurable length' began to reveal itself as early as the cantos of the later 1920s: that a structure and ideas taken up in one artistic period and mood inevitably become cumbersome to sustain once that period and its tastes have given way to others. The later cantos of *Don Juan* show signs of authorial fatigue, yet they were written only about five years after the poem's exuberant commencement; those five years, however, saw Byron move from being the fun-loving *cavaliere servente* of Venice to the political advocate who underwrote *The Liberal* for Leigh Hunt; and once he had embarked for Greece and actual freedom-fighting he could no longer adapt the poem to his concerns, loose though its structure had been. As early as 1915 Pound foresaw similar problems when he remarked that the poem would 'occupy me for the next four decades *unless it becomes a bore*' (italics mine).[24] It should not be surprising then that by the 1930s *The Cantos* had begun to buckle and snap under the strain of retaining some underlying consistency.

Pound must have been conscious from time to time of a restriction from which he would have preferred to escape. But the restriction had been imposed by no one but himself; and because of that sense of commitment to personal vision typical of rugged individualists (and usually called stubbornness) he had to stick with it or be forced to admit that his lifework was heading for failure. Thus devices in vogue in Paris of the 1920s – collage, stream-of-consciousness, wild expressionism, kinds of esperanto, synthetic mythologising – became devices Pound *had* to use in the 1940s and beyond, whether his readers still had time for them and whether they were actually proving effective in conveying his message – or even in embodying it. The implication one might draw from this is that aesthetic modernism itself became the chief problem of and for Ezra Pound: that by committing himself to the language and *signs* of Left Bank bohemia 1922 he prevented himself from ever returning to reasoned argument, smooth narrative line and indeed comprehensible English. His content became more jumbled and obscure – this no doubt in part because of his commitment to a fascinatingly experimental but ultimately irresponsible form. Thus sometimes we cannot quite tell which of his personae he is speaking through: Odysseus, Malatesta, John Adams, Confucius or himself. Nor can we be quite sure what he is driving at. The long passages of documentation of the history of the Monte di Paschi Bank of Siena seem partly unnecessary and certainly unpoetic; and the famous lines against *usura* may be rhetorically ravishing but they are subverted by their attachment to vitriol against the Jews. In the spirit of his part of the century Pound had become a propagandist rather than a persuader; thus he leaves us no opportunity to say, 'Yes, but . . . '. His poem lets in air, not breath; and it would be left to interviewers of the broken and senile octogenarian to inform us that, when all was said and done and the great errant masterpiece abandoned, its creator concluded that the real antagonist of his poem (and world) was not *usura* so much as common greed, and that this was a property belonging to all men, not just Jewish bankers or their Anglo-Saxon fellow-travellers.[25]

There is a sense in which, long before his incarceration for treason, Pound's career inevitably led into a trap: the trap of his determination to be a modernist *voyant* and make poetry NEW; of his commitment to be on the cutting-edge of economic and political thought; of his messianic urge to hector his country out of the many boneheaded stupidities and philistinisms of which he accused it; of his status as outsider, especially after his move in 1925 from cosmopolitan Paris to the relative backwater of Rapallo; of his marriage to an English rose when simultaneously and contradictorily engaged in a kind of crusade against England and the English. Forced to adopt some place to admire in this world he chose Italy, a land of surpassing art and beauty which there was ample tradition for him to embrace. But out of a mélange of macho, futuristic, reactionary and simply antithetical reasons, the Italy he chose was specifically the totalitarian state of 'the Boss', Mussolini, whom he sought to elevate into an embodiment of the necessary modernist man-of-action, natural successor to a Renaissance *condottiere* like Malatesta or minstrel-warrior like Bertans de Born. This was folly, of course. Whether treasonous or insane as it was declared to be, it was certainly disturbed. At the same time it seems important to ask if it was not also instructive: if indeed Pound's development and folly did not in many ways sum up the spirit of his age, specifically that particular 'new age' which had broken loose in the Left Bank of the 1920s. More than Hemingway with his retreat into anti-intellectual machismo, Eliot with his reactive orthodoxy, Joyce with his detachment into play of language, or Yeats with his sheltering in the occult, Pound remained attached – indeed, symptomatic, however wild. Perhaps it is after all most in his wildness, the very *un*safety and pathological bent of his rhetoric and action, that he represents a 'cracked looking-glass' of a period characterised by Depression, a Second World War, genocide, the Cold War and threat of nuclear holocaust. A wild, unsafe, pathological period, the mid-twentieth century was as comfortless in *its* content, as disjointed in its forms. Seen in this light, perhaps *The Cantos* really are what Pound hoped they were: the great composite document of the forces which had led up to and would lead out of the *vortex* of 'the Pound era'.

The last phase of his very long career was divided between Italy and St Elizabeth's Hospital, Washington, D.C., where he was held as insane after his indictment for treason. The two locales sum up the essential fracture in Pound's mature view of the world. On the one hand was the *paradiso*: a beautiful landscape rich in mythic elements, radiant with light, free, unpressured, a feast to the senses, an atmosphere filled with unearthly music, with the promise of love or – even better – the capacity to provoke memory and desire for blessed moments in one's own or even an archetypal past. On the other was the *inferno*: a madhouse enclosure pathetically stripped of natural or artistic associations, gloom-ridden with bureacratic regimes, unfree, manipulated, a pressure on the nerves, an atmosphere filled with the cacophony of voices of ambition and greed, with a threat of war of psychological violence always menacing in the background and the capacity to reduce man from his instincts for higher creativity into mere materialistic wage-slavery, money-grubbing or – worse –

violent revolution or theft. Italy was of course not entirely the one nor St Elizabeth's the other; but in Pound's Manichaean representation of his world they grew more or less to be depicted thus – at least until the very end of his career when, released from St Elizabeth's, he returned to Italy and found it no longer the land full of hope for the future that it had seemed to him under 'the Boss'. Pound's characterisation of Italy as blessed arose in part from associations with his youth: his exuberant days of first expatriation in Venice; his romantic journeys to Sirmione in the early years of his relationship with Dorothy; his wanderings with Olga Rudge to find manuscripts of Vivaldi shortly after he settled in Rapallo. Italy as home to Dante, Cavalcanti and Malatesta was locus for some of Pound's greatest heroes; it was also near enough to Provence to have some of the atmosphere he had loved through his studies and early walking-tours of troubadour byways. To some degree, as for Stendhal, Italy seems to have represented for Pound what he had wished to find in France yet had missed in the sound and fury of Paris of the 1920s. At any rate, Paris had been too northern for him: apparently he had not been in good health there.[26] Besides, instinct told him that if he remained in the centre of things as impresario for a generation he would never get his great poem written.

So to Rapallo. Pound might rationalise self-exile to this Mediterranean resort town by reference to his long-held belief that great art had emanated originally from the south, from these blessed sunclimes and their ancient sexually symbolic rites of the sun's passing and rebirth. There is plenty in *The Cantos* to suggest this, from allusions to the Eleusinian bringing of Persephone from the underworld, to legends of Adonis and Tammuz, to the Cathar love-feasts around Mount Ségur and what Pound seems to have seen as their northern equivalents in Druid solstice ceremonies at Stonehenge. But while he could thus rationalise personal, aesthetic and even mythic reasons for his transplantation, it had obvious pitfalls. The first, as we have said, was isolation. A significant symptom of this, as with Byron, was the torrent of letters on every subject sent to correspondents back home (in this instance, America as well as England), written in every sort of accent and tone: native, foreign, crankish, aggressive, humourous. Like Byron's later expatriate letters, they show increasing radicalism and rejection of national policy; also a truculent defence of the genius of his great poem and scorn for the critics, publishers and poetasters who lacked the insight to see it. Apparent too is a tendency to justify the choice of expatriation and to laud Italy in consequence. This was perhaps intensified in Pound's case by the arrival of his parents from America to spend their twilight years near him in the foreign country. Here a temperamental (and perhaps class) difference between Byron and Pound arises; for whereas Byron is always amused at, yet ultimately fatigued by, 'Italian operatics', Pound seems increasingly (and uncritically) to adopt them. André Gide had once written of Pound's early exemplar Marinetti: 'He paws the ground and sends up clouds of dust; he curses and swears and massacres. . . . [He is] animated in the Italian fashion, which often takes verbosity for eloquence, ostentation for wealth, agitation for movement, freshness for divine rapture.'[27] The same could be said of Pound in the 1930s, in letters, prose pronouncements and the most offensive cantos. Excessive expressionism became the problem: Italian volubility merging with the old time American seer's desire to buttonhole the passer-by and give him the low-down, the 'real goods', the Truth about the secret conspiracy that has thrown everybody on hard times and would lead to war again unless he, and he alone, could hold it off.[28]

Pound travelled to America in 1939, convinced that he could explain the Europeans to his countrymen and prevent a new cataclysm. This act constitutes the best evidence of the extent to which his messianic self-image had increased in the 15 years since he had left Paris. Pound genuinely saw himself as the boy who could put his finger in the dike, as the student who could stop the movement of the tanks as they rumbled across Tienanmen Square. At his own expense he tried to do what he saw as his civic duty by going to Washington and talking to Senators Borah and Bankhead – though not the President, whom he was simultaneously insulting in prose as well as new cantos. It seems that in Italy, with his reading of John Adams and Jefferson, Pound had developed an inflated idea of who he was back in the Land of the Brave and the Free. Many years of priding himself on being grandson of a congressman, descendant of early settlers, reader of Henry and Brooks Adams and acquaintance of Henry James had apparently persuaded him that, if he were not exactly a member of the ruling class, he was at least a voice to be heeded by it. The expatriate is always, inevitably, a kind of ambassador for his country. Called upon repeatedly to explain it to foreigners, he sometimes half-forgets that no official body at home recognises his status or is even aware of his efforts. When last in America Pound had been only a low-level academic kicked out of his job. A few now had heard of him as a voice among avant-garde expatriate poets; but as he himself loudly complained, he was not seen on the pages of mass-circulation American magazines and was even less of a household name than his equally experimental and bizarre expatriate contemporary, Ms Stein. Inasmuch as he was known at all, it was as an eccentric – one with potentially upsetting ideas. The fact that one stop on his journey was to receive an honorary doctorate from Hamilton College may have persuaded him that he might expect kudos elsewhere. In fact, America both official and literary was lukewarm, if polite, about Pound; and he went back to Italy feeling, rather like James after his returns to the US, that he had hardly received the esteem he deserved considering his struggles and successes in what he viewed as the superior civilisation of Europe.

And then came the War – the event Pound most dreaded, a far worse re-run of the events that had crushed so many young men and artistic hopes and had helped render him manic 25 years earlier. Money was cut off: Pound's royalties, Dorothy's dividends, the elder Pounds' pension. Pound's expressionistic anger and *angst* increased; Mussolini's radio was available to the distinguished foreign '*poet e professore*' who had long sought to appreciate fascism, and money would be paid for each broadcast he chose to make. Thus fate provided the great act of *hubris* in a developing tragedy. Pound took the microphone. The jumbled 'modernist method' of his poem – the 'fragments shored against our ruin' – became the jangle of accents and languages, aesthetic, political and economic messages of *The Rome Broadcasts*, which – once war between America and Italy was declared – led to Pound's treason indictment. It is a pathetic irony that during this period, and chiefly through the broadcasts, Pound for the first time became the sole support of his family; and it is sometimes suggested that his motives for broadcasting ought to be seen as practical rather than treasonous.[29] Pound himself would never use this argument in his defence. His defence was that, far from committing treason, he was trying to save his country by pointing out that – as he saw it – the fascists represented the best hope against the same forces and values that were decaying it: usury, Judaeo-Christianity, socialism, rampant commercialism and so on. In citing such elements of the modern world as the problem Pound was, as we have indicated, simply rehashing arguments common to James in *The American Scene*, the Adams brothers, Eliot in many of his prose pronouncements – indeed, the standard creed of the classic American expatriate in Europe who had always had a misanthropic, ultra-conservative streak, like Osmond, and a desire to preserve and collect the best of European tradition and impose it on that hopelessly uncultivated chaos that was 'American City', like Adam Verver.[30] But there is something radically different in Pound to these mandarin Bostonian fellows and forebears; and it was not just that he was willing to let his grouse against his country lead him into treason, which none of them – especially Eliot and James (both British patriots when the chips were down) – were.

Pound enunciated his objections in demotic language. Poorer and more backwoods than these others, he was also, instinctively, more proletarian. In this as well Pound was a more appropriate representative of the *Zeitgeist* than mannerly middle-class Eliot, for instance. The man-of-action overtook the man-of-contemplation in Pound. The polymath who had built his own furniture, composed an opera and played the bassoon was not to be restricted from his freedom to operate as a kind of slumming Villon or Huck Finn himself – personae that Eliot, like James, would not have dared to take up had he wanted to once he had established his footing on the respectable ladder of literary London. In the sneering and howling and cursing of Pound we get a rage to break out of bourgeois nineteenth-century order only glimpsed so far in this study in Maugham's portrayal of Strickland, the amoral artist of *The Moon and Sixpence*. And as in Maugham, the ultimate salvation for Pound is not mannered Anglo-Catholicism or a return to Jamesian drawing-rooms but a return to the seeker's quest on the road, the pursuit of the light – of elements of a new *'gnosis'* amid the great storehouse of Western and Eastern knowledge: the path of Larry Darrell. Here is the reason that Pound should have become an inspiration to Allen Ginsberg, despite his anti-Semitism. Pound and Ginsberg are both Darrells, as was their precursor Walt Whitman: they are seekers of the sensual and beautiful, in art, human form and nature; drop-outs from civilisation as ordered, with its materialism, greed, munitions-making, commercialisation of the arts, government coercions and lies, class and behavioural restrictions. They are questors for exuberant moments – for true freedom, whereas so many American expatriates in Europe, certainly Eliot and James, were in escape from freedom, in pursuit of a narrowing order, superior definition, consensus about manners and matters of the spirit. For all his censoriousness Pound is not ultimately a social dogmatist. He is, at the most basic level, simply reacting against those properties of modern life which prevent the individual from pursuing his sensual and aesthetic appetites. His vituperations are another manifestation of the urge which moved him to protect and promote so many fellow artists. They are the cries of pain of a Prometheus who, as Herbert Marcuse would tell us, is the antithetical face of the Orpheus-Narcissus type that simply wants to be left undisturbed to contemplate its own forms of beauty.

Substitute for the Jew in *The Cantos* the materialistic 'pig' of the 1960s, for the British munitions-makers the 'masters of war' of the American military-industrial complex, for the hate for Roosevelt and Churchill that for Presidents Johnson and Nixon, for moments on the road near Beziers Kerouacian *satori* in Mexico, for the jangled baggage of myth the intrusions of Old Testament tales in Bob Dylan, for beatific experiences of sex and revelation in Sirmione the drug-induced euphoria of hippies at, say, Woodstock; then one can see how the spirit of Pound remained relevant to the (essentially American) modernist period well beyond its dramatic early mani-festations in Paris of the 1920s. Pound's universalism and Europeanism marks him off from Whitman; the breadth of his knowledge across time adds an element of scholarship far tran-scending anything the Beats or hippies would take up (though it often partakes of the sort of imprecision that one might expect from these self-educated, proletarian successors to Jack London); never-theless, he is American through and through – more so, perhaps, at the end of his career when presiding over the so-called 'Ezuversity' at St Elizabeth's[31] than at the beginning when imitating the personae of Browning. His commitment to Europe – a Europe of heretics, artists, heroes and failures – is a typically American commitment to the underdogs and misunderstood: the beautiful losers, almost always male, who seem to become martyred by pusillanimous convention because of their very strength. Pound's heroes – de Born, Malatesta, even Bonaparte and Mussolini – are all in their way public versions of Kerouac's great male 'buddy' and embodiment of Nietzschean vitality, Neal Cassady; and returning to the argument that Pound was in part in flight from American (and later British) over-mothering, we might see him playing out on a European stage a version of D. H. Lawrence's characterisation of the classic pattern of American lit-erature: white (read American) male escapes the domesticating female to go hunting or exploring in the woods with dark (in this case European) pathfinder . . .[32] Thus Pound as Natty Bumppo or Huck Finn travels off with his version of Chingachgook or Nigger Jim (the composite European artist of his imagination, made up of aspects of Homer, Dante, Wyndham Lewis, Joyce and so on) to discover a new 'reality of experience' and bring it back home, not as cunning to survive the new continent so much as visionary art to provoke its cultural (re)naissance.

It is beyond question that Pound was in many ways a failure. Much of his opus was unreadable when it as written and has since only become more so. This is in part a problem endemic to Modernism (who can 'understand' Jackson Pollock?); but in literature it is probably more true of Pound than most – certainly than Eliot, perhaps only marginally less than Stein and late Joyce. But the spectacle of Pound's quest, the extremity of his aspiration and the drama of his folly make him one of the most instructive cases in expatriate pathology; and in the midst of the spectacle some of his creations – 'The Pisan Cantos' perhaps most of all – have moments of beauty and insight which are more moving and representative than in any other poetry of the century. 'What thou lovest well remain /... shall not be reft from thee.' What Pound loved best was Europe: selected creations of its art and tradition, old and new. Not for him to stand in front of Siena Cathedral, like James, and feel only the vague pleasing sensations of a *homme moyen sensuel* who pauses in the midst of shopping. For Pound even more than for Henry Adams at the portal of Chartres, the experience of Europe was an education into the spirit of another age: an age of glory and story, of faith and anagogical pursuit. This he tried devotedly to convey to his era, both in Europe and more insistently in America; for, as expatriate, Pound was always more of a time-traveller than a Jamesian gamboller through European space. The homeland of his soul finally was some river in Confucian China or grove in Dionysian Greece; some road in Aquitaine where Prince Henry Plantagenet had ridden, or Mount Ségur before the pope's armies had come. He would travel with Dante and Virgil to Hell in order to bring back Promethean light. He would give himself up in a divine immolation if it would bring leafy Persephone back to this earth. Somewhere in the past we had lost the golden age, the most ecstatic and natural civilisation for the spirit. Was it in Florence when the Medici bankrupted the city? In England in 1694 with creation of the Bank? In America in the 1830s when banking interests began to overshadow the government? All these times? Pound the crusader had to look, get the 'low-down' and – having discovered what he thought was the problem – combat it root and branch. But then these roots and branches wove around him, dragging him down into an incoherence which nearly destroyed his idealistic vision and condemned him in his last years to a feeling that he had 'botched the job'. Thus he retreated into silence – the final expatriation, as it were, from what had always been his most consistent homeland: the realm of the Word.

7

Greene

Graham Greene, if an expatriate at all, is the expatriate as embodiment of the *mal du siècle*. Great romantic aspirations decay with him into seedy realities. The high-mindedness of characters out of James (along with Conrad, his most revered precursor[1]) has vanished or is revealed as pernicious, as in the case of the Bostonian idealist, Alden Pyle, in *The Quiet American* (1955). On those occasions when characters behave nobly in Greene, it is often in large part a result of accident, boredom and/or desire for change after a career of 'sinful' self-indulgence. This is true of the whisky priest in *The Power and the Glory* (1940), the colonial official in *The Heart of the Matter* (1948), the world-famous architect in *A Burnt-Out Case* (1960) – indeed, the typical mature Greene 'hero'. And if Jamesian faith in self-conscious amelioration has vanished, so too has Byronic/Stendhalian enthusiasm for the grand immoral self-assertive gesture. Man will never be 'liberated' fully any more than he may attain a reliable level of civilisation. Nor in the midst of bleak prospects is he likely to draw comfort from ideological nostrums or Kulchur *à la* Pound. To survive in the modern world he must simply adapt to it, gaining what pleasure he can in a fugitive way. But while he does this, the Greene hero, like his author and unlike so many Existentialist or Beat contemporaries, retains a shred of idealism in secret: though the world has become soullessly materialistic and 'Americanised', he will never be reconciled to its necessary creed of self-serving pragmatism.

In this, the Greene hero shares something in common with Pound, different though he may be in his faith and in the aesthetic milieu in which he appears.[2] The private mutterings taken to a public level, the protest against the onslaught of capitalist economics, the attention to sufferings of small anonymous victims ('The enormous tragedy of the dream in the peasant's bent /shoulders . . .')[3] – these provide a constant susurrus under the apparent existential indifference. Where Pound's personae scream, Greene's mutter under their breath. Both are alienated from contemporary 'progress'; but whereas Pound, the 'last oarsman'[4] of Romantic self-expression, remains wildly unbuttoned like Walt Whitman to the end, Greene, the truer modernist in point of view, makes his personae voice their grouses with public-school caution and act if at all with the circumspection of spies. Greene heroes are not larger than life. Smaller obviously than the megaphonic Poundians, they are smaller too than the focal characters of his countryman Maugham, who came from an era before imperial certainty had been fully shattered. Maugham and his Ashendens travel the world viewing colonialists in the Far East or pre-jetsetters on the Côte d'Azur with a high British/European standard still in the background; at home the rebellion of Charles Strickland or elopement of the principals of *The Circle* only prove that Jamesian manners dominate – to the extent that they are becoming oppressive. In 'Greeneland' by contrast, the manners are gone: so gone that at home there is no longer much point in rebelling against them. Meanwhile, abroad, the Far East and Africa and Latin America that Greene and his narrators travel is without standards. It is a corrupt world: neither British/European nor American in prosperity, though those imperial presences have clearly meddled with it, nor pristine in its primitivism any longer. That has been violated to the extent that often what one finds is a worst of both worlds: a Hell of materialism without sufficient materials and of spiritualism without God: a 'heart of darkness' run by latter-day Kurtzs in unholy alliance with former tribal tyrants who terrorise their own kind with the white man's cast-off weapons.

Paradise is infernal. Instead of Gauguin's realm of Edenic colour which Maugham discovers in the South Seas, Greeneland – the Haiti of *The Comedians* (1966), for instance – is all hideous garishness, like a sub-Gauguin by Crowley.[5] Even the South of France, where Greene follows Maugham in the end, turns out according to his portrait in *J'accuse* (1982) to be a paradise deformed by modernist scourges of gangsterism and greed. In general, the world Greene travels appears so often to be unbeautiful and unjust that we must ask if, unlike the others in the study, he has gone in quest of Byzantium at all. Isn't he finally as much in pursuit of degradation? Doesn't his mid-twentieth-century disillusionment require that he disbelieve from the first in the possibility of a 'better place'? The way I state the question implies the answer. In Liberia, Mexico and Vietnam Greene is attracted – as in Duvalier's Haiti – to the *un*civilisation he will find. Part of the reason for this comes from his early struggles as a writer in England of the 1930s: World War and Depression had created a proletarian bias in the new generation of educated youth, from Auden and company at Oxford to the Cambridge communists; thus Greene, despite origins as reputable as James's or Maugham's (indeed, partly because of them), turns his back on his class and takes for his study the fallen – the 'people of the abyss'. Later, when successful enough to go travelling for copy, he does not seek out an Italy of the so-phisticated set: this is for dandies like his Oxford contemporary and critic Harold Acton (later a model for Waugh's Sebastian Flyte).[6] He does not ape the Byron of Ladies Melbourne and Blessington (the subject of an extended biography by his schoolmate Peter Quennell) but the Byron of the prostitutes of Venice and Suliote con-men of Missolonghi; not the Stendhal of grand premières at La Scala, but the Stendhal of Julien Sorel and Ferrante Palla – those scrambling, clever, lower-middle-class types whose values are a cross between Robin Hood purpose and cynical self-destructiveness.

In terms set out at the beginning of this study Greene is in some part a 'retrograde' expatriate; thus his affinity for Conrad. Lord Jim hovers behind his Scobies and Fowlers, and Marlow of *The Heart of Darkness* (perhaps Greene's favourite book) behind his narrative point of view. But Greene never became a real retrograde expatriate like Malcolm Lowry or B. Traven. His stint as an intelligence officer in Sierra Leone during the Second World War was his only official period of living abroad before expatriation to France in the 1960s. Well into the middle phase of his career he remained principally a traveller: one who went away to bring copy home to England, in the manner of Lawrence, Forster, Waugh and others discussed and dismissed in my introduction. In both of these categories, however, Greene turns out to be a misfit. As a retrograde expatriate he is *tempted* to melt down his overcivilised northern nature (consider the opium-smoking narrator of *The Quiet American* or the hotel-owning one of *The Comedians*) but does not even end up extolling the idea, like Lawrence of *The Plumed Serpent* (another favourite book).[7] Meanwhile as a traveller he is *tempted* to go away merely to discover a better form of Englishness; but he does not finally adopt an overtly Anglo-critical position like Forster nor backslide into Little Englishness like Waugh. Yet more than Maugham he has the public-schoolboy's fear of pretension; thus he avoids the High-Art-And-Culture-seeking purpose of *Childe Harold, IV*, Stendhal in his Count Mosca vein, James of the travel pieces or Pound as arbiter of the NEW. When he settles in France finally there is not a little of the bad-tempered tax-exile about it. Nor is this leavened, as in Maugham's case, by eager pursuit of new material – such as the Elliott Templetons.

Greene does not cleave to France as Byron or Stendhal to Italy, James to England or Maugham to a cosmopolitan 'beachcomber' set. It is almost as if he settles there out of general indifference or even disgust at the alternatives. Among the transients of the Côte d'Azur he can live as close to *nowhere* as possible. Nor is this *nowhere* to be translated 'Utopia'. The small flat at Antibes, in contrast to Villa Mauresque, becomes a *point de récul* only: a resting-perch for a bird of flight, a citizen of no country, a wandering Catholic who – believing as he must in the Fall – can conceive of no 'better place' on this earth at last: only Heaven can provide that. And this may be the key to Greene as both expatriate and writer. Heaven is what he is after – if he is after anything better. One must add the qualification because, though the great Catholic novels like *The Power and the Glory* suggest that his imaginative trajectory is toward a realm of the saints, several novels of the 1960s and later put this into question, raising the possibility that – on this earth – a communist or at least some form of socialist alternative might provide equivalent or better hope. Greene has gone on record to say that he would rather live in the Soviet Union than the United States.[8] His vision of Hell on earth is inextricably tied to the squalor he sees arising from irresponsible capitalism. He tacks an impassioned speech in favour of Marxism on to the end of his most brutal account of Third World suffering, *The Comedians*; in *The Human Factor* (1978) he has his hero defect to Moscow like Kim Philby (whom Greene would seek out to befriend);[9] and in *Monsignor Quixote* (1982) he raises Marxist dogma to a level equivalent with Roman Catholic in the dialogues between his hero and his Sancho Panza. In later years, Greene even called his own faith into question – all of which suggests a man slouching back towards an earlier, Leftish, quasi-existentialist despair that hope can be found in an imaginative hereafter, let alone on this blighted earth.

Greene's homeland finally may be the unhappy but typically mid-twentieth-century intellectual's dead-end of alienation. By the 1960s he had certainly come to subscribe to this position summed up by religious philosopher R. C. Zaehner, a contemporary who may also have had links to the Cambridge 'traitors':

> We [the British and Europeans] are a sick society. . . . We, following the USA, are the real materialists, much more than the Communist bloc, for, though some of us may pay lip-service to spiritual values, basically we care for nothing but material welfare and material comfort. We have grown flabby and rotten inside.[10]

It seems unsurprising – indeed, quite consistent – that a man holding such views (and having always been a traveller) should have at last turned his back on his country, and its principal ally, and taken up ambiguous residence in the nation least committed to the Western alliance, France: a nation which has long traditions of scepticism about orthodox (and by now all too Anglo-Saxon) Western values and with a highly-developed Catholic, socialist and of course literary culture of heresy. As with James and Maugham, we are told that Greene from his youth had been attracted to French writers more than any other besides English;[11] and his attitudes by the time of his expatriation have much in common with those of French Catholic novelists like Bernanos, whose *Monsieur Ouine* Professor Zaehner singles out as the perfect picture of the spiritual plight of the times. According to Ouine (whose name means 'yes' and 'no'), we are nowadays 'ruled not by God, nor by Science, but by Satan'. We have plunged into a new dark age in which 'with the progressive de-moralization of man you will see all manner of beasts emerge whose names men have long since forgotten, assuming they had ever been given one'. Greeneland, alas – the realm to which Greene expatriates us and himself ultimately – has already begun to swarm with these creatures; meanwhile, its creator, like Ouine, looks on by his own confession with 'a splinter of ice' in his soul.[12] It is a cruel prospect: a cruel creation: much crueller than we are used to in the great English novel before Greene's period. Yet if such a creation is to be redeemed it may be less through an adopted Catholic hope of Heaven than through an essentially British urge-to-survival, self-deprecatory wit, practical intelligence and sense of common decency.

These values may suggest the 'goodness tempered by a lively irony' and 'making the best of a bad job' we have seen Maugham extolling. If so, it should not be surprising. These are the values of the public schoolboy *in extremis*; and Greene no less than Byron or Maugham feels and incorporates the effects of his education in his works. He went to Berkhamsted where his father was headmaster.[13] His career there was marked by emotional conflict: between the stern standard of his father and the sometimes subversive activities of his friends. Fearing that he might have homosexual tendencies and alarmed by what seemed a nervous breakdown, his parents sent him to a psychoanalyst. Despite this, young Greene continued to feel anxiety so acutely that when he went up to Oxford he played Russian roulette.

Such a pastime may suggest a dull boy trying to excite himself and impress others and/or a budding moralist longing to brood over the great issues of Fate and Death; but less portentously, it simply shows how desperately unhappy Greene was. His mild-mannered mother remained as remote as his intimidating father; yearning for love drove him into obsession for a Roman Catholic girl who worked in Blackwell's bookshop; when she refused to grant him the favour he desired (in his Werther-like mood this may be how Greene would have described it), he became a convert in order to marry her. With marriage, depression and death-daring abated, evidences of a disturbed state of mind still find their way into his first published novel, *The Man Within* (1929). The book's protagonist, a young smuggler, feels unsuited to his manly, dangerous profession because of an over-fine education; his father, a smuggler-chief of repute, sent him to learn Latin and Greek so that he (the father) 'could brag about it'; after the father's death, the young man is liberated from the school by a new smuggler-chief, who is younger and more charismatic than the father, if less 'bullying' and 'clever'. The young man follows this new chief for a time, adulating him to the point of hero-worship; then an angry desire to realise his own identity rises up, provoking him to betray the smugglers and take flight. He finds refuge with a woman whose ethical purity makes him fixate on her like a lodestar; but he worships her too much to have sexual relations with her and relieves his frustrations with an establishment moll. In the end his betrayal of his fellow smugglers results in the death of his beloved; and in a last-ditch effort to live up to a confused sense of honour he commits suicide.

The complexity of emotions and motives here is reflected in a style of interior monologue – this is the decade of *Ulysses*, *The Waste Land* and *The Cantos*; and we are reminded that the Oxonian newly-wed is determined to make an heroic progress as a 'serious' writer. This distracts. Nevertheless we can see many aspects of the mature, realist Greene emerging: disquiet with father-authority figures; suspicion of schooling and institutions in general; desire for romantic excitement, yet betrayal of romance and thus inner dreams; guilt and remorse over this; finally a self-centredness which leads almost inevitably to detachment from human affections, however emotionally compelling. The Greene protagonist becomes driven; the world turns by necessity hostile; simple love recedes like the image of Penelope waving to Ulysses from the shore. The 'Departer' of Maugham is here but in more haunted form. Melancholy Childe Harold becomes part-criminal, part-saint; the half-betrayer who is half-betrayed; the lover who is at home with neither in- nor outlaws. This is the 'figure on the carpet' in Greene: certainly the early Greene up to *The Power and the Glory* which raises the hunted, haunted, betrayed and self-betraying fugitive to the status of saintly, if not Christly, avatar. On the way we see him in contemporary journalistic form as the Eastern European Socialist revolutionary Czinner in *Stamboul Train* (1933) and the Spanish loyalist operative pursued through an indifferent England in *The Confidential Agent* (1939). Sometimes the hunted becomes the hunter, as in the latter book; sometimes pursuit becomes a hunt for one's own identity as well, as in *The Ministry of Fear* (1943). At other times the fugitive impulse necessitates flight back to, rather than away from, home: Czinner's case is an example here as will be the whisky priest's. Along the way the early Greene protagonist customarily finds a population of *déracinés* and *aliénés* who, if not exactly like himself, reflect related aspects of the *mal du siècle*. Thus in *Stamboul Train* we have the Jewish currant-dealer who travels ostensibly on business but also out of wariness about staying too long in any one part of a Europe seething with latent anti-Semitism; the lesbian journalist who hops trains to pursue 'scoops' like Czinner but also to keep or to catch an evanescent beloved; the theatre-struck, classless, Americanised girl who hurries about trying to get nightclub jobs but all the while dreams of finding a Mr Right to let her settle and be looked after.

As the troubled 1930s descend into the maelstrom of the 1940s Greene adds to this existentially restless mix the involuntary pursued and pursuers – agents, double-agents, spies and refugees – two faces of which are represented by Anna Hilfe and her brother, Germans in England for opposite reasons in *The Ministry of Fear*. Significantly, most of these characters are foreign. Indeed, apart from the protagonist of *The Man Within* (set in the vague time of Victorian romance in which Greene had been steeped as a boy), the focal fugitives and *déracinés* are rarely English, a fact which in itself might indicate the author's alienation from national identity even while apparently happily married and living and working between Oxford and London. The important exception to this is Anthony Farrant of *England Made Me* (1935), a character said to be based on Greene's rogue brother Herbert[14] and first of the ne'er-do-well Englishmen abroad whom the mature author would render so memorably in Wormold of *Our Man in Havana* (1958). Farrant has held low-level commercial appointments in various corners of the decaying Empire, from Aden to Shanghai. Now he is in Stockholm where he cadges a job through his sister (nearly incestuous brother–sister relations feature with Byronic prominence in early Greene) as body-guard to the industrial magnate Erik Krogh. Farrant is a charming conman; he has no experience of being a bodyguard and is out of his depth but doesn't know it. He wears on Old Harrovian tie though he never went to Harrow, and behaves according to type if we believe the public-school joke that Harrovians are cads. He goes to his death because he gives information about Krogh to a legitimate Old Harrovian, the journalist Minty. Minty is a decent chap but a ne'er-do-well too; he pretends to himself that his shabby life has the 'touch of nobility' of 'the exile's dignity', and he writes letters home trying to make out that he's had great success abroad. The assumption here is that any Englishman worth the name would never give up the delights of the whores on Wardour Street or the Lyons Corner House were it not for the imperial necessity of gaining riches elsewhere. Some related streak of national false pride is part of what makes Farrant betray Krogh. Krogh for his part is the one true internationalist in the book: curious about all cultures and as eager to make money in Chicago or Amsterdam as in his native village north of Stockholm. He is young Greene's not unsympathetic rendering of the 'true holders of the balance of the world' (Byron's description in *Don Juan*):[15] not the class-proud or nationalistic, the would-be Bonapartes or Wellingtons, but 'Jew Rothschild and his fellow Christian Baring'.

The mature Greene would not be favourably disposed to financiers or the rich of any kind; and the faint whiff of anti-Semitism we sometimes get from his books may have to do with Poundian hatred of *usura* as well as age-old Roman Catholic and English middle-class distaste. Thus the picture of Krogh seems a little eccentric; but so too does the tone and style of *England Made Me* as a whole. The novel was Greene's most serious since *The Man Within*; and like that book, it seems to have been written with one eye cocked to high modernist techniques and concerns – interior flashback and concentration on the 'haves and have nots', for instance. But first with *Stamboul Train* and shortly with *A Gun for Sale* (1936) Greene was also writing books reflecting popular taste for cinema and the thriller – the so-called 'entertainments' (as distinct from highbrow 'novels') which show that their author had become caught between conflicting impulses in the literary *Zeitgeist*: whether to be 'great' in the Leavisite, Jamesian, Poundian sense, or to be a fluent money-spinner like Maugham or, say, J. B. Priestley.[16] In time Greene would resolve this dilemma in a way which more or less mirrors the decline of high modernism into more accessible modes; and this end is previewed in his beginnings. Early novels where he is most self-conscious of great literary models – *It's a Battlefield* (1934), for instance, with its obvious debts to Conrad's *The Secret Agent* and James's *The Princess Casamassima* – are nowdays opaque; whereas the entertainments remain '*clair, précis, net rapide au but*'[17] — in short, quite readable. The famous Greene is the serious author of the four 'Catholic' novels of the middle period: *Brighton Rock* (1938), *The Power and the Glory*, *The Heart of the Matter* and *The End of the Affair* (1951). But the most memorable Greene may turn out to be the less high-minded, more 'fallen' writer of those books where novel and entertainment at last merge: books written after the break-up of his marriage and essential departure from England, from *The Quiet American* to, say, *Travels with My Aunt* (1969). Here the mature author, confident to the point of being devil-may-care, proceeds with no eye cocked to modernist critics any longer but with a bitter-sweet lust for the unromantic truth. The mode is black comedy: farce impregnated with meaning and meaning never free of farcical elements. The masterpiece of this phase is *Our Man in Havana*, that serious send-up of subjects and styles Greene had been labouring to master at least since *England Made Me*; and just as Wilde is now remembered for *The Importance of Being Earnest* more than for his symbolist 'many-coloured things', so Greene may remain most unforgettable for this deceptively light-hearted book.[18]

But we jump the gun here. In *England Made Me* the signal expatriate theme may be this one of the potentially pernicious behaviour of certain Englishmen abroad: specifically, a clubbable public-school type, whether phoney or real – Greene's version of Wilde's Algy and Jack. The title of the book indicates the problem, but it would not be fully developed until a dozen years later in what many regard as Greene's most profound novel, *The Heart of the Matter*. Here Farrant and Minty become the quite dangerously meddling and tiresome Wilson and Harris, and the bogus Old Harrovian tie becomes the *Downhamian* magazine which links the two together in a hot country of uneduated black wogs. I use the offensive phrase to indicate the prejudice which lurks under Wilson's and Harris's apparently innocent exteriors. Wilson is a poetaster who makes love to the wife of the colonial police-chief, Scobie, because he imagines her the only civilised person in the place; Harris is a simple non-participant in any local life he can avoid, except that of the English colony's club.

The blithe double-dealing of Anthony Farrant is institutionalised in the status of Wilson as an MI5 agent who has been sent out to spy on the locals – the first of what would become a stock character in Greene: the English (or Western) intelligence operative whose effect on the un-Western world is quite evil. Wilson's activities contribute to the demise of Scobie, the death of his black 'boy', the failure of his marriage and of the affair that succeeds it, as well as the loss of his promotion to Commissioner (in the moral context of the novel the least serious consequence). But whereas the victim of Anthony Farrant's double-dealing was a man of dubious morality, Wilson's victim, despite his private sins of conscience (not least adultery, a personal problem for the maritally vagrant Greene at this stage), is a paragon in his world – indeed, an object of envy for Wilson because of his outward calm and of scorn for Harris because of his racial tolerance ('He loves [the natives] so much . . . he sleeps with 'em').[19] Scobie is Greene's embodiment of what the Englishman abroad ought to be, at least in the colonial context. After 15 years in a West African port he has lost all desire to return to England, or even ersatz Englands elsewhere such as South Africa. England to him has become a place which measures value on the false bases of trendy cultural chat, how one mixes at the club, career advancement and a patriotism which remains largely blind to the fine qualities in 'wogs', whether German sea-captains, the Vichy French across the border, a Syrian trader, a fallen woman, a shabby priest or one's black 'boy'.

The book is set in the Second World War and reflects Greene's growing concern that humane values are being lost amid aggravated national and class allegiances. Scobie, being Catholic, sees beyond such narrow identities. He is a man-of-conscience who broods over the ethical implications of all his acts. He is a hero because he does not let his morality be subject to any outer force, not even to his self-interest. Both as policeman and private man he is in a quest to understand, balance and be just. His journey in conscience is remorseless and as thankless in its way as the flight of the whisky priest through a hostile Mexican state in Greene's last pre-war novel; and as in *The Power and the Glory*, the hero must become a martyr – he must redeem himself, not only in his own eyes but in those of humbler souls who have put their trust in him. In Scobie's case these include his 'boy', Ali, and the woman, Helen Rolt, with whom he has had an affair. Both he has betrayed: Ali through a momentary lapse back into the white man's suspicion of the black; Mrs Rolt through temporarily abandoning her on the return of his wife, who he thought had left him for good. These betrayals, like the whisky priest's drinking, underline Scobie's humanness: they are proofs that nobody can be perfect on this earth, any more than any place can be Heaven. As the 'better place' can only exist in the soul so the Christly man can only be realised through acknowledgement of one's own sinfulness. This Scobie signals by committing an act which, ironically, is one of Catholicism's cardinal sins: he kills himself by his own hand. He has not been able, like the whisky priest, to take the more acceptably Christly course of allowing himself to be captured by his enemies and martyred. Nevertheless, his sacrifice is viewed favourably by Greene: like the whisky priest's, it constitutes the ultimate decent act a man can perform in a world that he knows he alone cannot put right – that indeed his own attempts at goodness have only rendered more complicated. Scobie's death makes existence superficially more easy for those who survive him: Wilson, Harris, his wife, the Syrian trader and Helen Rolt. Greene, however, parts company with them with Scobie; for unlike the down-trodden in *The Power and the Glory*, none of these – least of all the public schoolboys – seems likely to resurrect the martyr in his soul as inspiration to finer ethical behaviour.

An indication of Greene's personal 'goodbye to all that' may be made in the title of his next novel, the last to be set entirely in England, *The End of the Affair*. After this he moves substantially to Greeneland – Scobie's elective 'nowhere' of the Third World. *The End of the Affair* was written simultaneously with the end of Greene's marriage; his next novel, *The Quiet American*, contains an exchange of letters between the itinerant journalist Fowler and his wife back in England, a Roman Catholic who has refused him a divorce. The pain of break-up is evident in much of Greene's work of this period; and as with so many writers, especially in this century,[20] it appears to have been a stimulant. The urge to travel and expatriate gains momentum from the demise of domestic life in England, as in the cases of Byron and Maugham; so too does a corrosively critical streak, especially toward one's own kind. Old contexts are being broken; the individual must scorch the earth of easy comforts and become his lone, mature self at last. Also as with Byron and Maugham, the process has a sexual concomitant in Greene. His ex-wife would remark that he never should have married and that his name might have been Otis P. Driftwood;[21] as with his focal characters from Anthony Farrant to Scobie, his true sexual tendency was to casual affairs, occasionally with prostitutes, sometimes with women of foreign origin, often with those younger or of a lower class than himself. The liberation of this tendency, however painful at first underlies his wanderings of the next two decades, as it does his characters'. Scobie's preference for West Africa is tied up with his sentimental attachment to Ali and his sexual one to Mrs Rolt; Fowler's inability to leave Vietnam has everything to do with the sex and sentiment in his relationship with Phuong, a girl whose simple pleasingness makes her into a kind of dusky version of the Jamesian 'heiress to the ages' – a 'lady' whose 'mind is so fine that it cannot be violated by an idea'. Perhaps more than any of Greene's characters, Phuong embodies the quality in the Third World which most attracts him: its freedom from the duplicities of old Europe and the worse naïveté of young America. But like the silent wish-creatures of Byron's Eastern tales – the loyal page of *Lara* or all-giving Haidée of *Don Juan* – she is also a projection of the author's longing for a beloved who is a perfectly tractable free spirit.

Such a paragon is not captured easily; and the allegiance of Phuong becomes the key to the novel's moral pattern and plot. Fowler's bondage to an old, dead marriage is one symbol of the First World's inadequacy for her; a French colonialist's collection of Parisian pornography is another. But the great enemy of Phuong's authentic pristineness is the doctrinaire idealism of the 'quiet American', Pyle, who offers her what neither of the Old World representatives can or would: a hygienic, suburban marriage. Intelligence agent and dangerous innocent, Pyle is a further development of Wilson of *The Heart of the Matter*; and his effect on the milieu he has entered will be even more destructive. Not only does he threaten the sexual arrangements of an older, apparently wiser Englishman, he sets about to destroy the lives of scores of natives by supplying bomb materials to a renegade general who he imagines will provide a 'third force' between the old colonialists and insurgent communists. Pyle has picked up this subversive purpose by reading the works of an American journalist-turned-political-theorist named York Harding. Harding, as Fowler sourly points out, once spent a few weeks in Vietnam and from that experience wrote a book to prove that the country – like all such Third World old colonies – can only find its salvation through American-sanctioned 'national democracy'. Pyle believes in Harding with the same starry-eyed credulity as his puritan ancestors believed in the Elect, or some contemporary teenaged girl believes in the American dream as advertised by Hollywood. Pyle is clean-cut: he doesn't smoke, hardly drinks, eats sandwiches made with vitamin-spread, reveres his parents (his father is a professor of science who had his picture on the cover of *Time*) and doesn't go in for the loud-mouthed machismo of some of his more typical compatriots. Unlike Wilson he is a decent chap; but much more than Wilson he is a meddler – from his transcendentalist forebears he has inherited a purpose that Wilson's public-school code could only find pretentious: to save the world. The old colonialists may have exploited their subject populations but they developed a comfortable symbiosis of master and servant with them – so the argument goes. The new meddlers, these evangelical Americans, want to *cleanse*; and neither 'Fowlair' (as a French policeman calls him) nor Greene can abide that.

Of two American girls sitting in a Saigon café, Fowler reflects: 'It was impossible to conceive either of them a prey to untidy passion: they did not belong to rumpled sheets and the sweat of sex. Did they take deodorants to bed with them? . . . They were charming, and I wanted to send them home too.'[22] This perhaps reveals the narrative prejudice more than any other passage in the book; and indeed, such sexual resonances may always provide the best clue to a writer's real affinities. Byron is attracted to the looseness of women in Venice just as he was repelled by the primness of his wife back home; Stendhal is mesmerised by *émigrée* contessas, James by the American virgin abroad, Maugham by renegades like Strickland and Darrell, Pound by artsy vagabonds like Olga Rudge. Greene's Scobie may love his English Catholic wife but he is drawn sexually to the fallen Helen Rolt; and Fowler's recoiling from the squeaky-clean American girl is a logical obverse to his attraction to the opium-pipe-preparing Phuong. The American girls' penchant for cleanliness is a cosmetic analogue to Pyle's unreal idea that a new world order may be created doing away with all the injustices of the old. But the world is built on injustice, just as sex involves sin and sweat; without the latter there would be no fertility; and those who try to do away entirely with the former are a species of intellectual eunuch – like children grown up without fully matured parts. This is the message of *The Quiet American* and the explanation for Greene's recurring distaste for manifestations of American culture. It was there in his film criticism of the 1930s: notably the article about Shirley Temple which resulted in a libel trial and closure of a magazine he edited.[23] It would be there too in his portrait of the Smiths in *The Comedians*: a plump middle-aged couple from Wisconsin who come to Haiti to spread their preposterous save-the-world creed of vegetarianism. In these Americans, as in Pyle, a decadent Anglo-European narrator is forced to recognise latent courage and strength: as Pyle saves Fowler's life despite the latter's world-weary protests, so the Smiths stand up to Duvalier's murderous police where Brown simply tries to avoid them. But to the end the distaste remains: for as Fowler sets in motion the events which lead to Pyle's death once he has discovered the American's subversive activities, so Brown gives the last word to a Franco-Haitian communist despite his concession that the Smiths have been oddly 'heroic'.

It may be instructive here to contrast Greene's response to his American abroad with Maugham's in *The Razor's Edge*. Pyle, after all, has much in common with Larry Darrell: he is young, attractive, reasonably well-off, sincere, admiring of knowledge and avid for it; he declines to engage in duplicitous or exploitative sex and is eager to 'save' what he views as a damsel-in-distress – Phuong in this respect being analogous to Sophie Macdonald. But whereas Darrell's lonesome travels are in pursuit of a personal gnosis, Pyle's pursuit is terribly impersonal finally. His idealism is messianic, and messianism in the guise of anyone but a true messiah can only be a gross presumption. Pyle may be right in himself for himself, like Darrell; but he has no right to impose his brand of rightness on the world – an act Darrell would eschew. To do so is evil. It is evil because, however desirous these young men may be for knowledge, they must recognise that innocence can never really know the world: that indeed, it may take several lifetimes of experience to learn all the fine moral distinctions. Unlike his English precursor Wilson, Pyle has enough reverence for maturity to long for a mature model/mentor; however, the manifestation of it he imagines in Fowler evaporates and the man's disengaged attitude strikes him finally as complacent and corrupt. Ironically, it is Pyle-as-paragon who is the descendant of Scobie, while Fowler is a new version of Wilson. Fowler brings Pyle to grief for the same reason in part as Wilson did Scobie: the appearance of virtue in the paragon is simply too much to take for a more normal, self-interested *homme moyen sensuel*. There is a cardinal difference between Pyle and Scobie: the American's virtue masks criminal altruism while the Englishman's masks all-too-human confusion. Still, the result of Wilson's and Fowler's betrayals is the same: Wilson inherits Scobie's wife; Fowler regains Phuong. In each case we see the triumph of self-interest over high moralism – a resolution that the Catholic in Greene must remain compelled to take. Only

God may be just and survive in this world; men who try for perfection are committing sins of pride. Don't try, Greene implies; only slouch toward engagement when forced by events. Act like a human, not a hero or god: that way lies only fatal, self-destroying delusion.

John Carey has remarked that Greene's anti-Americanism is as traditionally English 'as oak beams and inglenooks': 'The big democratic smile of America made him cringe: it must, he felt sure, hide something corrupt.'[24] This is certainly fair comment. We see in Greene the urge irresistible to cultured Europeans to send up American pretensions: the umbrage almost necessarily taken in an era when the Land of the Brave and the Free finally exposes its Jamesian sense of superiority to a world disrupted by European wars. Maugham, as we've seen, displayed a touch of this; but he had sufficient gratitude to his hosts of the Second World War – and perhaps cunning about their importance as buyers of his books – to apologise for his English inadequacy before depicting them in *The Razor's Edge*. For an American reader this makes his errors in speech quite forgivable. Greene's similar errors (and there are many in *The Quiet American* as in later books) are more jarring because his intent in depiction is so much more critical. Why, the American must ask (as English readers of *An International Episode* did of James), should we credit an uncomplimentary picture of ourselves from an author who evidently does not know our culture fully? Has he really done his homework, or is his work just evidence of a decaying world order's grouse against the new force rising to supplant it? When Greene singles out *Time* magazine as a symbol of the new order's intellectual gimcrackery, as he does in *A Burnt-Out Case*, we are tempted to question his accuracy – would *Time* have bothered to put the architect Querry on its cover? or even Pyle's father, as alleged in *The Quiet American*? Isn't Greene simply taking an easy pot-shot at a recognisable label of the culture he irrationally despises? And might not his spite finally have to do with flaws in his own nature? – with the animus of the schoolboy against a too decent, upright headmaster-father? of the lover of travel against middle-class 'traps' of marriage and mortgage? of the inveterate identifier with fugitive outsiders against all organisations and establishments? of the adulterous sinner against normative morality? Isn't Greene's anti-Americanism simply anti-authority adapted to the post-war world-order, an extension of the *non serviam* this sour Lucifer felt on his fall from the grace of his marriage and ease of his former place as a conventional, middlingly successful climber of the ladder of literary London?

This would be an understandable American view; but as with the English reaction to *An International Episode*, it would have to do with national false pride as much as with real justice. We have noted that Greene portrays some aspects of his Americans favourably; nor does he hold much of a brief for their foils Fowler and Brown, though both are of his age and type and narrate their respective books in the first person. We have noted his dim view of the antics of some Englishmen abroad and of Frenchmen such as the Saigon porn-monger. Thus we might offer in his defence a version of the argument Jack London made when accused of depicting a Jew unfavourably in one of his fifty-odd books: 'I have made villians out of Englishmen, Germans, Yugoslavs, Mexicans, Arabs, West Indians, Chinese, so why should Americans be excluded?'[25] This might seem adequate, so far as it goes. But given Greene's anti-authority (read anarchic) instincts, it would be hard for him to view the masters of the post-war world with the same sympathy that he devotes, in his lifelong sentimentality, to victims. One American whom he treats with signal sympathy is the hippy vagabond Tooley in *Travels with My Aunt*: an *un*dangerous innocent buffeted from one affinity to another depending on whether the prevailing wind blows from her CIA-agent father, her would-be artist lover, a black marijuana dealer or the book's narrator, the retired suburban bank-manager Henry Pulling. Tooley is a guileless fool, a type Greene has always favoured, often in black form – Ali and his descendant Deo Gratias in *A Burnt-Out Case* – and frequently in female – the shop-girls abandoned in *England Made Me* and *Brighton Rock*; indeed, many of his heroes are similar types writ morally larger – this could be said of Scobie as well as such ambiguous cases as the bogus 'Major' Jones in *The Comedians*. What Greene rarely favours is the establishment figure: the type who controls the levers in this fallen world; thus his characteristic suspicion of intelligence operatives, government ministers, police chiefs, bureaucrats of all kinds – all Satan's agents, if we take Monsieur Ouine's view. This, however, must be qualified too; for even the lieutenant who pursues the whisky priest to his death is given a human rationale. And to conclude on this matter of Greene's anti-Americanism, we should note that toward the end of *Travels with My Aunt* it is Tooley's father, the CIA agent, who saves Pulling from the Paraguayan police when that guileless fool has made the mistake of blowing his nose on a handkerchief the colour of the ruling party's flag.

Travels with My Aunt seems at first glance the most wonky and

meaningless of Greene's entertainments: a deliberate attempt to in-
gratiate himself with a generation of Dionysian youth, as ill-advised
in its way as Pentheus's pursuit of orgiastic rites in *The Bacchae*. In fact,
this light-hearted excursion after anarchic pleasures takes a place in
Greene's opus analogous to, say, *As You Like It* in Shakespeare's or
(in a bloodier vein) *The Charterhouse of Parma* in Stendhal's. After the
grousing is over – after the corrosive critic has blasted his empire-
loving countrymen, the 'third force'-seeking Americans, the ruthless
French legacy in old colonies, his own shortcomings as a moral
Catholic and the inadequacy of all ideologies in this unpredictable
world – what is left? What does he want that is positive? Greene
propels his bank-manager into a milieu of smugglers, sexual ad-
venturers, 'life-givers' as he calls them, who live in the vulgar phrase,
'by the seat of their pants'. Tooley at one point gets him high on pot
and rattles on in a way that makes him imagine that 'the whole
world was travelling' and indeed that *that*, not the arriving, is the
point. His aunt has already convinced him that desultory anecdotes
about the eccentric in life and love are more interesting than the
purposeful little homilies and well-bred conversations he has known
back in his London suburb. Though he misses that world with its
narrow certainties, in the end he breaks from it to live in the curiously
Victorian 'lotos land' of Asunción, where he takes over his aunt's
lover's smuggling enterprise and marries the poetry-loving daughter of the Customs chief. On the whole *Travels with My Aunt* takes what
seems evil in more serious books and sees it as good – or at least *for*
its good – and the only really sour, threatening notes come from
outbursts on the part of the little Englanders Pulling has left behind
or actions by jack-booted authorities elsewhere. The book is a triumph
of transvaluation in this way: Greene puts us in Ouine's world but
shows it to be less Satan's than God's. 'The long summer afternoon
of freedom' dreamed of by idealist anarchists is the political faith
here, not socialism; 'All You Need Is Love' becomes the religion
rather than the exacting rituals of Catholicism.[26] It is a view as re-
flective of modish Left thinking in its era as the communism of *It's a
Battlefield* was of that in the 1930s or the anti-Ike-ism of *The Quiet
American* of that in the 1950s. But like the 'Summer of Love' and
rock-songs that inspired it, this 'flower-child' view couldn't last. The
'magical realism' of the South America where Pulling ends up turns
into the nightmare reality of terrorism in Greene's next book, *The
Honorary Consul* (1973); and by the end of the 1970s Greene has gone
back to a characteristic crisis of conscience over the political activi-

ties of his own kind in *The Human Factor*.

Greene's schoolmate Claud Cockburn has remarked that when he was at Oxford Greene 'joined the Communist Party, quite cynically, "with the far-fetched idea of gaining control and perhaps winning a free trip to Moscow and Leningrad" ';[27] and it would be hard not to feel a splinter of bogusness in the successful and wealthy author's identification in the 1970s with terrorists and traitors. Like Byron in Italy, Greene as expatriate thrives on travelling with the opposition; befriending admirers of Che Guevara is his version of consorting with the *Carbonari*; the renegade from the First World establishment becomes a hero among its exploited by declaring that he is able to confirm its injustice from the inside. He enhances his author-ity by claiming the Shelleyan position as the 'true legislator of mankind'; Byron versus Castlereagh, Blücher and the Austrians become Greene versus MI5, the CIA and BOSS. But, unlike Pound, Greene does not let his outbursts take over so much as to make him seem a 'mad' traitor; unlike Byron, he does not become anathema to a literary establishment – indeed, his status as lion is if anything increased by his expatriation. This may be in part because Greene's bouts of *lèse-majesté* have always had a fashionable resonance: as the Otis P. Driftwood persona reflected popular film, so the anti-Vietnam War and pro-Third World attitudes have had their film-world and journalistic partisans. The 'radical chic' breast-beating of *Salvador*, whether in book form (Joan Didion) or film (Oliver Stone), takes inspiration from Greene as do high-minded English productions of the 1980s such as *The Killing Fields* or *The Mission*; and it might be argued that Greene has been an important force in keeping moral concern alive in an aesthetic era of the 'lowest common denominator'. Part of the reason for this may be that, unlike Pound, Greene renovated his modernism with 'entertainment', thus ensuring that his work remained accessible. This may be a factor in his 'greatness' overall; but if so it comes at a price, as with Maugham. Sometimes in later Greene books the plots begin to creak with the all-too-familiar mechanisms of thriller and spy genres (*The Honorary Consul* and *The Human Factor* respectively). After many decades, too, certain recurrent motifs become monotonous: the middle-aged focal character teetering on the edge of Chandlerian self-disgust (but without Philip Marlowe's wit); the moral anguish of conflict between the desire to drift and the call to religious or professional duty; the girl who is loved and left; and the tear-jerking finale in which, as a reviewer of Greene's official *Life* has said, 'the sentimental idea of happiness is replaced by the equally sentimental idea of unhappiness, with its agreeable, self-important thrill of doom'.[28]

Like most of the others considered in this study, Greene's career was propelled first by an urge to eclipse an overbearing parent and have 'the last word'.[29] Adolescent quest for identity became adult mania for authority; rejection of parent became rejection of country and finally of all dominant sociopolitical orders. In the end Greene revels in levelling his curse at both houses, East and West, in *The Human Factor* while leaving the door open for a Catholic 'third way'. But this is half-hearted; for in his Wilson–Fowler irritation with perfection, he needs to violate all romanticism, even religious, and foment a more 'real' break-out of cruelty. Thus his God-figure in *Doctor Fischer of Geneva or the Bomb Party* (1980) is a full-blooded cousin of Monsieur Ouine: a Jehovah and Satan, who ends up as a carcass with 'no more significance than a dead dog'.[30] Fischer is immensely wealthy and powerful. He lives among the supposed *crème de la crème* in an international enclave which might as well be Monaco or the Greene/Maugham sector of the Côte d'Azur. He commands his world with an authority as legendary as that of the best-selling writers; his circle is made up of toadies as much as theirs; he despises them and finds his only pleasure in studying their vanity and greed. The origin of Fischer's cynicism is that his wife abandoned him years before because he could not love properly. Here we detect Greene's residual remorse for the failure of his marriage; and in the novel overall we see an emergent disquiet with his destination as expatriate. What has the quest for Byzantium led to at last but apotheosis as a kind of Osmond, cloistered in a ghetto of fashionable philistines, whose conversation does not even rise to the level of antique-dealing but settles on whether to buy Japanese shares or German? The novel is of course a portrait of Switzerland which Aunt Augusta of *Travels* describes as 'only bearable covered with snow' and Byron once called 'a curst selfish, swinish country of brutes, placed in the most romantic region of the world'.[31] But Greene has never written a novel merely as an exposé of a place, any more than he has ever created a focal character who does not partake of himself in some way; thus Geneva is surely a composite locale for high European expatriation and Fischer the representative type of contemporary success, even Greene's own. (As a matter of fact, Fischer has remarkable similarities to Maugham in his dotage at Villa Mauresque, ranting that Syrie had ruined his life and rejecting his daughter and her husband out of a Lear-like obsession that they were after his money.[32])

Geneva is French-speaking; and taking the sadism of *Doctor Fischer* along with the invective against Nice in his next published work, *J'accuse*, we might conclude that Greene came to despise his adopted homeland with as much fervour as he once satirised English public schoolboys or messianic Americans. This may be. Still, the impression of France one gathers from details strewn through Greene's books of the 1950s and 1960s is of a culture more in tune with its 'sin', more beautiful and civilised, more free of hypocrisy, more fun and finally, above all, less disappointing – perhaps because one did not expect so much from it in the first place. Through Fowler Greene defends the French over the Americans in Vietnam; in *Loser Takes All* (1955) he celebrates his attraction to the Côte d'Azur; in *The Comedians* he suggests – surprisingly – that French failure in the Third World has not been as great as that of the Anglo-Saxons. The revolutionary Philipot reads Baudelaire; the communist Dr Magiot keeps Hugo next to Karl Marx on his shelves. The French have provided answers as well as problems, this seems to say: they may have wreaked horrors yet they have left a transcendental vision that Greene can relate to – not the high-minded, puritan type of an Emerson, nor even Tennyson's sentimental sensuality, but the bitter-sweet music of a poem like *'L'Invitation au voyage'*:

> *Mon enfant, ma soeur,*
> *Songe à la douceur*
> *D'aller là-bas vivre ensemble.*
> *Aimer à loisir,*
> *Aimer et mourir*
> *Dans un pays qui te ressemble . . .* [33]

Lines from Baudelaire to his Creole mistress echo through *The Quiet American*, *Loser Takes All*, *A Burnt-Out Case* and *The Comedians*, until they die away in Greene's memoir *Ways of Escape* (1980). Why? Several elements which compelled Greene-as-expatriate are summed up in this *'fleur du mal'*: desultory love of a dusky erstwhile prostitute; an urge to travel, almost anywhere; the pain of departure; homesickness, generalised regret; the longing to arrive at an ideal – an *idéal* which the writer knows, even as he pens these splendid lines, will turn out in the *real* world to be a mirage: a mirage beckoning toward oblivion under some burning Third World sun; to terminal flight to a 'heart of darkness', like Rimbaud's. But where else, the Greene reader is left to ponder, may one escape when

Byzantium is taken over by the Fischers and his 'Toads'? To the suicide which follows his final 'bomb' party, a version of Greene's own youthful pastime of Russian roulette? Or to the second alternative left to the weary decadent according to the formula of the French of the *fin-du-siècle*: the foot of the cross?[34]

8

A Vanishing Breed

We are rapidly becoming a United States of the World; thus expatriation in the great tradition hardly exists any more. To a certain extent it need not. Through our television screens and other media, to say nothing about the multinational populations of the great cities of the West, we are exposed to much of the variety for which previous generations had to go abroad. Without stepping out of our sitting-rooms we are able to 'totalise' the societies we live in and apprehend the possibilities for 'transcendence' on a collective as well as an individual basis. I use the terms here of the Structuralist successor to F. R. Leavis, Terry Eagleton, in his study *Exiles and Émigrés*.[1] According to his thesis, the great writers in English in the modernist period were one Pole, three Americans, two Irishmen and a working-class English *déraciné* (Conrad, James, Pound, Eliot, Yeats, Joyce and D. H. Lawrence). This was because native English writers, unlike their predecessors of the nineteenth century, had become increasingly stuck in parochial class genres and considerations: the lower-middle class (Shaw, Bennett, Wells) pursued naturalism with its sociopoliltical concerns, while the upper-middle class (Woolf, Forster, Waugh) responded with imaginative-élitist works preoccupied with aesthetics and ethics. The 'exiles and émigrés' (as Eagleton calls his magnificent seven) were able to 'totalise' their pictures of English life because they always had 'alternative' frameworks in mind. For the same reason they were more easily able to see the potential for 'transcendence' both within and beyond that life. Not stuck in narrow cultural *données* or fixed class or accents, they could free themselves more readily in language and form. They could remake the world in English, as it were – open it up – precisely (indeed, perhaps *only*) because of their experience as *déracinés*.

To 'totalise' and 'transcend' in this way was a – perhaps *the* – principal purpose of literary modernism: to universalise; to beckon forward, beyond. It is part and parcel of the spirit of an age that opened it up, made it NEW, in art, music, politics, religion and so on,

151

producing avant-garde 'isms' of all kinds and exploding – sometimes with obscene glee – all the known narrownesses of the past.
Modernism in this way was the culmination of the old Romantic
impulse to liberation – indeed, to all forms of that word which
oscillates from the glorious to the pejorative: from Liberty to libertine.
But modernism, as I've pointed out frequently in this study, is in
decay – has been, despite the Terry Eagletons, for some time. In the
post-modern era literature itself may be in decay, serious modernist
literature at any rate. Why? As there was a bogus element in Romantic
tendencies to myth-making, glorification and special pleading, so
there is too in modernist messianic preoccupation with new forms,
with social reorganisation and tireless consideration of psychological states, with the mirrors behind mirrors and endless worlds within
worlds of the possibilities for story-telling and writing itself. Borges,
the unexpatriated modernist, shows how a writer in the later twentieth
century could quite easily 'totalise' *ad absurdam* from his own study
or the university library down the road. But will his post-Joycean,
metaphysical 'labyrinths' endure as models for communication in
the post-modern age? Will there even be writing as we've known it
in the age following post-modernism; or will *post* itself become the
significant word so that, once we get through a reactive phase and
come to what can now only be designated post-post-modernism, we
will be *post* literature algether?

   If so, this may come as a result of the same forces which have led
to the decay of what I have called a great expatriate tradition: linguistic
amalgamation; esperanto, 'newspeak', mid-Atlantic English,
Franglais; the decline of idioms and their replacement with forms of
slang so quickly arising, transforming and vanishing that they have
little permanent reason to be recorded; film, television, rock-music,
ubiquitous and all-devouring journalism; computerisation; the spread
of capitalist materialism throughout the world and consequent
pushing of spiritual pursuits to the crackpot periphery; a general
Americanisation (United States of the Planet) in which democratic
ideals and opportunity for all (an extension of Stendhal's beloved
Bonapartist *'carrières ouvertes aux talents'*[2]) erodes the distinctions and
– yes – *prejudices* on which the great tradition as we've known it was
substantially based. Criticism, I have quoted Wilde as saying[3], would
be the vehicle through which race-prejudices would be eradicated
from the world finally. Wilde saw this as good: he was part of the
grand liberal consensus in which all writers discussed here – even
Pound, that critic *in extremis* – were essentially working, as were

Eagleton's seven greats of the modernist movement or Leavis's three (or perhaps five or six, depending on whether one includes Austen, Dickens and Lawrence) of the English novel. Consider any of the major works discussed in this study: *Don Juan, La Chartreuse de Parme, The Portrait of a Lady, The Razor's Edge,* 'The Pisan Cantos', *The Heart of the Matter*; consider the *magna opera* of Eagleton's seven or Leavis's lauded 'Gwendolen Harleth', *The Ambassadors, Nostromo* or *Hard Times* and what does one have but fictive schemes of criticism which seek to 'totalise', to 'universalise' the human aggegate by systematic attack on race-prejudices? prejudices at large, and not least – especially in the case of my expatriates – the prejudices of one's own type, class and country?

A writer who didn't approach his material in this way was, in the Romantic-Modernist period, by definition not *great*. He may have had seriousness of purpose, an exact eye, a fine style and so on, but he lacked the liberal-transcendental greatness of soul: the essentially reforming, or at least ameliorating, sociopolitical-imaginative intent. But now in the post-modernist phase comes reaction. It was building through the expressionism of the 1920s and appeals to an urge equally basic in the writer-artist's psyche: the impulse to narrow, to particularise, to define; and by narrowing to focus on the essentials of self, kind or tribe, to create an apologia which is in a real sense anti-universal, anti-liberal, critical in order to enunciate and defend the prejudices of type; to redefine them in a period when their eradication has seemed to go too far, threatening to make the world into a kind of indeterminate mélange (United States of the Lowest Common Denominator). Thus in the post-modernist era we are hard-pressed to find big-hearted literature as we've known it: literature that strides forth with open eyes and welcoming arms for the new, or the old, but anyway the exotic and/or beautiful and *different*. The narrowing little English concerns of a Waugh or an Orwell (Eagleton's representatives of the English malaise in the mid-twentieth century) are one expression of this, as are similar tendencies in lauded successors like Kingsley Amis, for whom the very idea of 'abroad' is regarded with a sneer; a suspicion that woolly-headed, culture-philistine, liberal pretention lurks at the base of it. What individual of sensibility nowadays would want to travel to Maughamish destinations – let alone to the more retrograde outstations of Greeneland where one seems as likely as not to be taken hostage or blown up in some incomprehensible political upheaval?

And even in the First World, doesn't travel nowadays bring a resolve that, on balance, one would rather stay at home? Consider Martin Amis's view of America (the 'moronic inferno') in *Money* or Saul Bellow's of Europe (half-Bloomsbury, half-Auschwitz[4]) in *Mr Sammler's Planet*. Consider any number of lesser novelists' equally critical responses to sojourns in one-time destinations of the Grand Tour, nowadays disfigured by busloads of oriental tourists, pollution yet simultaneously ultra-hygienic, American-style hotels, as well as the perennial pickpockets and gyp-artists. We live in an era in which writers look with increasing disdain on the potentials for 'totalising' and 'transcendence': indeed, they do so with as much verve as reforming modernists enjoyed debunking the heroic pretensions of their Romantic precursors. Paul Theroux, an example of the expatriate urge degenerated into a style and content as self-indulgent and this-worldly as in a Jeffrey Archer best-seller, laments in his picaresque *My Secret History* the passing of African colonies into independence: at that moment, barefoot girls who once gave sex to white Western-ers for free began to demand money for it.[5] Phuong of *The Quiet American* subtly becomes a petty, would-be Imelda Marcos; so that now, even the Tahitis of the Maugham fantasy or the 'hearts of darkness' where Greenemen have found their 'hearts of the matter' have lost their charm. While camera-clickers mar the vistas around the 'monuments of unageing intellect' of Childe Harold's south Europe, so yuppification has spread its money-grubbing tentacles even to the soul of passionate, primitive Latin America of the last great 'Greeneland' books; and the sensitive writer, reader, sensibility altogether must increasingly retreat behind walls – university or 'community watch' enclaves – drifting further away from liberating ideals, trying to forget the poor Arabs or Latinos clamouring for 'a piece of the action' outside, reading books (probably 'faction') or watching TV journalism which testify to our growing preference for the narrow: our new conservatism.

We still have our Anglo-Saxon and French travellers – Theroux himself has covered Patagonia, the 'mosquito coast', China and the British beaches as well as the above-mentioned Africa; English contemporaries like William Boyd are not far behind him. We have had, too, recent cases of those who trade one *patria* for another — to a certain degree Auden and Isherwood fit into this category as did the francophone Belgian authoress Marguerite Yourcenar. But these latter-day expats, many of whom joined in the exodus of White Russian and Jewish *émigrés* to the New World, have been citizens of – even discoverers of – that new *patria* less than inhabitants of a super*patria* (one might even call it the modern nether-world) that recognises, generally with disparagement, a dominant element of the American in it, but remains dreaming in its soul of a lost European 'better place'. Yourcenar, for instance, beats a path back in her fiction to a freer, more fluid and chaotic (some might say 'Americanised') Europe of the sixteenth century (*The Abyss*) or even of Roman times (her *Hadrian*); whereas Nabokov, great exemplar of the *émigré* in exile in the New World, draws the bulk of his irony in a work like *Lolita* from the impact between a European point of view and the new, enwombing American vulgarity. The dying echoes of pursuit of Byzantium – the classic Byzantium of *pays mediterranées* – remain in the later Lawrence Durrell, writing and rewriting his *Alexandria Quartet* in various forms; and the ghost of Henry Miller's love of Parisian *pissoirs* runs through much cosmopolitan American semi-literature, including Erica Jong's animadversions on the construction of the German toilet bowl.[6] But we see here from both sides – European to America, American to Europe – a merging and mixing ultimately bent on destroying the concept of *patria* to such an extent that the condition of classical expatriation can no longer exist, even if there were such antiquated creatures as to continue to set out looking for it.

The urge which drove our 'great expatriates' toward Byzantium, the longing for a finer, more vital existence among 'monuments of unageing intellect' and for more sympathetic milieux in which to pursue various forms of self-realisation, quite often now seems to produce a reverse: a burrowing inward, back into one's own culture, one's 'roots', the past and its concomitant, an Osmond-like process of exclusion. From this point of view James remains the keystone of this study: the central arch from which one must descend as to which one once ascended. Whereas his early books from *Roderick Hudson* to *Portrait* reflected the Romantic century's urge to become more cosmopolitan and open – an urge which among his own countrymen had led to European travel and works by Irving, Cooper, Hawthorne and other predecessors[7] and among Europeans had produced not only Byron and Shelley but all the radical *déracinés* of the mid-century (Hugo, Wagner, Marx) – so his later works culminating in *The Golden Bowl* show the progressive Modernist decay of the urge into an elaborate defining, a closing of doors. Thus the later James prefigures the ultra-sedentary Proust; or among compatriot successors the disaffected patrician Gore Vidal, locking himself away in the mannerly Venice of his ancestors; or the Harold Actons of the British set around Florence. With these and lesser contemporaries, we see among other forms of narrowing (modernist cultural-aesthetic élitism being replaced by post-modernist parochialisation into gay, feminist, black, Jewish, 'magical realist' and so on precincts) nostalgia for a vanishing expatriate grandeur itself: for a 'tradition' evanescent when it existed and almost entirely illusory now. Shakespeare and Co. in Paris has long since decayed from the centre of avant-garde expat publication into a tourist trap attracting Anglo-Saxon ex-students eager to catch a trace of the days of Pound, Hemingway, Djuna Barnes, Nancy Cunard and the whole Left Bank crowd of the 1920s who themselves had gone abroad in part to capture a cosmopolitanness invested in the city by previous, more upholstered bohemians like Edith Wharton and George Moore – the *déracinés* of a more *belle* epoch.

The great expatriates have always shared qualities with their lesser fellow-travellers. No doubt there is a standard type; perhaps he can be seen best in works of the least 'great' figure studied here, Somerset Maugham. Synthesise him out of the three books set partly in 'self-releasing' Paris: *The Magician, The Moon and Sixpence* and *The Razor's Edge*. He is a romantic with some kind of familial discontent – against the mother like Byron, the father like Stendhal, or perhaps both subconsciously as one suspects of Pound and Greene; or perhaps even against a wife and children. Travel releases him from the world of smothering domesticity: travel most likely to a sunnier clime – a 'land where the orange tree grows'. He is in reaction against narrow nationalism as against narrow family; but he may merge with a native colonial type for a time to gain his identity abroad. He may be tempted to trade one *patria* for another too; but this will only be temporary, only a phase, however prolonged, finally to break fully the hold that his national traits have over him. Ultimately his going away produces mature detachment; this allows him to see his own kind more clearly, with decreasing emotional over-involvement and self-liberating antipathy. His goal is personal, transnational self-realisation. He is an existentialist at the core, though probably in a pre- or post-existentialist mode, being in the first case a nineteenth century dandy-*décadent* or in the second a mid-twentieth-century 'Beat'. Unlike the classic existentialist he is not de*moral*ised entirely: he does not flirt long with suicidal despair, because the impulse which led him to expatriate originally pushes him onward, forever looking, questing, for the more perfect landscape, the more civilised city, the more appealing woman – in short, the atmosphere in which he can apprehend the 'better world' that he wants to be a citizen of, and that his essentially critical art is always working to bring into focus.

Classically in the period, for Europeans and Americans, this process has led from Paris or London to Italy: from the most civilised cosmopolites man has yet created to the most aesthetically bounteous country. But in the end the process tends to flag. A kind of entropy sets in. Perfection once glimpsed seems to move beyond the horizon; and the expatriate must move on after it or – if it actually seems to have been reached – move on in any case. For what alive person – what writer anyway (all writing depends on 'irritability', as Jack London said[8]) – can remain in the *paradiso* for ever or even for very long? There must be a fall: from Eden, from grace. The writer must become Prometheus or Satan ('*non serviam*'):[9] the bringer of light to his kind which does not yet have it or the rebel against the Godly order that restricts self-expression even in Heaven. The expatriate in this way is fated either to return home or to travel on to places he knows cannot be 'better' (which may, indeed, turn out to be pandemonium); otherwise he becomes static and his peculiarly 'transcendental' power to 'totalise' will vanish. In all we have discussed here – Byron, Stendhal, James of *The American Scene*, Pound with his increasing Americanness at St Elizabeth's, Maugham and Greene in their oscillation back toward trivial yet familiar English comic writing – we see the tendency to turn back, even the desire to go home again. But after the great questing outer push and myriad rich discoveries of years abroad there can be no satisfactory homecoming. Destiny beckons elsewhere. Byron moves on to Greece though he knows it will prove treacherous; Stendhal returns to Civitavecchia and dashes up to Rome whenever possible; James becomes a British citizen though he has long since lost his illusions about Englishness; Pound returns to Italy and becomes depressed by its irrelevance to the post-war world order; Maugham and Greene settle into liveable compromise with the *déracinés* of the south of France.

The south, the sun, the phallic has been a motif of the great expatriation in all these cases except for James, that peculiar part-Tiresias, part-eunuch; but as our 'greats' grow old the heat and light and rise of the blood flickers; Byzantium as worldly destination grows dim and the homeland of the Work – of one's literature and its relation to posterity – is what is essentially left:

Once out of nature I shall never take
My bodily form from any natural thing,
But such a form as Grecian goldsmiths make
Of hammered gold and gold enamelling . . .
(W. B. Yeats, 'Sailing to Byzantium')

Death, of course, is one identity of this 'homeland'. Yeats's vision of
the art-incorporating-artist which 'keep[s] a drowsy emperor awake'
and sings of 'what is past or passing or to come' is a glorious veil
dropped before that terrible secret – or perhaps the secret itself after
the veil has been torn away. Perhaps one can achieve eternal life by
'sailing to Byzantium' in great art; all that is assured, however, is
that – in the sailing – one must learn to bid ever 'Adieu, adieu, my
native shore . . . '. The bittersweet love of farewell, homesickness, the
poésie des départs, allied with the prospect of approaching some exotic
better place, runs through the work of the last great expat discussed
here as through the first. And what is the lyricism of Pound in *The
Cantos* but memory and desire of transcendental moments of revelation such as might have been apprehended by the sacrificial
heroes of Eleusis as they entered the mysteries? The light of the
Himalayas or the South Seas for Maugham, or of Milan and its lakes
for Stendhal – recalled in winter, in darkness, in the infertile north,
isn't this likely to shimmer and transform, until it comes in some
sense to seem the light beyond the grave? Aren't all these spirits
(again with the exception of the oddly neuter James) seeking subliminally to enter an unreal world beyond; to penetrate to the
other side, as it were, the eternal, and find it to be a landscape that
one's soul can dwell in, thus conquering finally the fear of grey
blankness, which is death?

An expatriate career is by definition a journey from the place of
one's birth to that of one's death. One is born where one must be but
would like to die where one chooses. The choices of where one goes
have by logical extension something to do with death and after-
death. They have to do in a Christian (or post-Christian) culture
with, perhaps, getting oneself as close to Heaven as one can during
one's period here on earth. Byron on a soldier's pallet in Missolonghi,
Stendhal on his cosmopolitan street, James at home in London styling
himself 'Napoleone', Maugham in abject splendour at Cap Ferrat,
Pound mute in Venice, Greene dreaming of an otherworldly ballroom
in his 'Aunt's' mansion in Asunción – in arriving at these chosen
places all had bid hail and farewell to birthplaces and former resting-

perches so many times as to be, one suspects, in as close a state of preparation to bidding farewell to this world as one may get. So is the whole process of expatriation perhaps a version of what Arthur Symons saw as the chief motivation for his group of writers in *The Symbolist Movement in Literature*?[10] to find a means to escape or explain death; to evade the pain of it; to know the experience of farewell and loss so well that the shock when it comes will seem no more earthshaking than some 'momentous decision' to expatriate taken years before? To give up family and country is a metaphor for death surely – or at least for finding a new life. And so, on the positive side, expatriation of course must be seen as not death-related at all but a vital act in favour of rebirth. This would be the argument of Henry Miller, that 'plenipotentiary from the realm of free spirits', who was 'never more "at home" ' than when rootless; who sought to bring Walt Whitman's identification with the transcendental All out of America and into old Europe; who concentrated on 'the moment, the expanding moment that is heard forever'; and whose mind, thus writing, was intended to become 'a huge divan smothered with cushions and [whose] life one long snooze on a hot, drowsy afternoon'.[11]

Miller is to some degree what the urges of all these other expatriates might have led to if fully liberated. What he lacks is their sense of form, both as regards the outer world and the self, thus their varying degrees of formalism in writing. Form to him was death, free expression life; and to the extent to which other authors, past or contemporary, approached free expression he lauded or denigrated them as 'life-givers' or 'death-eaters'.[12] Among contemporaries, Lawrence fell into the first category, Joyce and Proust into the second; among the greats of the past Villon and Rabelais belonged to the first, Virgil to the second. Of our expats, Miller might have seen Byron as restricted by senses of class and duty; he certainly would have rejected his attachment to eighteenth century forms though he might have extolled *Don Juan* for its license. Stendhal he would have approved of for his lust, appetite and travel, and for the ruthlessness with which he lambasts the 'mental asphyxia' of the high life of Paris – a life Miller was mercifully (by his standards) never exposed to, owing to his utterly proletarian bohemian persona. This social identity leaves him ill-equipped to judge James who belonged to the drawing-room as exclusively as Miller did to the street; but had he done so, Miller (as intimated in my chapter on James) might have admired the Master's courage to go on and on with psychological detail, almost to the point of metaphysical revelation. Maugham he would have 'seen through' as a 'phoney': a man stuck in a closet of deceptive grandeur, hiding the fact of his faecal nature as of his phallic excitements. However, with Maugham he has something intensely in common. For what is Miller but the literary realisation of the wild, self-expressive beast of an artist whom Maugham creates in Charles Strickland? And what was Miller's massive rebellion against American domesticity and mores but an outspoken version of the resentment Maugham felt toward Edwardian strictures and not least the petty social tyranny of women such as he associated with his ex-wife?

'America is essentially a woman's country', Miller says at one point in his complaints about it.[13] This mirrors Maugham's picture of the London in which Strickland is caught; it also mirrors the America embodied in Isabel Maturin which Maugham's great expatriate Larry Darrell wanders away from. (Miller is in fact an unhousebroken version of Darrell: a self-educator through eclectic reading, proletarian jobs, 'self-releasing' Paris and transcendental religious ideas. He had been exposed to theosophy from his early twenties, he practised psychoanalysis in the 1930s and had his works praised by the most prominent European exponent of the new religion of self-realisation, Count Keyselring.[14]) It also echoes Pound's complaints about the American literary milieu, dominated by 'old maidish' editors scared of anything but Victorian forms and conventional subject matter. Where Pound blasted against this with torrents of classical allusions and images, Miller – to us a phrase appropriate to the author of *Tropic of Cancer* – shit upon it; and between Pound and Miller, almost exact contemporaries, there is superficially closer affinity than between Miller and any other discussed here. Both left America and revelled in the literary Bohemias of Europe for similar reasons; but Pound in his fascism seemed to want to restructure the world, whereas Miller in his anarchism wanted to end structure altogether; and Miller was finally an inveterate wanderer of *this* earth whereas Pound increasingly inhabited other times. In this Miller may at last have most in common with Greene, though he would have rejected the Oxbridge Englishman's attachment to the well-made novel and his neurotic quest for answers amid old 'isms' and new ideologies (Catholicism and communism). Both actually liked dwelling among the low-down, the company of whores and the 'beat' life-rhythm of drug-takers. They shared an essential taste for the seedy, also a compulsion to find *satori* in whatever way, even at the expense of living 'disreputably'.

Thus Life *chez* Miller. Domestic existence means being in 'a polished mausoleum in which [one's] misery and suffering [is] kept brightly burning'. It means to 'die of malnutrition of the soul' or at best to become preoccupied with 'malignant diseases', real or imagined, and suppressed social rage and neuroses. Nowhere, alas, was this worse than in America, where spiritual decay had advanced in inverse proportion to material progress:

> I couldn't help but think of the old ones in Europe [he writes upon returning to Brooklyn and seeing his parents]; they had not only managed to do without these comforts [refrigerators, gas ranges, central heating] but, so it seemed to me, they remained far healthier, saner and more joyous than the old ones in America. America has comforts; Europe has other things which make all these comforts seem quite unimportant.[15]

This is a new version of the classic American cry, heard in Pound, James on Hawthorne and so on, for the properties of culture the New World is lacking. But it is also a cry against something James, like Eliot, ultimately eschewed in pursuit of culture in Europe. They, quite Americanly in an upper-middle-class way, sought the social milieu of a fixed society and place – a sort of better Boston, thus their attachment to London. They wanted, as I've said, greater *order* as an antidote to what they saw as an excessive freedom in America, leading to chaos. They were in rebellion in part against an excessively inclusive tendency in the transcendentalism of their backgrounds (thus Eliot's narrowing into an Anglo-Catholic faith) and an excessive 'totalising' in the development of their country (thus Eliot's anti-Semitism and both men's narrowing focus on the 'better sort' of White Anglo-Saxon Protestant society). They dabbled with French and other European cultures and ideas only at the higher levels. They were after universalism only in the rarefied individual consciousness. They were, in short, snobs: conservatives; believers ultimately in no 'better place', thus apologists at last for a world order such as had existed in their youths; Pax Britannica deteriorating if it must into Pax Anglo-Saxonia, but not if you please into a too-robust Pax Americana.

Miller and his half-expatriated followers among the 'Beats' – Burroughs in Morocco, Kerouac seeking *satori* in Paris, Ferlinghetti 'bringing it all back home' to North Beach in San Francisco – were in revolt against this, as against those half-steppers between Jamesian-Eliotic conservatism and themselves: the middle-class Hemingways and Fitzgeralds of 1920s Paris. Miller and his kind were with the radicals Pound and Stein in wanting to make their art formally *new*; they were with the self-immolating Harry Crosby in wanting to record every detail of their being and consciousness. And thus they all lead beyond the limits of literature *per se* – toward the solipsism of self-analysis; toward that point of breakdown of form and attention to the outer, beyond which no consciousness can reach. And so we have to turn back – as for instance Greene, as I've argued, successfully did – toward the conventional, the comprehensible, the (perhaps) non-*great* literary *à la* Leavis (though Leavis, as we have said, had foreseen the dead-end toward which solipsistic modernism might lead in his criticism of Joyce and Proust). And in turning back there must be reassessment of many things escaped: bourgeois society, domesticity, Edwardian Britain and not least the material Moloch of America. Some Europeans, as noted, had become expatriates to the latter even as the existential 'Beats' escaped it. Miller himself went back, albeit unwillingly, at the same time as Auden and Isherwood arrived there by choice, and many others – Mann, Brecht, even Maugham – did by necessity. And what did these Europeans find in the great, welcoming, all-embracing land which so many of its best found sadly lacking? We know why they went: freedom from dictators, class systems, restricted mores, religious narrowness, formal dogma, an inability to make money easily and as they wished, fundamentally (though only superficially, as Miller would contend) less *Liberty*. But was this New-World 'better place' sufficiently 'better' on close inspection to make them want to stay permanently?

Probably most Europeans in America in the 1940s, like most Americans in Paris in the 1920s, never intended their expatriation to be endless. Mann, Brecht, Maugham, bitty travellers like Waugh (*The Loved One*) all avoided over-great consciousness of the country or vented their satirical attitudes and returned to Europe at the earliest convenience. But some didn't, notably some who settled (as many did) around the newest metropoles of the country growing up in California. Miller himself gravitated finally, and happily, to Big Sur. Isherwood, unlike his friend Auden who stayed in New York and went back to his old college at Oxford to die, settled in L.A. along with Gerald Heard, Aldous Huxley, Raymond Chandler (a special case),[16] various movie writers, composers and artists, latterly David Hockney and others. All appeared to find a congenial home there which eventually eroded their attachment and desire to go back to the old. Why? In the first instance, it seems that California appeared to them to be an America beyond the materialistic and matriarchal domesticity of the rest of the country. In the 1940s when they arrived it seemed a wild, young place still, where society had not yet taken firm root; and where it had pitched its tent or built its little clapboard houses it seemed to have done so in a bohemian way that promised something entirely new: a sort of aesthetic, exuberant, unascetic Walden-by-the-sea – a 'Little Good Place', as Isherwood would put it, where man could be at one with a beneficent nature and realise his potential in body and spirit in a way which had not been known in the West since ancient Greece. California provided a hope at this stage of a society which at its worst might constitute an aggregation of Maugham's beachcombers, in both their rough South Seas and their sophisticated Côte d' Azur aspects. And on top of this, for better or worse, there existed Hollywood – that city-state of the great Eastern Moloch transplanted, where writers could earn vast sums for little effort and which, despite its lowest-common-denominator philistinism, still carried the potential (as it seemed all America had always) to create unexpected masterpieces one day.

As it had been for Jack London's friends in Carmel at the turn of the century and as it would be for Jack Kerouac's in the Bay Area in the 1950s, California was the new American Bohemia: a sort of Left Bank, Tuscany and Greek island combined, looking west in Yeatsian-Joycean Celtic style to the 'land beyond the wave'. Could a more perfectly 'totalising', 'transcendentalising' landscape have beckoned? Miller, who had found in Paris his 'only home' and who had 'never known the meaning of peace until [he] arrived in Greece', found in Big Sur another potential 'navel of the human spirit', another escape from the 'cultural rigmarole' which in the American East generally turned writers into academic experts who 'slowly degenerate[d] into full-fledged chimpanzees'.[17] In *Big Sur and the Oranges of Hieronymous Bosch* he 'invokes' a new type of man 'as wild and unpredictable as this wild and lonely coast where he finally anchors': a spirit who though cultured in 'medicine, folklore, magic, anthropology, languages', really craves above all a 'virginal world, a world unspoiled by man'. Here indeed is what America offered – had offered always and only at its best – to the Europeans drawn to it. If Byzantium and all we have attributed to it was what they could find by travelling back to civilisation's origins in its Mediterranean south-east, *this* is what they could find by going to its pristine furthest west: 'New land, new figures of earth. Dreamers, outlaws, forerunners. Advancing toward the other world of long ago and far away, the world of yesterday and tomorrow. The world within the world.'[18] Nor is it merely the verbally diarrhoetic Miller with his theosophical metaphysics who invested this Californian coast with a messianism of place. The (by comparison) verbally constipated Isherwood describes a 'stunning baptism of the surf' in his expatriate exposition of California, *A Single Man*, set in the megalopolis of the south. 'Giving himself to it utterly', he writes of his Brit expat hero, 'he washes away thought, speech, mood, desire, whole selves, entire lifetimes; again and again he returns, becoming always cleaner, freer, less . . .'.[19]

Of course Isherwood had theosophical tendencies too, as we have said. Larry Darrell-ism had not led him to India but led India to him in the person of Swami Prabhavananda, whom Miller also met on coming to California.[20] And though Isherwood's style is fastidious and as far from Miller's compulsive ramblings as one might get, we see instantly in his use of the present tense, in his emphasis on *here* and *now*[21] and 'eternal return', a kindred insistence on existential awareness and self-transformation – what Miller with his more unbuttoned American messianism calls ' the task of genius . . . to keep the miracle alive, to live always in the miracle, to make the miracle more and more miraculous, to swear allegiance to nothing, but live only miraculously, think only miraculously, die miraculously'.[22] This is what leads both to California, or at least what leaves them there: a sense that 'the miraculous' remains immanent – indeed, remains eternally present for those who will recognise and take it. This sets the place off from what Isherwood calls 'the past' of England, a place in his view of damp and darkness, of material discomfort and dogmatic values, mitigated only by 'heartbreakingly insecure' and 'snug' nursery pleasures – a dim, vanishing, 'dear tiny doomed world' where child is nurtured by nanny.[23] California coastal Bohemia, on the other hand, was created by 'pioneer escapists from dingy downtown Los Angeles and stuffy-snobbish Pasadena' – from middle-class dogma and domesticity, in short – who wanted to create in the 'woodsy atmosphere' of the canyons 'a subtropical English village with Montmartre manners; a Little Good Place where you could paint a bit, write a bit and drinks lots'. Of these founding fathers of 1920s Paris dragged west (or of an anti-Paris created by an impulse similar to what had led many to the Left Bank), Isherwood continues affectionately:

They saw themselves as rearguard individualists, making a last-ditch stand against the twentieth century. They gave thanks loudly from morn till eve that they had escaped the soul-destroying commercialism of the city. They were tacky and cheerful and defiantly bohemian; tirelessly inquisitive above each other's doings, and boundlessly tolerant. When they fought, at least it was with fists and bottles and furniture, not lawyers. Most of them were lucky enough to have died off before the Great Change.[24]

As Pound's pioneer Americanism strained toward an old NEW bohemianism amid 'monuments of unageing intellect' in London-Paris-(beachcomber) Rapallo, so these pioneers of the far west pressed for a new old free-spiritism in the most classically beautiful landscape of the New World. Each was in revolt from material modernism – Americanisation as well as tight-assed (cf. Miller) northern Europe. But as war demolished Pound's nostalgic Euro-bohemian vision, so in California, as Isherwood tells us : 'The Change began . . . . The world-war-two vets came swarming out of the East with their just married wives . . . . One by one, the cottages which used to reek of bathtub gin and reverberate with the poetry of Hart Crane have fallen to the occupying army of coke-drinking television-watchers.'[25] Freedom goes into eclipse: the 'long summer's afternoon' in 'the land where the orange tree grows'. The new California wives explain to their men that 'breeding and bohemianism do not mix'. Tract houses are cut into hills that on a clear day had a kind of 'Andean' splendour; the water becomes (or seems to become) polluted; smog, radio-blare, endless parking-lots and 'the magic of the think-machine gods' with their endless statistical analyses invade. Upper-class Walden-seekers arrive from the East and carp about the motels, the fast-food stores, the plastic-fantastic optimism, the zombie-like attitudes – and suddenly Isherwood in Californian chauvinist reaction rises to an unexpectedly passionate defence:

'You sound like some dreary French intellectual [his hero says] who's just set foot in New York for the first time! . . . A motel-room isn't a room, it's the Room . . . it's a symbol – an advertisement in three dimensions if you like. . . . We've reduced the things of the material plane to mere symbolic conveniences. And why? Because that's the essential first step. Until the material plane has been defined and relegated to its proper place, the mind can't ever be truly free. . . . The Europeans call us inhuman – or they prefer to say immature, which sounds ruder – because we've renounced their world of individual differences, and romantic inefficiency, and objects-for-the-sake-of-objects. All that dead old cult of cathedrals and first editions and Paris models and vintage wines. . . . The Europeans hate us because we've retired to live inside our advertisements, like hermits going into caves to contemplate. . . . Essentially, we're creatures of the spirit. Our life is all in the mind. That's why we're completely at home with symbols like the American Motel-Room. Whereas the European has a horror of symbols because he's such a grovelling little materialist . . . .[26]

One's eyes open in surprise. Though there may be residual irony here, the declaration sums up why Isherwood – a classical expatriate, if never a *great* one – could remain in California, along with the drug-taking Huxley, where a yearner after upper-class Euro-English country-house exclusivity like Waugh could only sneer and beat a hasty retreat. 'How delightful it is, to be here!', Isherwood's persona enthuses at a beach-side gymnasium where Californians pursue their cult of the body with perfectly frank narcissism. 'If only one could spend one's entire life in this state of easy-going physical democracy! Nobody is bitchy here, or ill-tempered, or inquisitive.'[27] But . . . But later, in hills which seemed a pristine 'primitive alien nature' when he arrived in the state he finds ubiquitous fast cars, encroaching suburbia and oppressive awareness of the city spreading its tentacles up from below. 'It will die of over-extension', he laments at this all-too-American materialist entreprise; 'it will die because its taproots have dried up; the brashness and greed which have been its only strength. And the desert, which is the natural condition of this country, will return.'[28] So he foresees the apocalypse of what Auden, after a trip to L.A., described as 'the Great Wrong Place'.[29] Yet still for Isherwood (or his persona) it is 'Home'. Still he wants to sneer at his unexpatriated countryman: 'I [am] blissfully happy here, and never never will I set foot on [your] dreary little island again.'[30] But as with Byron in Italy or Greece, the original attraction dims. His mind drifts back to 'the beach months of 1946. The magic squalor of those hot nights, when the whole shore was alive with tongues of flames, the watch-fires of a vast naked barbarian tribe – each group or pair to itself and bothering no one, yet all part of the life of the tribal encampment'.[31] Now 'the glory has faded', to be replaced by 'the sad fierce appetite of memory, as it looks back hungrily on that glorious Indian summer of lust'. Childe Harold's Greece of poetic awakening gives way to swamp fever and the money-grubbing of the once 'noble savage' Suliotes; and in the end Isherwood can't help but see the point of the reaction of one of his oriental students:

> She says she won't marry a Caucasian. She says she can't take people in this country seriously. She doesn't feel anything we do here *means* anything. She wants to go back to Japan and teach. [32]

Among the less-great expatriate writers – Miller and Isherwood as I use for example – one finds all too often that the best espouse a flaccid universalism while the worst are full of parochial intensity. They may satisfy at some times some of the Leavisite standards for greatness – 'changing the possibilities of the art for practitioners and readers', being 'significant in terms of the human awareness they promote', having 'rich matter to organize', 'subtle interests', 'strength of analysis of emotional and moral states', and so on[33] – but they lack Jane Austen's ability to respond closely and without prejudice to the mores of 'the best society' or Austen's middle-class successors – Dickens and Lawrence, for instance – to respond to the personalities and structures of bourgeois and / or proletarian classes with sympathy, taking into account how those classes view themselves. The task of the great writer is to go beyond self, high and low, and (to mix in Eagleton's terms once more) 'totalise' and apprehend the possibilities for 'transcendence' for a *whole* society. Thus Leavis praises *Nostromo* for its attempt to make all the significant parts of a social organism work together for an essential (and not merely material) benefit; and Eagleton considers *Brideshead Revisited* flawed by nostalgia for a narrow, élite world which eschews identification with values or aspirations outside itself. If Waugh is not great because he is parochially upper-class and Orwell similarly limited by lower-middle-class focus, then Miller must be *un*great too because he only really cares about his own kind of 'lonesome traveller' (usually macho, but also including Anaïs Nin);[34] and Isherwood, with his sometimes appalling misogyny and his invective against 'the [middle-class] Enemy', is too narrowly gay. The novels of both, furthermore, fail the Leavisite test as dramatic patterns of forces and characters working through plot toward a new and better relation to one another: for *Tropic of Cancer* is a memoir tarted up (or down, if you prefer) with sex and metaphysics; and *A Single Man*, like *Berlin Stories*, is much the same, with 'I' dressed up as 'George' and the autobiographical reportage obscured behind the Englishman's fastidious sense of style and storytelling (beginning, middle and end).

Beyond the Leavisite standards of greatness, more is missing in these authors as great expatriates. Their finis as beachcombers on the California coast cuts them off substantially from that essential of Byzantium: the 'monuments of unageing intellect'. To this they might object that (a) there is no earthly reason why admiration of great art and culture can't proceed in California as well as anywhere, in the Getty Museum or in finely printed small-press books; and (b) what they may lose in immediate contact with a great past they may gain in spiritual attachments, to the theosophical 'sixth race' growing up in California or the endless surge and resurge of the Pacific.[35] But these arguments remained flawed, not least by the specious element of anti-materialism which underlies them. Isherwood's diatribe against the European's obsession with his little *objets*, his property as opposed to the American's tacky yet 'symbolic' motel room, glosses over what Henry James recognised about European materialism versus American and embodied in the collector's enthusiasm of Osmond and of Adam Verver. In Europe the object is an accretion of years, perhaps centuries, of history and significance; so too is a property – so that Osmond's Roman coins or the Touchetts' country house represent 'monuments of unageing intellect' themselves: 'spiritual' entities, each at its best a kind of Holy Grail, contemplation of which can lead the sensitive spirit to higher attainment both in society and the self, whether in the 'Great Good Place' of Europe or – at least theoretically – wherever that 'Good Place' can be properly transported. Isherwood himself seems to intuit this when he calls his vanishing Californian Bohemia a 'Little Good Place', and 'English village' with 'Montmartre manners'; and Miller's 'Beat' successor Lawrence Ferlinghetti recognised it implicitly in his partly successful move to import the ethos of Left Bank Paris to 1950s San Francisco. But these are only intimations. In Miller and Isherwood and lesser expatriates of various coteries there remains a limiting alienation from much of the ethos of the past, thus its materialism, because that ethos seems forever tainted by bad spiritual associations – the élitism and contempt of aristocrats or the petty greed of the middle-class 'Enemy'.

Pound, perhaps curiously, is less afflicted by this: he simply claims as his own the parts of the past he approves of. Byron and Stendhal do much the same; the 'Enemy' for them seems most often the present – a present of degenerate usurers in Pound's case, of rapacious Lord Elgins in Byron's and restored Bourbon philistines in Stendhal's: all those who imperilled the proper associations, as they saw it, of particularly admired 'monuments of unageing intellect'. In these three expats, each of whom exhumed in their works personae and tales from the past, we can see that the most reliable form of expatriation finally might be that which takes one out of contemporary life altogether: expatriation in *time*. Nowdays with the United States of the Universe upon us this has become so apparent that even pop culture has its burgeoning genres of historical romance and science fiction; and no less a pop idol than Mick Jagger once told an interviewer that he spent his leisure time reading a biography of Bernard Baruch as it provided a more reliable mode of escape than reading contemporary 'faction' or watching TV.[36] Expatriation in space, in short, has reached its limits. In its last gasp, as in Greene, it has tended to produce manic travel to every corner of the Third World. But this process proves futile; for as Greene shows, everywhere one encounters a creeping First World malaise. Thus such 'ways of escape' become just that: temporary, semi-touristic voyages having the effect of narcotics – distracting, exciting for a moment, but wearing off and leaving the traveller to return to the same old problems of self and society that can never be transcended wholly in this world. The process becomes even more clear in Greene's *manqué* American successor Paul Theroux, though in his manic travels the problems of self and society seem more readily overcome or ignored, for he seeks and attains repeatedly a guiltless self-gratification that Greene might have regarded as a moral blight on the age; and his most consistent *problem* seems to be that others are not always as obliging of his desires as a picaresque *homme moyen sensuel* might want. Expatriation *chez lui* becomes banal.

Other successors to Greene – Joan Didion, for instance – implicate themselves more on the level of nerves and conscience in the problems of the Third World (see her novels *A Book of Common Prayer*, *Democracy*[37] and so on); and Didion's is an important case to consider beside those minor expats who sought or found their Left Bank in Californian Bohemia. Being native to the state, she knows that in order to 'totalise' and 'transcend', the first proper step must be to the Spanish-speaking south whose problems are rolling up to her 'civilised' world's border and spilling over in a trickle that may soon become a torrent. But Didion's sensibility remains narrow, if fastidious; and her concerns are really the parochial ones of an upper-middle-class California Episcopalian Anglo trying to maintain orderly domesticity. She may be a minor descendant of James in this way – something Theroux (though he comes from Boston) is not. But though she goes beyond James in space and in class subject-matter, she is not *great* like him in her ability to present and explore her own 'civilised' kind in every detail of its operations. Indeed, in comparison with the world James evoked, one wonders if civilisation as such really exists where Didion places it – in West L.A. – or whether what one is seeing isn't some kind of mock-up, as phoney in its way as the Tudor house-fronts of an old Hollywood movie set. Whatever the answer to that, the fact that the argument turns back to James at this point emphasises, I think, his centrality to the standard implied in this study, for better or worse. More than any other, James created an entire world – specifically one which revolved around the 'international theme': these problems of expatriation. If it was a narrow world – too restricted in class, space and perhaps even time – at least it was a *whole* one, complete in itself: a world to which its creator had unlimited commitment and did not seek to escape out of satiety or boredom.

In his narrow sphere, James wanted to *know*. He was inexhaustibly curious. He would never have booked an airplane to almost anywhere on earth *à la* Greene and successors because he was sick of himself and his writing. Nor would he have ever looked on his writing as they would: as principally a profession – a way to make money. This separates him, along with Pound, from the rest: from Byron and Stendhal with their disdain for the sedentary occupation, though less so Maugham; for he remained curious too, endlessly avid for vignettes and religiously committed to his stint at his writing-desk every morning. Thus Maugham – or perhaps Maugham as an extension and correction of James – may in the end constitute the most *serviceable*[38] example of the great expatriate writer, derivative and low-brow though he may seem. The fact that he is both serious *and* readable is crucial here. Amid all the high-minded Leavisite standards, the requirements to 'totalise' and 'transcend' stated by Eagleton, Maugham slips through with something more – with qualities highly valued in that other critical tradition of English letters: the more cavalier, even 'upper-class' (Eagleton's term) tradition of style over morals. Wit, charm, formal ease and grace, the ability to entertain – even as austere a personality as T. S. Eliot recognised the call of these in the end; for what are his plays – *The Cocktail Party*, for instance –

but a marriage of the (poetic) *problem* with wit? One might argue that in becoming essentially an upper-class Englishman, Eliot was collapsing at the altar of a narrowing dandyish standard: that he was giving up his original expatriate virtues of being able to 'totalise' and 'transcend'. There is something to this. But then perhaps Eliot recognised instinctively that modernist universalism could only lead to the dead ends of his friends Joyce and Pound (*Finnegans Wake* and *The Cantos*); and that in the post-modernist era some form of narrowing was inevitable – indeed, necessary – if coherent sensibility were to be restored.

Not that Maugham with his wit and Britishness was narrow. *The Razor's Edge*, as I've argued, may be one of the great books about *American* expatriation. In one sweep it takes in many of the impulses essayed here: from the high Jamesian in Elliott Templeton, to the low *à la* Miller in Larry Darrell's proletarian career, to the mystic *à la* Miller and Isherwood as stated, to the scholarly *à la* Pound. Added to this is a compelling Romantic sense of the Grand Tour as central educative and motive force to a career of ultimate action; for though Larry does not go off to a soldier's end like Byron nor to a diplomat's like Stendhal, he gives up writing and ease to take up a form of 'service' perhaps more appropriate to his origins and era – driving a taxi in New York – committing thereby a version of Byron's *auto-da-fé* at Missolonghi and dying away into obscurity for us like Stendhal with his *crise de cardiac dans la rue*. The point of *The Razor's Edge* in any case, as of Byron's and Stendhal's lives, is the great, questing expatriate act of *departure*. It is all in the travelling, perhaps, not in the destination after all: all in the *sailing* to Byzantium, not in the 'holy city' itself, which remains a medallion at the end, a beckoning ideal. Larry has lived in a garret, read, seen, worked, made love, been in love, lost in love, gained enlightenment, been betrayed; and through all, he has learned the relative values of Beauty, Truth and Goodness. He has written his slim volume relating great minds of the past to his present; and finally, having escaped the material world of his kind, he turns back to face it again, to be narrowed again perhaps, *un*totalised, *un*transcendentalised, *un*bohemianised – we don't know. We only know that to have stayed on in the free-spirit-land of expatriation would have meant to become increasingly detached: more fully, until terminally deracinated, like Pound; or perhaps progressively more absorbed in the new *patria* – no doubt Paris in his case, unlike London for Eliot and James. But the Paris of Larry's time and type was principally 'self-releasing' and meant to be so: not meant to be a final destination. In the classic, established, more cavalier tradition, the destination was Mediterranean – the Côte d'Azur, Tuscany, Rome: the end-point geographically for most of those discussed here, even the unrepentantly northern, social, upper-class other face of the Larry Darrells, the Jamesian Elliott Templetons.

Notes

CHAPTER 1. THE EXPATRIATE TRADITION

1. I state this ambiguously on account of the fact that the dictionary defines the word principally as a verb.
2. In *The Critic as Artist*. See my *Wagner to 'The Waste Land'* (London: Macmillan, 1982) pp. 46–7.
3. In Robert McAlmon, *Being Geniuses Together* (London: Hogarth Press, 1984) pp. 203–7 and elsewhere.
4. In Gillian Hanscombe and Virginia Smyers, *Writing for their Lives* (London: The Women's Press, 1987).
5. Ibid.

CHAPTER 2. BYRON

1. See Edward John Trelawny, *Records of Shelley, Byron and the Author* (London: Folio Society, 1952) p. 28.
2. Letter to John Hanson, 16 April 1809, to be found in Leslie Marchand, *Byron: A Biography* (New York: John Murray, 1957) vol. I, p. 175.
3. In ibid., pp. 31, 60–1 and elsewhere.
4. Letter to John Cam Hobhouse, 29 July 1810, to be found in Peter Quennell (ed.), *Byron, A Self Portrait: Letters and Diaries, 1798–1824* (London: John Murray, 1950) vol. I, pp. 75–6.
5. Reproduced among other places in Leslie Marchand (ed.), *Lord Byron: Selected Letters and Journals* (London: John Murray, 1982) pp. 320–1.
6. See Elizabeth Longford, *Byron* (London: Hutchinson/Weidenfeld and Nicolson, 1976) p. 18; also Andre Maurois, *Byron* trans. Hamish Miles (New York: Ungar, 1930) p. 123.
7. See Enid Starkie, *Baudelaire* (London: Faber and Faber, 1957) p. 319.
8. Letter to Robert Adair, 4 July 1810, to be found in John Murray (ed.), *Lord Byron's Correspondence* (New York: John Murray, 1922) vol. I, p. 9.
9. Frederic Raphael, *Byron* (London: Thames and Hudson, 1982) p. 55.
10. Letter to Francis Hodgson, 13 Oct 1811, in Quennell, *Byron: A Self Portrait*, vol. I, p. 121.
11. The name originally given the hero in *Childe Harold's Pilgrimage*.
12. Letter to Francis Hodgson, to be found in Rowland Prothero (ed.), *The Works of Lord Byron: Letters and Journals* (London: John Murray, 1898–1901) vol. II, p. 100.
13. Final stanza of *The Corsair*.
14. See Prothero, *Works of Lord Byron*, vol. II, p. 105.
15. *Byron: A Portrait*, p. 137.
16. Marchand, see *Childe Harold's Pilgrimage*, Canto III, stanza III.
17. Ibid., Canto IV, stanza CXXXVII.
18. Ibid., stanza CLXXIX.

19. Though Caroline Lamb has him dying by drowning in her *roman à clef*, *Glenarvon* (1816).
20. The Earl of Oxford's family name was Harley. A famous collection of pamphlets in family possession went by this name; and when Lady Oxford produced a brood of children whose handsome features bore no relation to her husband's, they picked up the sobriquet as well.
21. See among others, letters to Hobhouse and Douglas Kinnaird, 19 January 1819, and to Murray, 6 April 1819, in Marchand, *Selected Letters and Journals*, pp. 184–91.
22. The German poet's opinion of Byron is record in George Bancroft, 'A Day with Lord Byron', in *History of the Battle of Lake Erie and Miscellaneous Papers* (New York, 1891). Byron dedicated two of his dramas to Goethe, *Sardanapalus* and *The Deformed Transformed*. Goethe's opinion was that *Don Juan* was a poem of such wit and looseness that it could have only been written by an Englishman. Byron cited Goethe's high opinion of the poem in his defence of it to his sceptical friends (see Letter to Murray, 26 May 1822, in Marchand, *Selected Letters and Journals*, p. 288).
23. *Don Juan*, Canto XV, stanza XL.
24. See, among other places, Maurois, *Byron*, pp. 433 and 480.

CHAPTER 3. STENDHAL

1. In his travel books, *Rome, Naples et Florence* (1817) and *Promenades dans Rome* (1827). See David Wakefield, *Stendhal: The Promise of Happiness* (Bedford, Beds.: Newstead Press, 1984) p. 103; also Robert Alter, *Stendhal: A Biography* (London: George Allen and Unwin, 1980) pp. 182–3.
2. Stendhal, *La Vie de Henry Brûlard* in *Oeuvres intimes*, ed. Henri Martineau and Victor del Litto (Paris: Pleiade, 1961) p. 11.
3. *L'Histoire de la peinture en Italie* (1817). The dedication even includes a reminder to the Emperor that Stendhal was 'the soldier you buttonholed at Gorlitz'.
4. Lord Broughton (John Cam Hobhouse), *Recollections of a Long Life* (London: John Murray, 1909) vol. II, pp. 52–6.
5. The introduction to *The Cenci* is an essay on the figure of Don Juan, including various versions: Molière's, Mozart's, Byron's and others. See Stendhal, *The Abbess of Castro and Other Tales*, trans. C. K. Scott-Moncrieff (New York: Liveright, 1926) pp. 165–74, esp. p. 169 for Byron. Stendhal conveyed the same views more forcefully in letters written at the time of composition of his Cenci tale. See *To the Happy Few: Selected Letters of Stendhal*, trans. Norman Cameron (London: John Lehmann, 1952) pp. 348–50.
6. Stendhal, *Souvenirs d'egotisme*, in *Oeuvres intimes* (Paris: Pleiade, 1973) p. 1398.
7. Stendhal makes this remark in *Racine et Shakespeare* (1823). See Wakefield, *Promise of Happiness*, pp. 22 and 53.
8. Stendhal claimed in various works to have met Shelley, including 'Rome, Naples et Florence', in *Oeuvres completes* (Paris: Cercle de Bibliophile, 1967) pp. 183 and 447. It is very doubtful, however, that

this was the truth. In early books of this kind the down-at-heel author was not only a plagiarist but a liar.

9. This is how she referred to her happy interlude with Byron in the autumn of 1812. Certainly it was one of the most idyllic moments of the poet's life. See, for instance, André Maurois, *Byron*, trans. Hamish Miles (New York: Ungar, 1930) ch. XVII.

10. Stendhal took his favourite phrase from Oliver Goldsmith's *The Vicar of Wakefield*. It appeared first, in English, on the title page of the second volume of his *Histoire de la peinture en Italie*. Its most prominent reappearance would be on the last page of *La Chartreuse de Parme*.

11. This has been a commonplace in Stendhal criticism for decades. See for instance, Robert Alter, *Stendhal: A Biography* (London: Allen and Unwin, 1980) pp. 13 and 98.

12. For a discussion of Marcuse's views, described in his book *Eros and Civilization*, see my *Art, Messianism and Crime* (London: Macmillan, 1986) ch. 2.

13. The phrase is not Stendhal's but T. S. Eliot's in describing Henry James in his essay 'On Henry James' which appeared in the James number of *The Little Review*, August 1918.

14. See my *Wagner to 'The Waste Land'* (London: Macmillan, 1982) pp. 73–4.

15. After the July Revolution of 1830 Stendhal was sent to be French consul in Trieste. However, remembering his Bonapartist views expressed in *Histoire de la peinture*, the Austrian authorities refused him the post and he was transferred to the little port-city of Rome, where he remained, except for extended medical leaves, until his death in 1842. From the time of his arrival in Trieste his letters contain constant complaints about his boredom in these relative backwaters. Stendhal needed great cities and was only happy in Italy in his last years when he left his duties in the hands of a vice-consul and went to enjoy the high life in Rome.

16. I have reverted to the English title here as I have depended on the translation of Margaret Shaw (London: Penguin, 1990). Ms Shaw has chosen to Italianise the names – Fabrizio for Fabrice, for instance. I have followed her in this.

17. Geoffrey Strickland quotes from James's *Literary Reviews and Essays* (New York: Twayne Publishers, 1957) p. 156, in his *Stendhal: The Education of a Novelist* (London: Cambridge University Press, 1974) pp. 251–2.

18. Ibid., p. 252.

19. Paul Bourget, *Stendhal: Discours prononcé le 28 Juin 1920 a l'inauguration du monument* (Paris: Champion, 1920) pp. 17–18; quoted in Joanna Richardson, *Stendhal* (New York: Coward, McCann and Geoghegan, 1974) p. 297.

20. Leon Blum, *Stendhal et le beylisme* (Paris: Ollendorf, 1914) pp. 2–5, 304–7; quoted in Richardson, *Stendhal*, pp. 296–7.

21. Stendhal's relevant discussion of these matters might be found in *Racine et Shakespeare*, which staked out his position in contemporary battles about the identity of French Romanticism.

22. Stendhal, *Vie de Henry Brûlard*, p. 3. See also discussion by Gita May

in her *Stendhal and the Age of Napoleon* (New York: Columbia University Press, 1974) p. 16.

23. Stendhal, *Vie de Henry Brûlard*, p. 14. See also Wakefield, *Promise of Happiness* p. 86.
24. May, *Stendhal*, p. 16.
25. Wakefield, *Promise of Happiness*, p. 66–7.
26. For discussion of the idealistic anarchist tradition, see my *Art, Messianism and Crime*, ch. 5.

CHAPTER 4. HENRY JAMES

1. See F. R. Leavis, *The Great Tradition* (Harmondsworth, Middx: Penguin, 1972) p. 151.
2. In numerous places. For discussion see F. W. Dupee, *Henry James* (New York: Doubleday, 1956).
3. In *Boon* (1915), which included a vicious satire on James in retaliation for James's criticism of Wells in his essay 'The New Novel'. For discussion of the James–Wells controversy, see ibid., pp. 199–200.
4. James told the tale of his famous 'injury' in *Notes of a Son and Brother* (1914); the relevant passage is quoted and discussed in ibid., pp. 39–41. Another view of the matter may be found in Harry T. Moore, *Henry James and his World* (London: Thames and Hudson, 1974) p. 25.
5. See ibid., p. 19: 'James had a lifelong and rather secret admiration of Napoleon I, whose presence he felt during his boyhood days in the Paris of the Second Empire. The glory and power of the Napoleonic past had come to vivid life for James upon his first visit to the magnificent Galerie d'Apollon in the Louvre, which had so impressed him that it figured much later [in *A Small Boy and Others*] as the scene of a dream he always remembered as "the most appalling yet most admirable nightmare of my life".' His prejudice in favour of Bonapartists vs the *ancien régime* is implied in his treatment of the views of young Mme de Bellegarde vs the behaviour of her husband and his family in *The American*; also in his description of the apartment of Mme de Vionnet in *The Ambassadors*.
6. See Van Wyck Brooks, *The Pilgrimage of Henry James* (London: Jonathan Cape, 1928) p. 5.
7. Ibid., p. 15.
8. James puts this phrase in the mouth of a reactionary American expatriate living in Paris in *The Portrait of a Lady* (Harmondsworth, Middx: Penguin, 1963) p. 213. Might this have been the source of London's concept and title for his 1906 novel?
9. See the discussion of Christof Wegelin, *The Image of Europe in Henry James* (Dallas, Tx.: Southern Methodist University Press, 1958) pp. 46–7; also Brooks, *Pilgrimage*, pp. 39–40, where James's passage from *Hawthorne* is quoted in full.
10. By Colin Haycraft, who tells me that the formulation comes from the late Cambridge scholar, Michael Swan.
11. The influence of popular melodrama on James may have been sub-

stantial, particularly when young. It appears from *A Small Boy and Others* that he spent many happy hours going to entertainments of this kind when the James family lived in New York. The experience may explain some of the more strained aspects of later plots and of course his own enthusiasm to succeed in theatre in New York in the 1880s and in London in the 1890s.

12. Henry James, *The Golden Bowl* (New York: Dell, 1963) p. 259.
13. See my *California Writers* (London: Macmillan, 1983) p. 104.
14. The phrase in Ezra Pound's. See 'The Rest' (originally collected in *Lustra* (1915)), in *Collected Shorter Poems* (London: Faber and Faber, 1984) p. 93.
15. See Moore, *James and his World*, pp. 44–5.
16. See ibid., p. 101.
17. Dupee, *James*, p. 102.
18. In a letter to his brother William, quoted in Moore, *Henry James and his World*, p. 59.
19. Not all agree with this assessment, of course. Leavis, for instance, considers the book one of James's major achievements.
20. This phrase again comes from Pound, in *Hugh Selwyn Mauberley*.
21. I take the famous phrase of Virginia Woolf deliberately. Her concept and work was undoubtedly inspired in part by James's tendency toward abstraction.
22. See the preface to this novel, included in Henry James, *The Critical Muse: Selected Literary Criticism*, ed. Roger Gard (London: Penguin, 1987) p. 513.
23. See ibid., p. 428.
24. See ibid., p. 303, in a letter discussing *Lady Windermere's Fan*.
25. See my *Wagner to 'The Waste Land'* (London: Macmillan, 1982) p. 125.
26. See the preface, included in *The Critical Muse*, pp. 547–62.
27. 'Among forms, moreover, we had had, on the dimensional ground – for length and breadth – our ideal, the beautiful and blest *nouvelle*'. For discussion, see the preface to vol. XII of the 'New York edition' of James's *Novels and Tales* (New York: Charles Scribner's Sons, 1907–9); also Willard Thorp's foreword to *The Turn of the Screw and Other Short Novels* (New York: Signet, 1962).
28. See ch. 6 of my *Orthodox Heresy* (London: Macmillan, 1989).
29. The phrase is F. O. Matthieson's, from his *Henry James: The Major Phase* (Oxford: Oxford University Press, 1946).
30. See note 3 above.
31. See Martin, *Wagner to 'The Waste Land'*, p. 10.
32. Quoted in ibid., p. 114.
33. See the preface to *Portrait*, p. xiii.
34. With whom he shares initials. The comparison is a commonplace. See, for instance, Wegelin, *The Image of Europe in James*, ch. IV.
35. James, *The Golden Bowl*, p. 498.
36. See note 13, ch. 3; also Wegelin, *The Image of Europe in James*, p. 107.
37. The comparison is George Moore's. See Martin, *Wagner to 'The Waste Land'*, p. 110.
38. See Moore, *James and his World*, p. 115.

39. This is reproduced on the cover of *The Critical Muse*.
40. *The Ivory Tower*'s heroine, Rosanna Gaw, was to have been a new type of American girl who 'show[ed] the impact of James's late vision of his native country' (Wegelin, *The Image of Europe in James*, p. 165); but of course, the novel remained unfinished.

CHAPTER 5. MAUGHAM

1. See Maugham's chapters on these two writers in his *Ten Novels and Their Authors* (London: Pan, 1978). Extensive reference to both occur elsewhere in his works, notably Stendhal in *The Summing Up* (London: Pan, 1976) pp. 49, 60, 113, 140.
2. On James, see Maugham, *The Summing Up*, pp. 30, 64, 80, 114, 139, 144; also the section on James in 'Some Novelists I Have Known', included in *The Vagrant Mood* (London: Heinemann, 1952). According to Anthony Curtis (*The Pattern of Maugham* (London: Hamish Hamilton, 1974) p. 237), Maugham's 'greatest literary hostility was to Henry James'.
3. For the following quotes, see F. R. Leavis, *The Great Tradition* (Harmondsworth, Middx: Penguin, 1972) pp. 10, 12–13, 24–5, 33.
4. Ibid., p. 13. The quote in context is applied to Richardson, but the complaint is registrered against the others copiously elsewhere.
5. Ibid., p. 183.
6. Ibid., p. 207.
7. Ibid., p. 276.
8. Ibid., p. 30.
9. Maugham, *Ten Novelists*, pp. 145, 148. Maugham, sounding remarkably like Leavis, quotes Matthew Arnold on the need for 'high seriousness' as a standard.
10. Wilson's 'The Apotheosis of Somerset Maugham' first appeared in the *New Yorker* in June 1946; reprinted in *Classics and Commercials* (New York: Farrar, Straus and Giroux, 1958).
11. Pound's phrase, ubiquitous throughout his critical pronouncements, became the title of a book published in 1934.
12. In Maugham, *The Summing Up*, p. 12 and elsewhere.
13. Maugham did take strong patriotic and anti-fascist views during the later 1930s and through the Second World War.
14. See Maugham, *The Summing Up*, pp. 166–7 and elsewhere.
15. See 'A Lesser Splash' in *The Sunday Times*, Books Supplement, 26 March 1989.
16. In conversation, Belsize Park, September 1989.
17. In 'Willie and the Men', *The Observer*, 2 April 1989, p. 45.
18. In Ezra Pound, *Hugh Selwyn Mauberley*. See *Collected Shorter Poems* (London: Faber and Faber, 1984) p. 187.
19. Where in fact he spent his last years and died.
20. See W. S. Maugham, *The Moon and Sixpence* (London: Pan, 1974) pp. 207, 212.
21. See Robert L. Calder, *Somerset Maugham and the Quest for Freedom* (London: Heinemann, 1972).

22. See Frieda Lawrence, *Not I, But the Wind* (New York: Viking, 1934) pp. 147–8.
23. See Maugham, *The Moon and Sixpence*, pp. 162–3, as well as many other places in his work of the years 1916–46.
24. Curtis, *Pattern of Maugham*, p. 225.
25. He did consult these expatriate mystics when in Hollywood in the early 1940s; but given that he had gone to India himself in 1938 expressly to gain material for the book, he can hardly stand accused of having pinched their ideas. On the contrary, their Eastern enthusiasms might be seen as a confirmation of contemporary interest in a scenario which had long been germinating in his mind.
26. As is apparent from his novels *Christmas Holiday* (1939) and *The Hour Before Dawn* (1942). The latter was originally a propaganda film.
27. See Maugham, *The Summing Up*, pp. 151–203, esp. pp. 194–5, 151–2, 183–4, 192, 199, 203.
28. See Robert Calder, *Willie: The Life of W. Somerset Maugham* (London: Heinemann, 1989) pp. 218–19, 321.
29. See Curtis, *Pattern of Maugham*, p. 30 and elsewhere.
30. See my *Art, Messianism and Crime* (London: Macmillan, 1986) chapter entitled 'Sixties' *Zeitgeist*, I: Mysticism.
31. Of *The Ambassadors* and *Portrait of a Lady* respectively.
32. See W. S. Maugham, *The Razor's Edge* (Harmondsworth, Middx: Penguin, 1963) p. 312.
33. Ibid., p. 71.
34. See W. S Maugham, *Of Human Bondage* (London: Pan, 1973) p. 469.
35. Curtis, *Pattern of Maugham*, p. 226. Curtis's judgement is intuitive, not textual.
36. Maugham, *The Razor's Edge*, p. 73. Isabel's phrase may be a comic jab at American pretensions when you consider that the 'backwater' Larry has settled into at that time is Paris.
37. See *The Collected Plays of W. Somerset Maugham* (London: Heinemann, 1952) vol. II, pp. 74–6, 78, 87.

CHAPTER 6. POUND

1. See *The Autobiograhy of Alice B. Toklas* (New York: Harcourt Brace, 1933). Quoted in John Tytell, *Ezra Pound: The Solitary Volcano* (London: Bloomsbury, 1987) p. 186.
2. In a review of 'The Letters of J. B. Yeats', in *The Egoist*, vol. IV (July 1917). Quoted in Alan Holder, *Three Voyagers in Search of Europe: A Study of Henry James, Ezra Pound, and T. S. Eliot* (Philadelphia, Pa: University of Pennsylvania Press, 1966) p. 60.
3. James's discussion of this matter may be found in *The American Scene* and Adams's views in *The Education of Henry Adams*. At least as dramatic were the fears of Henry Adams's brother Brooks that 'the old American blood is hardly reproducing itself', expressed principally in his *Law of Civilization and Decay*, which Pound admired. See Ibid., pp. 235–6.
4. In his *Autobiography* (New York: Random House, 1957); also in se-

lected letters, including in particular one written to his mother on 30 March 1904 (see Tytell, *Ezra Pound*, pp. 20–1.

5. 'In Durance' (originally in *Personae,* 1909), in *Collected Shorter Poems* (London: Faber and Faber, 1984) p. 20.

6. See W. B. Yeats, *A Vision* (New York: Collier, 1973) Introduction.

7. See Tytell, *Ezra Pound*, p. 63.

8. Lewis's comments on Pound are contained mainly in *Blasting and Bombadiering* and are quoted in Peter Ackroyd, *Ezra Pound* (London: Thames and Hudson, 1981) pp. 24, 36–9, 44, 57, 77–8.

9. In a letter to Katherine Heyman, a fellow Philadelphian and pianist for whom Pound wanted to act as impresario shortly after arriving in Europe. See Tytell, *Ezra Pound*, p. 58.

10. 'Men's lib' was a prominent subcurrent in the *Zeitgeist*. Joachim Fest remarks on 'advocates of Male Rights' and young Hitler in *Hitler* (New York: Harcourt and Brace, 1973) p. 37. Kenneth Lynn tells us of Hemingway's fear of over-mothering and effeminacy in his *Hemingway* (New York: Simon and Schuster, 1987).

11. Originally in *Ripostes,* 1912. See Pound, *Collected Shorter Poems*, p. 61.

12. 'To Whistler, American', ibid., p. 235.

13. 'L'Homme Moyen Sensuel', ibid., p. 240.

14. Originally in *Personae*, ibid., pp. 33–4.

15. See 'Portrait d'une femme' (note 11 above).

16. See 'The Garden' (originally in *Lustra,* 1915), ibid., p. 83.

17. See 'Salutation', 'Salutation the Second' and 'The Rest' (all originally in *Lustra*), ibid., pp. 85–6, 88–9, 92–3.

18. See above, also 'Tenzone', 'Further Instructions', 'Ité' and 'Salvationists' (all also in *Lustra*), ibid., pp. 81, 94, 95–6, 99.

19. See 'The River-Merchant's Wife: a Letter', 'Separation on the River Kiang' and 'Taking Leave of a Friend' (all originally in *Cathay,* 1915), ibid., pp. 130–1, 134–6, 137.

20. Hemingway summed up the dismay of many of Pound's literary friends when he wrote to him in April 1933: 'Since when are you an economist, pal? The last I knew you you were a fuckin' bassoon player.' See Tytell, *Ezra Pound*, p. 231.

21. In E. Hemingway, *A Moveable Feast* (New York: Scribner's, 1964). See the chapter entitled 'Ezra Pound and His Bel Esprit'.

22. In the 1930s, for instance, he remarked to George Santayana's secretary that he had married a 'beautiful picture that never came to life'. See Ackroyd, *Pound*, p. 36.

23. See Hemingway, *A Moveable Feast*, pp. 107, 108, 110, 143–4 for Hemingway's example's of Pound's guileless nobility to friends. See also Hemingway's remarks to Archibald MacLeish on Pound as 'a crazy and harmless traitor' who had 'foolishly swallowed fascism whole because he felt respected as a poet in Italy, something no one but an idiot with Ezra's type of ego would do' (quoted in Tytell, *Ezra Pound*, p. 275).

24. Pound's comment in a letter. See ibid., p. 127.

25. See Donald Hall's interview with Pound in *Paris Review* (Summer–Fall, 1962); also 'A Conversation between Ezra Pound and Allen Ginsberg', in *Evergreen Review* (June 1968).

26. See Tytell, *Ezra Pound*, p. 190.
27. See ibid., p. 106.
28. This was Malcolm Cowley's assessment in 'Pound Reweighed'. See Holder, *Three Voyagers*, pp. 235–6.
29. See Tytell, *Ezra Pound*, pp. 263–4.
30. In Henry James, *The Golden Bowl* (New York: Dell, 1963).
31. Pound had been collecting a group of acolytes for directed reading and 'loose tutorial discussion' since the early 1930s in Rapallo. See Tytell, *Ezra Pound*, pp. 218, 235, 305–6, 308–16.
32. Lawrence's theory is contained in his *Studies in Classic American Literature* (1915; London: Penguin, 1990) and was developed further by Leslie Fiedler in *The Return of the Vanishing American* (London: Paladin, 1972).

CHAPTER 7. GRAHAM GREENE

1. Greene acknowledges Conrad's influence in his memoir *A Sort of Life* (1971); of an early, disavowed novel he writes: 'All that was left in the heavy pages of it was the distorted ghost of Conrad.' (See Graham Greene, *A Sort of Life* (London: Penguin, 1972) p. 147.) On Henry James he wrote a chapter for the English Novelists' Series in 1936.
2. Pound was one of the modernist poets Greene was particularly interested in as a young man. Years later he would incorporate a line from Pound's 'Villanelle: the Psychological Hour' in *The Quiet American* (London: Penguin, 1962) p. 53. He also quotes Pound's 'The Seafarer' directly in *Doctor Fischer of Geneva or the Bomb Party* (London: Penguin, 1980) 87.
3. The opening lines of 'The Pisan Cantos'.
4. Jean Cocteau's description.
5. See the description of paintings by Haitian artists in *The Comedians* (London: Penguin, 1967) p. 69; also my discussion of *The Moon and Sixpence* and Crowley in Chapter 5.
6. On Acton and Greene, see Norman Sherry, *The Life of Graham Greene* (London: Jonathan Cape, 1989) pp. 121, 128, 148.
7. He read the novel when it was published in 1926 and developed a desire to go to Mexico from that time (see Sherry, *Life of Greene*, p. 662). But Greene's Mexico would have little to do with Lawrence's heroic vitalist fantasy.
8. In a letter to *The Times*, 4 September 1967.
9. He went to Moscow to interview Philby shortly before the latter died.
10. See my *Art, Messianism and Crime* (London: Macmillan, 1986) ch. 8, for discussion of Zaehner, these ideas and their effect on the 'drop-out cults' of the 1960s.
11. As David Pryce-Jones points out in his little book *Graham Greene* (London and Edinburgh: Oliver and Boyd 1963).
12. Greene's famous remark, 'There is a splinter of ice in the heart of the writer', comes from Greene, *A Sort of Life*, p. 134.
13. Greene's own memoirs are a principal source here as well as Sherry's official *Life of Greene*.

14. Greene's own admission in *Ways of Escape* (London: Penguin, 1980) p. 31.
15. See Byron, *Don Juan*, XII, 5.
16. Priestley believed that Greene had him in mind in the cockney novelist Mr Savoury, whom he sends up in *Stamboul Train*.
17. These are the qualities of fine French prose according to the critic Catulle Mendès (see my *Wagner to 'The Waste Land'* (London: Macmillan, 1982) ch. 1).
18. Wilde may be an influence on Greene in his light-hearted vein. In *Travels with My Aunt*, the eponymous lady has the same christian name as Lady Bracknell in *The Importance of Being Earnest*; both Aunt Augustas are imperial presences in the lives of their nephews, and both turn out farcically to be their nephews' mothers. Greene even includes an animadversion on the name Ernest, which without the Wilde reasonance might seem out of place. See Graham Greene, *Travels with My Aunt* (London: Penguin, 1971) p. 57.
19. See Graham Greene, *The Heart of the Matter* (New York: Viking, 1948) p. 6.
20. I discuss this in *California Writers* (London: Macmillan, 1983) ch. 4, section 2.
21. Interview with Vivien Greene, August 1977. See Sherry, *Life of Greene*, p. 665.
22. Graham Greene, *The Quiet American* (London: Penguin, 1962) pp. 159–60.
23. See Sherry, *Life of Greene*, pp. 619–25. The libel case coincided with Greene's trip to Mexico (which resulted in *The Power and the Glory*). He had some hesitation about returning to England for fear of being arrested; and this trauma may have contributed to his anti-Americanism, his suspicion of First World institutions and his rather perverse sense that one might after all be safer in some backwater of the Third World. At any rate, the incident directly precedes the epoch of his serious wanderings.
24. In *The Sunday Times*, 16 April 1989.
25. See Martin, *California Writers*, ch. 2, section 2.
26. See Martin, *Art, Messianism and Crime*, ch. 5 and elsewhere for discussion of anarchism and the 1960s. Pulling remarks of his development: 'I discovered in myself for the first time a streak of anarchy' (Greene, *Travels*, p. 52). Later he is pleased to hear the sound of a Beatles' tune wafting over the fence in his garden (ibid., p. 139).
27. See 'Legwork vs. brainwork' in *The Observer*, 16 April 1989.
28. Ibid.
29. At the time of writing, this is the title of Greene's final book, a collection of stories (London: Reinhardt, 1990).
30. See Greene, *Doctor Fischer*, p. 141.
31. See Greene, *Travels*, p. 95; also my *The Sayings of Lord Byron* (London: Duckworth, 1990) section entitled 'Home and Abroad'.
32. For discussion see the final chapters of Robert Calder *Willie: The Life of W. Somerset Maugham* (London: Heinemann, 1989).
33. See Greene, *The Quiet American*, p. 14; *Loser Takes All* (London: Pen-

guin, 1971) pp. 21, 90, 121; *The Comedians*, pp. 133, 173. A general atmosphere of the *'poésie des départs'* hangs over much of Greene's other work; see, for instance, *Travels*, p. 188.

34. The phrase comes from Huysmans in *A Rebours*. See Martin, *Wagner to 'The Waste Land'*, ch. 1.

CHAPTER 8. A VANISHING BREED

1. Published by Chatto and Windus, London, 1970. See especially the Introduction.

2. At the end of his excursion around Europe following the Second World War Edmund Wilson concluded that bureaucratic careerism derived and perverted from this source had been a major cause of decay of both socialist and democratic ideals. See *Europe Without Baedecker* (London: Secker and Warburg, 1948) pp. 229–34.

3. See ch. 1, n. 2.

4. This is Malcolm Bradbury's phrase in *The Expatriate Tradition in American Literature* (British Association for American Studies, 1982) p. 39.

5. See Paul Theroux, *My Secret History* (New York: Ballantine Books, 1989) Part 3: 'African Girls'.

6. Several of Ms Jong's sub-Miller, hopped-up feminist, Therouxish picaresque books are applicable to the discussion here, including in addition to her famous *Fear of Flying* (1973), *How to Save Your Own Life* (1977) and *Parachutes and Kisses* (1984).

7. This is discussed very adequately by Bradbury in his *Expatriation Tradition in American Literature*, specifically in ch. 2, 'The Romantic Experience, 1776–1860'.

8. See Stoddard Martin, *California Writers* (London: Macmillan, 1983) p. 213, note 81.

9. The Luciferian motto of Stephen Dedalus before he expatriates at the end of James Joyce, *The Portrait of an Artist as a Young Man*.

10. See the conclusion of this famous and influential (especially to Eliot and Pound) study: Arthur Symons, *The Symbolist Movement in Literature* (London: Heinemann, 1899).

11. See *The Henry Miller Reader*, ed. Lawrence Durrell (New York: New Directions, 1959) pp. 3, 17, 20, 44.

12. See 'The Universe of Death', ibid., pp. 203–27.

13. Ibid., p. 96.

14. See 'Chronology', ibid., p. 386.

15. See 'Reunion in Brooklyn', ibid., pp. 95–133.

16. He was an American citizen to begin with, though brought up in England. (See Martin, *California Writers*, ch. 4, section 3).

17. See *Miller Reader*, p. 71.

18. 'Big Sur Invocation', ibid., pp. 77–9.

19. Christopher Isherwood, *A Single Man* (London: Methuen, 1964) p. 138.

20. See *Miller Reader*, pp. 383, 385–6.

21. See Isherwood, *A Single Man*, first paragraph.

22. *Miller Reader*, p. 62.

23. See Isherwood, *A Single Man*, pp. 11, 112, 118.
24. Ibid., p. 13.
25. Ibid., p. 14.
26. Ibid., pp. 75–7
27. Ibid., p. 91.
28. Ibid., p. 93.
29. In an article on the thrillers of Raymond Chandler. (See Martin, *California Writers*, p. 212, note 72.)
30. Isherwood, *A Single Man*, p. 117.
31. Ibid., pp. 124–5.
32. Ibid., p. 142.
33. See beginning of ch. 5.
34. See '*Une Être Etoilique*', in *Miller Reader*, pp. 287–307.
35. See Stoddard Martin, *Orthodox Heresy* (London: Macmillan, 1989) ch. 4, section 4.
36. Interview transmitted on BBC2 during the Rolling Stones' 1981 American tour.
37. Joan Didion, *A Book of Common Prayer* (London: Weidenfeld and Nicolson, 1977), and *Democracy* (London: Chatto and Windus, 1984).
38. Maugham's own term about Elliott Templeton at the beginning of *The Razor's Edge*.

Index